Making a difference

Bob Fugere

Making a difference

NGOs and development in a changing world

Edited by
Michael Edwards
and David Hulme

Save the Children

For Bob,
warm regards,
Michael Edwards

EARTHSCAN
Earthscan Publications Ltd, London

First published 1992 by
Earthscan Publications Ltd
120 Pentonville Road, London N1 9JN

British Library Cataloguing-in-Publication Data

A catalogue record for this book is available from the British Library

ISBN 1-85383-144-1

Typeset by DP Photosetting, Aylesbury, Bucks
Printed and bound in Great Britain by
Biddles Ltd, Guildford and King's Lynn

Earthscan Publications Ltd is an editorially independent subsidiary of Kogan Page Ltd
and publishes in association with the International Institute for Environment and
Development and the World Wide Fund for Nature (UK).

Contents

Foreword

The origins of this book can be traced back to a conversation over an *aprés*-seminar beer at the University of Hull when both editors found that they had common concerns about the ways in which the recent popularity of NGOs, especially with official donors, was influencing the strategies that they pursued. In particular, we felt that the new emphasis on NGOs ('Northern', 'Southern' and at the grassroots level) required that NGOs recognise the need to analyse how they can progress from improving local situations on a small scale to influencing the wider systems that create and reinforce global poverty. Could NGOs really 'make a difference'? These discussions led to the mounting of an international workshop at the University of Manchester in January 1992 on *Scaling-Up NGO Impacts: Learning from Experience* that provided the basis for this volume.

Inevitably such a work is the product of contributions from a large number of people, not all of whom are credited in the text. In particular, we should like to acknowledge the contributions of all the participants of the Manchester workshop who presented papers and took part in discussion groups and plenaries. These have helped to shape our own thinking on the challenges that face NGOs as they approach a new millennium, and the thinking of the other contributors to the book. In preparing this volume we have been all too painfully aware of the differences in the resources available to participants from the 'North' and the 'South' and the way in which this has meant that the authorship of this volume has a 'Northern' bias. The Manchester workshop included a high proportion of papers, group discussants and participants from the 'South' but many have been unable to convert their contributions into finished papers because of the pressures on their time and the lack of supporting facilities. We have, perhaps, exacerbated these difficulties by opting for rapid publication. This decision was taken because of a desire to make the workshop's debates about future NGO strategy available to a wider audience at the first opportunity.

We should also like to acknowledge the financial support of a number of institutions that helped to make the workshop possible: these include Save the Children Fund (UK), the Institute for Development Policy and Management, the University of Manchester and the Overseas Development Administration.

At the University of Manchester especial thanks go to Debra Whitehead and Delphine Mills for sweating blood to make the workshop such a success. Katy Swan and Jo White undertook similar responsibilities for Save the Children. The successful preparation of the manuscript for this volume, to an exceptionally tight deadline, has only been possible because of the technical proficiency and inordinate good humour of Debra Whitehead in Manchester and Catherine Williams in London. Thanks also to Kumarian Press for granting permission to reproduce materials from D C Korten and R Klauss (1984) *People-Centred Development: Contributions Toward Theory and Planning Frameworks*.

Our sincere thanks to all those individuals and agencies that have helped us to see this book through to publication.

MICHAEL EDWARDS
London
July 1992

DAVID HULME
Manchester
July 1992

Contributors

Anthony Bebbington lectures at the Centre for Latin American Studies, University of Cambridge. He has recently collaborated with the Overseas Development Institute in London on a study of the role of farmer organisations in agricultural technology development.

David Billis is Director of the Centre for Voluntary Organisations at the London School of Economics. His particular field of interest is management and organizational change in British voluntary agencies.

Robert Chambers is a Fellow of the Institute of Development Studies at the University of Sussex. From 1989 to 1991 he was a Visiting Member of the Faculty of the Administrative Staff College of India, where he worked with NGOs and Government staff on the development of Participatory Rural Appraisal, conducting training workshops and developing training methodologies.

John Clark was at the time of writing his chapter for this volume Development Policy Adviser for OXFAM-UK. He is now International Relations Officer, working particularly on NGO relations, at the World Bank in Washington DC, USA.

Karina Constantino David is Executive Director of the NGO Harnessing Self-Reliant Initiatives and Knowledge (HASIK), Chairperson of the network Partnership of Philippine Support Service Agencies (PHILSSA), President of the Caucus of Development NGO Networks (CODE-NGO), and Professor of Community Development at the University of the Philippines.

Elsa Dawson was Field Director for Save the Children Fund-UK in Peru for seven years, from 1984 to 1991. She was then awarded a Visiting Fellowship at the Institute of Development Studies at the University of Sussex, and worked on a research programme sponsored by SCF-UK on 'NGOs, Scaling-Up and Partnership.'

Chris Dolan lectures at the Rural Development Facility, University of Witwatersrand, South Africa. His chapter is based on research conducted as a postgraduate student at the University of East Anglia.

Michael Edwards has spent the last ten years working for UK development NGOs. From 1984 to 1988 he was OXFAM-UK's Regional Representative in Lusaka, and then spent two years as Director of the PRASAD Foundation in India. Since 1990 he has been Head of Information and Research for Save the Children Fund-UK, based in London.

John Farrington is a senior research fellow at the Overseas Development Institute, London. He has researched extensively into farmer participatory research and is the coordinator of ODI's current work on NGO–government interaction in agricultural technology development.

Rip Hodson is a research fellow at the Centre for Voluntary Organisations, London School of Economics. Previously, he was the Chief Executive of ActionAid, for whom he worked at headquarters and field level for many years.

Mick Howes lectures at the Institute for Development Studies, University of Sussex. He is currently collaborating with the Bangladesh Rural Advancement Committee (BRAC) in the field of institutional development.

Tony Hall worked for OXFAM-UK in Brazil before joining the Agricultural Extension and Rural Development Department at Reading University. He is now Lecturer in Social Planning in Developing Countries at the London School of Economics, and has a continuing interest in Brazil.

David Hulme is Reader at the Institute for Development Policy and Management, University of Manchester. He has researched extensively into the operations of NGOs and government agencies in promoting rural development, particularly in the fields of rural credit, agricultural extension and land settlement. Recently he published *Sociology and Development: Theories, Policies and Practices*, Harvester-Wheatsheaf (with M M Turner).

Kevin Ireland worked for a number of years in local government in the UK before moving to Sudan with Save the Children Fund-UK. From 1987 to 1992 he was SCF-UK's Field Director for Thailand, and is currently engaged on a research programme sponsored by SCF on the 'European Dimension of the Sexual Exploitation of Children in South-East Asia.'

Beverley Jones, a teacher by profession, worked for two and a half years in education in the Sudan before completing a Masters in Education and Development at the University of Bristol. She now works for Christian Aid as part of their Horn of Africa Team.

P A Kiriwandeniya is Chairman of SANASA, the Federation of Thrift and Credit Co-operatives in Sri Lanka and Director of the Forum on Development – Kegalle. He has worked in the voluntary sector in Sri Lanka for many years and is a committed social activist.

Somthavil Klinmahorm has spent the last fourteen years working with local and international NGOs in her native Thailand. Most recently she has been the Projects Coordinator for Save the Children Fund-UK in Bangkok, where she was responsible for support to the Integrated Education Project which forms the subject of her chapter in this volume.

James Mackie has worked for VSO since 1982, first as a member of field staff in Sri Lanka, The Maldives and the Philippines, and for the past four years as VSO's Programme Funding Manager. Before joining VSO he wrote a geography PhD thesis at the School of Oriental and African Studies, University of London.

Joy MacKeith lectures at the Centre for Voluntary Organisations, London School of Economics. She is currently involved in a problem-oriented research project into the management problems facing UK based development NGOs.

Diana Mitlin is a research officer for the Human Settlements Programme of the International Institute for Environment and Development, London. Her special interest is urban development in Latin America.

John Parry-Williams spent five years teaching in Uganda and then worked for fourteen years as a Probation Officer in the UK. He returned to Uganda in 1988 to head the Social Work Team of Save the Children Fund-UK in Kampala. In 1992 he was awarded an MSc by the University of Lancaster for his work on the Child Law Review Committee, which forms the subject of his chapter in this volume.

Mark Robinson is a research officer at the Institute for Development Studies, University of Sussex. Until recently, he worked at the Overseas Development Institute, London, where he co-ordinated a major study on the effectiveness of NGOs.

Chris Roche works in the Research Department of ACORD, the Agency for Co-operation and Research in Development, London. He is presently working on *auto-evaluation* and developing methodologies for participatory evaluation.

M G Sattar heads the Research and Evaluation Department of the Bangladesh Rural Advancement Committee (BRAC). He has many years of headquarters- and field-level experience with BRAC.

David Satterthwaite is a research officer for the Human Settlements Programme of the International Institute for Environment and Development, London. He has published extensively on urban problems in developing countries with particular reference to Latin America.

Part I

Introduction

1

Scaling-up the developmental impact of NGOs: concepts and experiences

Michael Edwards and David Hulme

Introduction

There are now some 4,000 development non-governmental organisations (NGOs) in OECD member countries alone (OECD 1989), dispersing almost three billion US dollars' worth of assistance every year (Clark 1991, p.47). They work with around 10,000 to 20,000 'Southern' NGOs who assist up to 100 million people (ibid p.51). Yet despite the increasing scale of this sector, and the growing reputation that NGOs have won for themselves and for their work over the last ten years, their contribution to development on a global level remains limited. Many small-scale successes have been secured, but the systems and structures which determine the distribution of power and resources within and between societies remain largely unchanged. As a result, the impact of NGOs on the lives of poor people is highly localised, and often transitory. In contrast to NGO programmes, which tend to be good but limited in scope, governmental development efforts are often large in scale but limited in their impact. Effective development work on a sustainable and significant scale is a goal which has eluded both governments and NGOs.

One of the most important factors underlying this situation is the failure of NGOs to make the right linkages between their work at micro-level and the wider systems and structures of which they form a small part. For example, village co-operatives are undermined by deficiencies in national agricultural extension and marketing systems; 'social-action groups' can be overwhelmed by more powerful political interests within the state or local economic elites; successful experiments in primary health care cannot be replicated because government structures lack the ability or willingness to adopt new ideas; effective NGO projects (and not all are) remain 'islands of success' in an all-too-hostile ocean. 'If you see a baby drowning you jump in to save it; and if you see a second and a third, you do the same. Soon you are so busy saving drowning babies that you never look up to see that there is someone there throwing these babies in the river' (Ellwood, quoted in Korten 1990a). Or, as an Indian development worker once asked us in Rajasthan, 'Why help trees to grow if the forest is going to be consumed by fire?' In other words, small-scale NGO projects *by themselves* will never be enough to secure lasting improvements in the lives of poor people. Yet what else can NGOs do, and how can they increase their developmental impact without losing their traditional flexibility, value-base and effectiveness at the local level? Resolving this dilemma is the central question facing NGOs of all kinds as they move towards a new millennium.

Of course, an emphasis on *quality* in NGO work is never misplaced. Good development work is not insignificant just because it is limited in scale, and some might disagree with Clark's statement (in this volume) that 'maximising impact is the paramount objective of NGOs.' As Alan Fowler (1990, p.11) rightly points out, the roots of NGO comparative advantage lie in the quality of relationships they can create, not in the size of resources they can command. Some NGOs appear to have lost sight of this fact in a headlong rush for growth, influence and status, forgetting that 'voluntarism and values are their most precious asset' (Brown and Korten 1989). Simple, human concern for other people as individuals and in very practical ways is one of the hallmarks of NGO work. There is a danger that these qualities will go 'out of fashion' because of mounting concerns for strategy and impact, but in so doing the voluntary sector will lose its most important defining characteristic.

Nevertheless, all serious NGOs want to increase their impact and effectiveness, ensure that they spend their limited resources in the best way possible, and thereby maximise their own particular contribution to the development of people around the world. The question is, how are these goals to be achieved? We believe that there are many possible answers, but none which ignore the importance of macro-level influences in determining the success of people's development efforts at grassroots level. We find it inconceivable that NGOs will achieve their objectives in isolation from the national and international political process and its constituent parts. It is this interaction, this search for greater impact, that forms the central theme of this book. Although many contributors use the term 'scaling-up' to describe the goal of 'increasing impact', it should be noted at the outset that this does *not* imply expanding the size of NGO operations. There are many different ways in which impact can be achieved, and the contributions to this book have been chosen deliberately to reflect the wide diversity of approaches chosen by different NGOs at different stages in their development. There is no attempt to identify the 'best' strategy for achieving greater impact, still less to impose a consensus where none exists.

The term 'NGO' also embraces a huge diversity of institutions, though the chapters in this volume are consistent in differentiating between: international NGOs such as Save the Children and Christian Aid (commonly referred to as Northern NGOs or NNGOs); 'intermediary' NGOs in the South (SNGOs) who support grassroots work through funding, technical advice and advocacy; grassroots movements of various kinds (grassroots organisations or GROs, and community-based organisations or CBOs) which are controlled by their own members; and networks and federations composed of any or all of the above. Clearly, each of these 'NGOs' plays a distinctive role in development and faces a different range of choices and strategies when considering the question of impact. Added to this is the obvious importance of *context* in determining which strategies are chosen and how effective they are in practice, and the observation (made with particular force in Ireland and Klinmahorm's paper in this volume) that 'scaling-up' is often a spontaneous process rather than the result of a pre-planned strategy. These complications make generalisation difficult and dangerous.

Nonetheless, a conceptual framework is needed if any sense is to be made of such a wide range of case studies. There are at least five models of scaling-up we have considered in writing this introduction. The first comes from Clark (1991), who differentiates between 'project replication', 'building grassroots movements', and 'influencing policy reform' These distinctions are echoed by Howes and Sattar (in this volume), who separate organisational or programme growth (the 'additive' strategy) from achieving impact via transfers to, or catalysing other organisations (the 'muliplicative' strategy). Mitlin and Satterthwaite (also in this volume) comment that successful NGOs concentrate on 'pulling in' resources rather than expanding the scale of their own service provision, while Robert Myers (1992:379) makes the opposing case, defining scaling-up as 'reaching as many people as possible with services or programmes.' This is a limiting definition, but Myers goes on to make a useful distinction between 'expansion, explosion and association'. 'Explosive' strategies begin with NGO operations on a large scale and adapt programmes to local circumstances afterwards. In contrast, 'associational' strategies 'achieve scale by piecing together coverage obtained in several district (and not necessarily coordinated) projects and programmes, each responding to the needs of a distinct part of the total population served' (Myers 1992, p.380). In Myers's model the most obvious form of scaling-up is direct programme expansion. Robert Chambers (this volume) adds a further important dimension to the debate by highlighting what he calls 'self-spreading and self-improving strategies' – 'to develop, spread and improve new approaches and methods', gradually extending good practice through NGO and government bureacuracies until their entire approach is transformed, and rejuvenating the NGO sector by stimulating the formation of new, independent NGOs.

From all this, and on the basis of the experience recounted in the chapters that follow, it seems to us that the most important distinction to be made lies between *additive* strategies, which imply an increase in the size of the programme or organisation; *multiplicative* strategies, which do not imply growth but achieve impact through deliberate influence, networking, policy and legal reform, or training; and *diffusive* strategies, where spread is informal and spontaneous. These distinctions are important because each group of strategies has different costs and benefits, strengths and weaknesses, and implications for the NGO concerned. Different strategies may be more, or less, effective according to circumstance, and it may not be possible to combine elements of each one in the same organisation. We make some preliminary observations about these trade-offs in the conclusion to this volume. The value of a strong conceptual framework is that it can clarify the strategic choices available to different NGOs and help them to make the decisions appropriate for the specific realities they face.

For the sake of clarity, we have divided this introduction and the rest of the book into four sections, each representing a particular approach to scaling-up. Three of these approaches fall into the 'multiplicative' and 'diffusive' categories: working with government, linking the grassroots with lobbying and advocacy, and advocacy in the North. The fourth strategy – increasing impact by organisational growth – falls under the 'additive' approach. These categories are not intended to be wholly self-contained, and indeed as the chapters illustrate there is a good deal of overlap between them. In particular, when this volume was edited, we found that several examples combined support for local-level initiative with lobbying at the national level (see the chapters by Constantino-David, Dawson, Hall, and Mitlin and

Satterthwaite) so that Section IV covers both of these approaches and looks at their linkages. Nonetheless, a structure is needed to order the debate and to ensure a degree of clarity in the discussion.

Working with government

Traditionally, most NGOs have been suspicious of governments, their relationships varying between benign neglect and outright hostility. Governments often share a similarly suspicious view of NGOs, national and international, and their relationship, at least in Africa, has been likened to cat and mouse (Bratton 1990). It is not hard to see why this should be the case. Government structures are often rigid, hierarchical and autocratic. Power and control rest at the topmost level where programmes are designed and resources allocated. All governments are encumbered with authoritarian relationships with their citizens, for they are collectors of taxes, enforcers of the peace, and protectors of the social order (Copestake 1990). They have a natural tendency to centralisation, bureaucracy and control. NGOs, on the other hand, are (or should be?) distinguished by their flexibility, willingness to innovate, and emphasis on the non-hierarchical values and relationships required to promote true partnership and participation.

Nonetheless, there are sound reasons for NGOs to enter into a positive and creative relationship with the institutions of both state and government. Governments remain largely responsible for providing the health, education, agricultural and other services on which people rely, though this is changing under the impact of the 'new conditionality' and its attempts to expand the role of the private sector at governments' expense. The state remains the ultimate arbiter and determinant of the wider political changes on which sustainable development depends. Some would argue that *only* governments can do these things effectively and equitably – that any attempt, for example, to privatise services is bound to result in declining access to quality care for the poor. Whether or not this is true, it remains a fact that (in most countries) government controls the wider frameworks within which people and their organisations have to operate. While this remains true, NGOs ignore government structures at their peril. An increasing number of NGOs have acknowledged this and are working actively to foster change at various levels. International NGOs tend to restrict themselves to the institutions of government, working within ministries to promote changes in policy and practice. National NGOs, on the other hand, can take a more active role in the political process and the wider institutions of the state. Usually, this takes the form of subjecting these institutions to various forms of external pressure and protest, as in the case of social action groups in India lobbying the local Forest Department or Block Development Officer (a strategy covered under 'linking the grassroots with lobbying and advocacy' below).

A more direct approach is to work *within* the structures of government in an explicit attempt to foster more appropriate and effective policies and practices, which will eventually be of benefit to poorer and less powerful people as they filter through into action by civil servants 'lower down' the system. The aim here is to ensure that governments adopt policies which are genuinely developmental at national level – policies which will ultimately enable poor people to achieve greater control over their lives in health, education, production and so on. NGOs have attempted to do this via direct funding, high-level policy advice, 'technical assistance', the provision of 'volunteer' workers, or (usually) a mixture of these things. Many NGOs provide government with a 'package' of inputs which includes material support as well as people and ideas. It is important to remember that these strategies are *not* an attempt to 'replace' the state, but rather to *influence* the direction of government policy or support existing policies. 'NGOs cannot seek to replace the state, for they have no legitimacy, authority or sovereignty, and, crucially, are self-selected and thus not accountable' (Palmer and Rossiter 1990).

Although the case studies in this section of the book cover a wide range of approaches and contexts, their conclusions are strikingly similar. First, when the decision is taken to work within government, the constraints and difficulties of the government system have to be accepted as a starting point. Unlike in NGO programmes, good staff cannot be handpicked and supported with high salaries or generous benefits; systems and structures cannot be changed at will and resources are always in short supply. Motivation is often lacking because salaries are low and conditions poor. Public services are suspicious of change and often officers at lower levels in the hierarchy have been actively discouraged to experiment, innovate or take initiative. Inevitably, progress, if it is achieved, will be slow, and agencies must commit themselves to partnership for long periods of time. The chances of succeeding in this approach are increased if NGOs agree to work within the government system, right from the start. This increases the likelihood of sustainable reforms and enables the NGO to understand and deal with the constraints faced by the official system.

Second, personalities and relationships between individuals are a vital element in successful government–NGO partnerships. If these relationships do not exist, no amount of money or advice will make a difference. In addition, conflicting interests and agendas within government ministries may make dialogue and consensus impossible, undermining the efficacy of even the strongest NGO inputs. The whole notion of 'counterpart training' needs to be closely examined to ensure that NGO expatriate inputs really do have a lasting impact when faced with such a range of constraints. Even when good relationships do exist, this is no guarantee of success. This is partly because individuals are moved around the government system with alarming regularity (making influence through individual training and advice difficult to achieve), and partly because there is often a barrier between the 'pilot project' stage of co-operation (which is heavily dependent on a small number of likeminded officials) and the acceptance and diffusion of new approaches throughout the government hierarchy. The case of special education in Bangkok related in this volume by Ireland and Klinmahorm provides a graphic illustration of this problem. VSO has also had some success in making this transition by using what Mackie (in this volume) calls 'the planned multiplication of micro-level inputs' – the slow and careful evolution of different forms of support which are small in themselves but significant in the aggregate. Such approaches appear most likely to make an impact in smaller countries where NGOs have better access to key decision-makers. John Parry-Williams's account (in this volume) of legal reform in Uganda provides just such a case.

Third, NGOs are generally 'small players' when it comes to influencing governments, as compared to bilateral and multilateral donors such as the World Bank. It is these much larger agencies that tend to determine the ideological context in which policies are formed, a classic case in point being the 'new conditionality' of good governance and free markets which NGOs have thus far largely failed to influence (Edwards 1991). In addition, in a situation where donor funds abound and government needs are acute, NGOs which insist on detailed assessment of programmes and on long-term, low-input strategies may be labelled as 'unhelpful' and 'obstructive', a case in point being SCF's work at provincial level in Mozambique (Johnson 1992). There are many official donors (and NGOs?) who are willing to commit large-scale resources for immediate consumption or ill-thought-out interventions, with little acknowledgement of the longer-term implications of their actions. The impossible recurrent cost burdens imposed by vertical programmes in basic services are a good example of this problem.[1]

Certainly, greater success may be achieved if NGOs allow governments to take credit for progress in programme and policy development, regardless of their own influence in these areas (for an example of reforms in Primary Health Care in Indonesia see Morley et al 1983, p.13). Something similar may be happening in the much-vaunted District Development Programme supported by Britain's Overseas Development Administration (ODA) in Zambia (Goldman et al 1988). There is also evidence that concentration at central ministry level, and coalitions of NGOs reinforcing each-other's influence, can help to combat the impact of the larger donors (Edwards, 1989).

The relative influence of NGOs and official agencies on Southern governments is a useful reminder that this strategy needs to be approached with care. The decision to work with (but not for) government must be based on an assessment of the 'reformability' of the structures under consideration, the relationship between government and its citizens, the level at which influence can be exerted most effectively, and (for international NGOs), the strength of the local voluntary sector. NGOs must also calculate the costs and benefits of this strategy in relation to others. For example, it may be difficult to operate simultaneously as a conduit for government and an agent of social mobilisation, or to work both within government and as an advocate for fundamental change in social and political structures. There are also dangers in identifying too closely with governments, which may be overthrown or voted out (as in the case of well-known health activists in Bangladesh). Nonetheless, even under the most authoritarian governments there are often opportunities for progressive change. For example, the Ministry of Health in Pinochet's Chile developed a strong policy on breastmilk substitutes with help from NGOs. The example quoted by Clark (in this volume) of an OXFAM programme which worked alongside rigid government structures in Malawi is also instructive. There are certainly enough examples of NGO impact on government policy and practice to give hope for the future, so long as the conditions for influence are right.

The direct approach: increasing impact by organisational growth

For many NGOs the obvious strategy for increasing impact is to expand projects or programmes that are judged to be successful. Over the 1980s this approach has been pursued in the South, where it has led to the evolution of a set of big NGOs in Asia (see the chapters by Howes and Sattar and by Kiriwandeniya in this volume for discussions of two such cases), and in the North where many NGOs have dramatically expanded their operational budgets and staffing. Expansion can take

---

[1] SCF is currently carrying out a major research programme on the 'Sustainability of Health-Sector Development' to address these issues. Contact Anne LaFond at SCF for details.

several forms. It may be *geographical* (moving into new areas or countries); by *horizontal function* (adding additional sectoral activities to existing programmes, eg adding a housing component to an income-generating programme); by *vertical function* (adding 'upstream' or 'downstream' activities to existing programmes, eg adding an agricultural processing project to an agricultural production scheme); or, by a combination of these forms.

Apart from the strong common-sense appeal there is a logic in supporting direct operational expansion. At its foundation is the argument that any agency capable of alleviating poverty has a moral obligation to help as many poor people as it can. Added to this are the claims that, in a resource-scarce situation, NGOs can use existing resources more efficiently than other agencies (but, Robinson, in this volume, disputes this claim) and can mobilise additional resources. Successful past experience means that NGOs have already 'learned' what to do, so that they can tackle development problems with comparatively short 'start-up' times. For the NGO itself large-scale operational successes enhance credibility for other scaling-up strategies (eg lobbying domestic governments or international agencies is more effective for organisations that demonstrate a considerable operational capacity in the field). Finally, one can draw upon institutional theories arguing that organisational pluralism in service delivery creates choice and efficiency that makes poverty-alleviation more probable (Leonard 1982).

Those who espouse the direct expansion approach recognise that difficulties will be encountered, particularly in terms of how to manage organisational change (see the chapters by Hodson and by Billis and MacKeith for a detailed discussion of issues). The characteristics that are presumed to explain NGOs' comparative advantage in local-level poverty-alleviation – the quality of relationships with beneficiaries, their flexible and experimental stance and their small size (Fowler 1988; Tendler 1987) – all require modification or compromise as expansion occurs. If we conceptualise the internal features of an organisation in terms of its systems or procedures, its structure and its culture (values and norms), then we can identify the nature of these problems. Commonly, expanding NGOs assume that the systems or procedures developed in a locally 'successful' project or programme can be used on a wider scale, providing that internal structures are suitably modified. These modifications usually require: *i* the extension of the hierarchy that separates those who manage the organisation from those who manage field operations; *ii* increased functional specialisation between parts of the organisation, and; *iii* increased capacity to raise resources, both material and human. The need to raise significant additional finance almost invariably requires 'Southern' (and often 'Northern') NGOs to take grants from official aid agencies. This fosters upward accountability and may lead to NGOs being increasingly '... driven by the procedures ...' (Fowler 1991).

The impact of these changes on organisational culture can be dramatic, as Billis and MacKeith (in this volume) demonstrate. There is a shift from a task-orientation to a role-orientation; control from 'higher up' the hierarchy grows in significance; and professionalism subordinates commitment and 'mission'-related values. As Dichter (1989:2) warns, many NGOs encounter severe problems as they expand because they retain '... cultural predispositions to non-hierarchical structures and are often anti-management'. The NGOs that seem best able to avoid partial paralysis during such transitions are those directed by charismatic, and often autocratic, founder-leaders.

As expansion occurs, these changes in culture, structure and accountability may accumulate to change the organisation from a voluntary organisation (based upon the pursuit of a developmental mission) trying to shape events, to a public service contractor oriented towards servicing needs as defined by donors and national governments. Korten (1990) has provided examples of NGOs foundering with expansion and, in particular, has charted the evolution of the International Planned Parenthood Foundation (IPPF) from a path-breaking crusader on a forbidden topic to '... an expensive and lethargic international bureaucracy ...' (ibid:126).

For observers who adopt a more explicitly political form of analysis then the co-optation of expansionist NGOs by the status quo (both domestic and international) is not simply the result of changes in organisational characteristics. Rather, it is an outcome that is consciously sought by those who hold power as they respond to the growing popularity of NGOs. At the level of local and national power structures it can be argued that a strategy of service delivery expansion permits the alleviation of the symptoms of poverty without challenging the causes. From this radical perspective, NGOs are seen as eroding the power of progressive political formations by preaching change without a clear analysis of how that change is to be achieved; by encouraging income-generating projects that favour the advancement of a few poor individuals but not 'the poor' as a class; and by competing with political groups for personal and popular action.

A focus on international relations yields a different but equally distressing scenario. NGO expansion is seen as complementing the counter-revolution in development theory (Toye 1987) that underpins the policies of liberalisation, state withdrawal and structural adjustment favoured by official donors. NGOs are viewed as the 'private non-profit' sector, the performance of which advances the 'public-bad, private-good' ideology of the new orthodoxy.

It is no surprise to such radical commentators that strategies of operational expansion emasculate NGO attempts to serve as catalysts and advocates for the poor and lead to a focus on delivering health care, credit, family planning and housing while issues such as land reform, access to public services, civic and human rights, the judicial system and economic exploitation lose significance.

Given the strength of these counter-arguments in some contexts, the strategic decision to scale-up by additive mechanisms should never be seen as incontestable 'common sense'. At the very least, NGOs that are considering operational expansion need to plan for the stresses of organisational restructuring and cultural change; examine how dependent they will become financially on official donors and consider the consequences of this for accountability; study the trade-offs and complementarities with other strategies for enhancing impact; and analyse the implications of such a choice for the poor majority who are not beneficiaries of their projects or programmes.

Advocacy in the North

Rather than working directly *within* the structures they intend to influence, NGOs may choose to increase their impact by lobbying government and other structures from the outside. This is a time-honoured activity for NGOs around the world, particularly for Northern NGOs, some of whom focus exclusively on advocacy and have no 'practice base' overseas. The rationale for this approach is simple: many of the causes of under-development lie in the political and economic structures of an unequal world – in trade, commodity prices, debt and macro-economic policy; in the distribution of land and other productive assets among different social groups; and in the misguided policies of governments and the multilateral institutions (such as the World Bank and IMF) which they control. It is extremely difficult, if not impossible, to address these issues in the context of the traditional NGO project. Other forms of action are necessary, particularly on the international level where the biggest decisions are made.

However, success at this level has proved elusive. There are, for sure, some signs of impact, and Clark (in this volume) provides examples such as the international baby milk campaign, increasing environmental awareness, and better systems for food aid, to illustrate how effective and sophisticated NGO advocacy has become. One commentator goes so far as to claim that 'non-governmental groups managed by half a dozen professionals have shown that they can change the course of decision-making about a country they may never have seen' (Jha 1989). Northern NGOs have made some progress on the debt issue (playing a major part in lobbying for successive improvements in the terms on offer for debt-relief); on 'structural adjustment' (though here the influence of another multilateral agency – UNICEF – was more important than that of the NGOs); on international refugee issues (with NGO consortia persuading international agencies to adopt improved food regimes for refugees); and in primary health care (Save the Children Fund-UK in particular being a constant thorn in the flesh of UNICEF and WHO on the issue of sustainability in health-sector development).

NGO strategies in this field range from direct lobbying of key individuals within bilateral and multilateral agencies, through staff exchanges and working together in the field, to publications, conferences and participation in joint committees (such as the World Bank–NGO Committee). One of the most controversial issues here is the choice all NGOs must make between 'constructive dialogue' (the incrementalist or reformist approach) and 'shouting from the sidelines' (the abolitionist approach). Opinion differs widely among NGOs as to the usefulness of these opposing approaches, the choice resting on the degree to which the NGO concerned feels its 'target agency' is reformable over time. This debate has been fuelled by the increasing profile given to NGOs by neo-liberal thinking on 'governance and democratisation'. Most NGOs see their relationship with bilateral and multilateral agencies as a dialogue on policy, but the donors themselves are increasingly enthusiastic about NGOs as *implementers* of projects. This is true of both Northern and Southern NGOs, and indeed, some NGOs are perfectly happy with this trend. It gives them vastly-increased resources and enables them to 'scale-up' their work directly as never before (see Part III of this volume, on organisational growth). The international NGO community is deeply divided over this issue. 'NGOs have generally been used for the ends of the borrowing governments or the [World] Bank, and not as partner institutions with their own unique development purposes' (Salmen and Eaves 1989). The same internal World Bank report states that only 11 per cent of NGOs with whom the Bank co-operated in 1988-89 were used in the design phase of projects (Salmen and Eaves 1989). If this remains the case it is difficult to see how NGOs will be able to take advantage of the wider windows for international advocacy which Clark claims are opening up to them in the wake of the 'new conditionality', environmentalism, the end of the Cold War, and the increasing scale of NGO operations (Clark, this volume).

It is probably true to say that, while NGOs have succeeded in influencing official donor agencies on individual projects (such as the Narmada Dam in India and the Polnoreste Project in Brazil), and even on some programme themes (such as participation and the environment), they have failed to bring about more fundamental changes in attitudes and ideology, on which all else depends. Nagle and Ghose (1990) make the telling comment that, while operational guidelines on participation in project design will be useful to World Bank staff, many do not actually see the connection between 'participation' and 'development' that NGOs take as axiomatic. They do not, in other words, see *why* people should be placed at the centre of the planning process. Clark's optimistic assessment of the future of NGO advocacy in this volume needs to be tempered by an acknowledgement of the limited gains made thus far. Lobbying, alongside the other strategies examined in this book, has to be carefully planned and evaluated to establish what really works, and why. The importance of advocacy cannot simply be taken for granted. It is worth reminding ourselves that decades of NGO lobbying have not dented the structure of the world economy and the ideology of its ruling institutions, nor has it brought about the alternative vision of development that most NGOs ascribe to, albeit poorly articulated in practical terms. Indeed, one of the criticisms often made to NGOs by official donor agencies is that insufficient work has gone into developing workable alternatives to the policies NGOs oppose: alternatives which will guarantee rising living standards without the social and environmental costs imposed by current systems.

NGO contact with the wider structures they seek to influence is often too limited to effect any real change. By definition, NGOs are peripheral to the systems they are trying to change, and lack the leverage necessary to maintain their influence when there are other, more powerful interests at work (World Bank 1991). Although NGO lobbying networks do exist (organised, for example, around debt and environmental issues), they have yet to make a concerted effort to work together on a common agenda, a weakness highlighted by Chris Dolan in his contribution to this volume. In contrast to Clark, Dolan is sceptical of the future of NGO lobbying, arguing that, at least in the United Kingdom, development NGOs lack the shared vision and commitment to working together on a joint agenda which might make success more likely. They also have to deal with a more restrictive legal framework which makes 'political activities' a sensitive area.

In addition, the sheer size and complexity of international institutions is often overwhelming, even to large NGOs such as OXFAM and Save the Children Fund. Many NGOs do not understand the way in which multilateral agencies operate, though the specialist advocacy groups have developed a good knowledge of their targets. Even if the agency's structure and procedures are known, these organisations remain hierarchical, technocratic and often unwilling to listen. Multilateral and bilateral donors have been keen to set up internal 'NGO liaison units' in recent years, but it remains to be seen whether these are to facilitate communication or merely keep NGOs away from the departments that take significant decisions. The fundamental requirement for successful influencing is a degree of openness on the part of the organisation that is being lobbied; if this is not present, no amount of information or experience-sharing will induce changes in the system.

Many NGOs maintain that a practice base overseas is essential for successful influencing. There are organisations (such as the World Development Movement) in the UK which have no involvement in development practice, but they are not registered as charities; there are also charities outside the UK (such as Bread for the World in the USA) which are purely advocacy-based. For the majority of British development charities, however, there is no escaping the linkage between practical experience and influencing, for it is their practice base which generates the themes and the evidence (and therefore the legitimacy) for their related, but subsidiary, information and educational work. In his presentation to the Manchester workshop on scaling-up, Ahmed Sa'di of the Galilee Society for Health Research and Services made a powerful plea that NGOs put much more effort into research and information work based on grassroots views and experiences, in order to counter the 'knowledge produced by the official institutions which reflects the interests of the powerful' (Sa'di 1992). John Clark (in this volume) takes this one step further by admonishing NGOs for their failure to capitalise on their knowledge of grassroots realities in their dialogue with governments and donor agencies. As the role of Northern NGOs changes in response to the growing strength and range of Southern development institutions, they will have to develop new attitudes, skills and partnerships as they move from 'operational' work overseas to international advocacy in support of local NGO efforts – from 'projects' to 'information', as Clark puts it. How many NGOs recognise the need for such a transition, let alone being equipped to manage it successfully?

A consistent theme in the chapters that follow is the need for much stronger links between development efforts at micro-level, and NGO advocacy at meso- and macro-levels. Only when these activities are mutually supportive can lasting change occur. For example, the success of the Voluntary Health Association of India in influencing government policy comes only partly from its sophisticated use of the Indian media and parliamentary process, but also because it maintains very strong links with thousands of voluntary health workers and organisations around the country. In this way, advocacy is anchored in real experience and the messages transmitted to government have a power and legitimacy which is difficult to ignore. NGO agendas for advocacy must grow out of grassroots experience if they are to claim to 'speak for the poor.' Similar themes are raised in this volume by Dawson and Hall, who show how progress in particular cases was achieved in Peru and Brazil respectively through a combination of pressure 'from above' (national and international advocacy) and 'from below' (strengthening grassroots organisation and concrete initiatives), acting towards the same goal. In this analysis, development at local level and advocacy at other levels form complementary components of the same overall strategy. The key question (to which we return in our Conclusion) then becomes how to strengthen these complementarities so that action at each level informs and supports the other. Few agencies have achieved this, either in their own work or in the partnerships they have formed with other organisations working for the same objectives.

If it is true that advocacy will become a more important strategy for NGOs in the future, then legitimising this activity in the eyes of governments, official donor agencies and the general public (whose financial and moral support is vital) is going to be a vital task in the years ahead. Development education among the countries of the rich North will play a key role in generating widespread support for changing NGO roles, just as official donors will have to see NGOs as valuable, independent actors with something different and positive to offer. Unless this happens it is difficult to see how the NGO voice will be heard, let alone acted on, fatally undermining the credibility of this approach to achieving greater impact.

Linking the grassroots with lobbying and advocacy

Grassroots organisations (GROs) or community-based organisations (CBOs) that are managed by members on behalf of members, have been central to the activities of many NGOs. Such organisations can originate spontaneously from local initiative but '... while isolated instances of local institutional development can be impressive their cumulative effect is negligible ... what counts are systems of networks of organisations, both vertically and horizontally' (Uphoff 1986:213). As a consequence of this many Southern and Northern NGOs have recognised and adopted an intermediary role to accelerate the creation of local organisations (sometimes referred to as catalysis), to provide assistance in strengthening and expanding such organisations, and fostering linkages between them. This, it is believed, will lead to the proliferation of grassroots organisations that can, as a 'people's movement', have a beneficial impact on development policies and wider political processes.

The main emphasis for NGOs involved in such efforts is usually held to be the 'process' involved in supporting local initiative – awareness raising, conscientisation, group formation, leadership, training in management skills – rather than the 'content' of the programmes and activities which local organisations pursue. This is because such a strategy seeks the 'empowerment' of people – a much used and abused term that we take to mean the process of assisting disadvantaged individuals and groups to gain greater control than they presently have over local and national decision-making and resources, and of their ability and right to define collective goals, make decisions and learn from experience. While in its pure form such an approach would mean that NGOs should not influence GRO activities, many intermediaries mix catalysis with their other programmes and provide members with loans and services. Mitlin and Satterthwaite (in this volume) present a number of examples of such mixes. The relative weightings in such mixes – ie whether catalysis or service delivery is paramount – are usually very difficult to determine.

Many different ideas underpin strategies of grassroots organisation but all have in common the notions that disadvantaged individuals need to be stimulated into taking group action, that groups of the disadvantaged can have a discernible impact on the local situation, and that the combined efforts of grassroots organisations can coalesce into movements that have the potential to influence policies and politics at the national level. The conceptual bases for these ideas range from liberal-democratic notions of pluralism (for example Esman and Uphoff 1984) to radical formulations that see grassroots organisations as confronting (sometimes violently) oppressive social forces. Paulo Freire's ideas have been particularly influential on those agencies adopting the radical perspective, arguing the need to 'conscientise' the poor as an initial step in the process of identifying and ultimately challenging the social and political structures that oppress them.

Differences in the conceptual roots which intermediary NGOs recognise, along with local contextual factors, mean that approaches to supporting local level initiative vary considerably. Amongst agencies that seek to serve as catalysts for group formation there is a vast analytical gulf between those who believe that membership should be open to all in a 'community' (ie inclusive) and those who opt for exclusive organisational forms in which membership is open only to the disadvantaged. Depending on the ideas that guide an approach, the work of the promoter (facilitator, change agent, catalyst) may initially focus on the advantages of group action and the management of group activities or alternatively, concentrate upon an analysis of the social and political causes of poverty in a locality and the need for groups to see themselves as political actors. Group formation is usually recognised as a slow process (at least in public statements if not in practice) and one in which non-governmental intermediaries have a significant comparative advantage over state intermediaries, because of the quality of their non-directive, 'participatory' interaction with intended beneficiaries.

While a vast number of GROs can be seen as having the potential to achieve locally beneficial results, intermediary organisations are usually keen to create linkages between GROs (see Chris Roche's chapter on ACORD). In part this is to promote more effective local action (through exchanges of knowledge and access to pooled and external resources). Even more significantly, however, such linkages are seen as making it possible to take actions that are beyond the capacity of local associations. Karina Constantino-David (in this volume) examines the highly sophisticated networking and federating of NGOs that has occurred in the Philippines in an attempt to challenge national policies and establish new institutions. Linkages may be horizontal (ie networking between GROs so that they can exchange information and negotiate collective action) or vertical (ie federating GROs into a regional or national level organisational structure, in the direction of which all member organisations have a say and a vote).

From the foregoing arguments a strong case can be made for supporting and linking grassroots organisations: they 'empower', relate knowledge with action, are sensitive to local contexts, flexible and, when collectivities take collective action, can tackle regional and national level issues. In addition, and in contrast to other NGO activities, this approach may permit a degree of downward accountability so that NGOs which claim to represent the 'voice of the poor' may add some legitimacy to the image they seek to portray.

There is, however, a potential 'downside'. From a programme management perspective, there are difficulties in maintaining the interests of poor people in conscientisation, mobilisation and empowerment when they have pressing short-term needs. Hence, many intermediary NGOs incorporate a 'service' element, such as savings and credit schemes, in their approaches. The case study of BRAC (Howes and Sattar in this volume) provides an illustration. This helps to maintain member interest, but it can also be seen as contradicting the logic of empowerment and group autonomy. In some cases it leads to the beneficiaries of NGO mobilisation strategies reporting to independent researchers that they are recipients of service delivery programmes (Hashemi, forthcoming). There is also the practical problem of 'who' does the catalysis. Few NGOs have been able to tap into volunteers on a significant scale, and so they rely on paid staff. This places them in a position, not dissimilar to government mobilisation efforts, of having to maintain the commitment of change agents for whom mobilisation is a means to a livelihood.

From a political perspective a number of objections can be raised. For some, the assumptions of pluralism that underpin liberal configurations of mobilisation are misplaced. Genuine empowerment will generate responses from local and national elites, and the state, that range from intimidation to violence (as in the case of Thailand in the mid-1970s when more than 20 organisers of agricultural labourers' associations were murdered). There is thus an ethical dilemma for NGOs, about exposing staff and intended beneficiaries to violence, and a practical dilemma as to whether entrenched local and national elites need to be confronted more radically.

For those who adopt a radical view (for Bangladesh this position is examined in Wood and Palmer-Jones 1991:220–4) then NGO mobilisations are seen as supporting the status quo. They are 'diversionary' in that they take resources (finance, leadership, popular action) away from political parties and underground movements dedicated to fundamental political change, and they create false impressions of pluralism and change.

Have the results of mobilising strategies been as negative as the radical critics suggest? Much depends on the cases and regions one examines. In terms of the 'narrow' goal of providing tangible benefits to members, then Uphoff (1986:208) provides considerable evidence of success in South and South-East Asia. In terms of broader political change, claims have been made that networks of local organisations significantly helped the push for democracy in the Philippines (the fall of Marcos) and Bangladesh (the fall of Ershad). However, these have only been weakly substantiated. In Latin America, the evidence of local organisations working together to promote political change is clearer (Hirschmann 1984) in no small part because such organisations saw the local and national political arena as a major focus for their actions. Tony Hall's study of Itaparica (in this volume) provides a clear example of the way in which well-supported local initiative has influenced national and multilateral development policies in Latin America. Elsa Dawson's chapter illustrates the complementarities that can be found between strengthening local level organisations and advocating policy reform. The involvement of groupings of grassroots organisations in African development would appear, from the literature available, to be much more limited than in Asia or Latin America. The reasons for this are complex (Fowler 1991) but clearly a major factor in many countries has been the desire and ability of the state to control or eliminate any non-official mobilisation of the populace. Clearly contextual factors are of great significance in determining the feasibility and results of such approaches.

Commentators on the future role that NGOs should play in development are presently highlighting strategies for catalysing and federating local-level organisations. Clark (1991:102–19) sees such movements as reshaping national politics, redefining and ultimately 'democratising development'. Hirschmann (1984) sees 'collective action' as the means by which the economic and political well-being of the masses is most likely to be attained in Latin America. For Korten (1990:127) the key to future effectiveness is '. . . to coalesce and energise self-managing networks over which it [the NGO] has no control whatever' and '. . . involve themselves in the broader movement of which they are a part as social and political activist'. Developmental NGOs will not only forge linkages between grassroots organisations, but they will also forge linkages with other movements that have related missions – peace, environment, women, human rights and consumer affairs. In this grand vision NGOs become a force for dramatic social change that restructures class relationships and reforms global economic processes by non-violent, non-revolutionary means.

Organisation of the book

This introductory chapter is followed by two further background chapters. Mark Robinson's chapter presents a summary of the Overseas Development Institute's research on NGO effectiveness and reviews the implications for scaling-up. It finds that NGOs are effective in reaching the poor, but not the poorest, and that their unit costs are broadly comparable with those of the public sector. The chapter by Robert Chambers makes the case for diffusive strategies to enhance NGO impact.

The book is then divided into four sections, following the framework outlined in this chapter. The section on 'working with government' includes three case studies of specific projects (Klinmahorm and Ireland, Jones and Parry-Williams), a study of Voluntary Service Overseas (Mackie) and a summary of a large-scale research project into NGO-government interaction in agricultural technology development, drawing on cases from Africa, Asia and Latin America (Bebbington and Farrington).

Part III examines the strategy of scaling-up by organisational growth or operational expansion. Two of these chapters describe and analyse the growth of individual South Asian NGOs (Kiriwandeniya and Howes and Sattar). Although the Sri Lanka case study is based on a multiplicative strategy it is included in this section because it illustrates problems that arise when growth is achieved by using official finance. The two other chapters examine the management problems encountered by expanding NGOs with particular reference to northern agencies (Hodson, and Billis and MacKeith).

The next section focuses on 'strengthening the grassroots' and linking grassroots action with lobbying and advocacy, with case studies from Peru (Dawson) and Brazil (Hall), a review of initiatives in the urban sector (Mitlin and Satterthwaite), a description and analysis of NGO networking in the Philippines (Constantino-David) and a detailed examination of ACORD's experiences in supporting local level initiative in Africa (Roche). Several of these papers illustrate the advantages of linking local-level institutional strengthening with national-level policy advocacy.

Part V is comprised of two papers that focus on lobbying and advocacy in the North. Clark reflects on the lessons of experience gained from many years of advocacy work targeted at bilateral and multilateral development agencies by OXFAM, while Dolan draws pessimistic conclusions about the likelihood of British NGOs achieving the 'shared vision' and resource commitment that would permit them to make their lobbying more effective.

In the concluding chapter we summarise the lessons that can be generated from the materials that have been presented and identify the key issues that form a basis for future action and research on enhancing the developmental impact of NGOs.

NGOs and rural poverty alleviation: implications for scaling-up

Mark Robinson

Introduction

It is commonly believed that NGOs possess a number of characteristics which give them a comparative advantage over governments and official donors in implementing projects and programmes which aim to alleviate poverty. At the same time, it is recognised that NGO activities are generally small-scale and that they reach a relatively limited number of people. It is on the basis of a series of assumptions concerning the ability of NGOs to reach and benefit the poor through low-cost and effective interventions that arguments are made in favour of the need to 'scale-up' their impact in order to benefit larger numbers of the poor (Edwards and Hulme 1992).

Yet the evidence to support the view that NGOs possess a comparative advantage over government is weak and patchy. Most NGO practitioners can point to successful projects that have made a tremendous difference to the lives of the poor, but there is little systematic evidence which documents the strengths and weaknesses of NGOs and the reasons for their success and failure in different types of projects and environments. Variations in NGO performance will determine the extent to which scaling-up a particular type of intervention is both feasible and desirable since there is clearly little point in NGOs seeking to build larger structures on weak foundations.

These considerations formed the background to a recently-completed research project which set out to systematically evaluate NGO impact and effectiveness in rural poverty alleviation across countries and projects (Riddell and Robinson forthcoming). The study focused on a narrow range of projects which aimed at a sustained improvement in the economic status of the poor by raising incomes and creating new opportunities for employment, which in turn have the potential to bring about increased consumption, savings and investment.

This chapter presents the results of 16 detailed NGO project evaluations undertaken by the Overseas Development Institute (ODI), and discusses their implications for scaling-up NGO interventions. It begins by sketching the background to the study and provides brief descriptions of each of the projects. The chapter then analyses the results of the case study evaluations, listing both their achievements and limitations in alleviating poverty, and highlights the reasons for their success or failure. The final section examines the attempts of several of the NGOs to scale-up their impact and effectiveness, and concludes by identifying elements in their approach and organisation which require specific attention if these strategic objectives are to be realised in practice.

Background to the study

Sixteen projects in Bangladesh, India, Uganda and Zimbabwe which had an economic component were investigated. All were located in rural areas and centred on credit income generation, skills training and technical assistance, projects focused on social services and relief were excluded, even though such projects can mitigate some of the most pernicious effects of poverty. An attempt was made to strike a balance between projects which sought to promote off-farm employment and those with a focus on small-scale agriculture. Each of the projects selected also contained broader social objectives in seeking to increase participation, improve self-reliance or enhance social mobility. Two further considerations underlying the choice of projects were size (micro-interventions and very large projects were excluded) and the length of time that the project had been running.[1]

Four projects were selected in each country to reflect a range of organisational types, differing approaches to poverty alleviation, and different socio-economic and physical environments. The projects were representative of the broad range of ventures in this sector of activity, even if they did not represent an unbiased and randomly selected sample. The intention of the research was not to generalise about NGOs across the board, but rather to assess whether a small group of narrowly-defined projects had been successful in achieving their objectives. It also aimed to generate insights into the reasons for success and failure of specific types of intervention and to identify factors associated with project success.

In Bangladesh, the four projects selected were the Action Aid Development Centres (savings and credit) Programme which focused on off-farm income-generation; the horticulture and agriculture programme of the Gono Kallyan Trust (GKT); the fisheries programme of Gono Unnayan Prochesta (GUP) which helps the landless to develop disused ponds for fish cultivation; and the Caritas social forestry programme where the aim is to motivate the poor to grow more trees on their homesteads and public land (White 1991). The projects in south India were the Community Organisation Programme of Rural Development Trust (RDT) based on a revolving agricultural credit scheme; the CASA Phase III programme which is concerned with accessing subsidised bank credit for off-farm income generation; the Arthik Samata Mandal agricultural development programmes whose main thrust is on crop loans, grants for small-scale irrigation and land improvement schemes; and the Kanyakumari District Fishermen Sangams Federation (KDFSF) which aims at improving the marketing of fish caught by its members (Robinson 1991a). Similarities between the projects in both India and Bangladesh included a focus on group formation, an emphasis on the poor (especially the landless and women), and the provision of credit.

The four projects in Uganda were the Uganda Women's Finance and Credit Trust (UWFCT), which provides credit for employment and income generation to rural women; an engineering workshop under the West Acholi Co-operative Union, producing agricultural equipment for local farmers; the health component of the Multi-Sectoral Rural Development Programme which has attempted to fund its

---

[1] Eight projects had been in operation for ten or more years, five were less than five years old, and one had started less than two years prior to the evaluation. One project had ended more than five years previously while in another, particular areas or groups no longer received direct support.

activities through user fees and income-generating projects; and the technical skills training unit of the ActionAid Mityana rural development programme (De Coninck 1992).

In Zimbabwe, the four case study projects focused on rural enterprise and group work, but adopted very different approaches. The Catholic Church's Silveira House is one of the oldest NGOs in the country, and pioneered group approaches to credit for communal farmers in the pre-independence period; the Mzarabani farmer credit project provides an example of an NGO attempting to move away from a primary focus on relief to promoting development; the Campfire project represents an innovative approach to sustainable wildlife resource management; finally, the Simukai collective cooperative focuses on joint productive enterprises (Muir, 1992).

The approach developed for evaluating the impact and effectiveness of NGO projects in alleviating poverty was both participatory and in-depth. A methodological framework provided a common point of reference for the detailed in-country investigations (Riddell 1990). This was premised on a series of key questions concerning the extent to which objectives had been realised, the impact of the project on the economic status of the poor, the distributional effects on different groups of the poor, the contribution of factors external to the project, cost-effectiveness, its likely sustainability and potential for replication. Indicators to assess the impact of the project were provided by the beneficiaries, who used a range of economic and social criteria to gauge the changes that had taken place in their lives over the duration of the project. These indicators, together with the extent to which the objectives of the project had been achieved, formed the basis for determining whether the project had been successful or not (Robinson 1991b).

Results of the ODI studies

The evaluations produced a generally favourable picture of NGO achievement; 12 out of the 16 projects broadly achieved their objectives and had a positive impact in alleviating poverty. Only two failed to meet their overall objectives and made little headway in addressing the problem of poverty. The other two projects achieved some of their objectives but fell short on others.

These findings would appear to confirm the expectations of the general NGO literature, in that three-quarters of the projects were successful and had an impact in alleviating poverty. But their performance was much less consistent when it came to more specific criteria of impact and effectiveness. Three in particular stand out. First, even if they had an appreciable impact in improving the economic status of the poor, many of the projects failed to reach the poorest, and were of relatively marginal benefit to women. Second, in only a minority of the projects did the benefits significantly outweigh the costs of the intervention. Third, on the question of sustainability, relatively few of the projects demonstrated the potential to continue once the NGO ceased operating in the area. Some were heavily constrained in this respect by an adverse physical environment. Both of these factors have a close bearing on the potential of NGO project interventions for replication and scaling-up, which are addressed in a later section.

Types of benefits

The immediate benefits arising out of economic interventions were not restricted to increased incomes, even though these are central to improved economic status. Factors such as the stability and regularity of income were also important for the rural poor, especially in view of the fact that many experienced seasonal spells of unemployment. Improvements in consumption also provide a good indication of the range of benefits that stem from economic interventions. These included changes in food consumption patterns, not only in terms of quantity and regularity of food intake, but also a better quality diet and enhanced nutritional status. Other indicators of improved consumption included increased expenditure on education, health and non-food items, housing and amenities (sanitation, lighting etc.), investment in land, implements and livestock, and the acquisition of luxury goods.

In addition to economic benefits, there were a range of social benefits which are less amenable to quantification, but which were of great significance to the poor, especially in the South Asian context. These social benefits included reduced dependence on moneylenders and local political elites, greater independence in decision-making, lower seasonal out-migration, improved ability to cope with contingencies such as illness and natural disasters, greater political participation and awareness, reduced social discrimination, and increased self-respect and mobility for women. These and other factors were frequently cited by the poor when identifying and ranking the relative importance of the benefits arising from economic interventions (Robinson 1991b).

Distribution of benefits

It is widely assumed that NGOs are good at reaching the poorest (broadly those lacking land, livestock, assets and education) in the sense of involving them in development activities and raising their living standards. Although there were significant gains to the poor, the evaluations found that most projects failed to benefit the poorest, and even in those where some benefits did accrue, the improvement in the economic status of the poorest was modest. In most cases, the poor gained to a greater degree than the poorest, largely by virtue of greater access to land, livestock and assets. At the same time, there was little to suggest that the elites had benefited to any significant extent from the projects. This was the general pattern across the sixteen projects and, perhaps more surprisingly, in all four countries.

These results also need to be seen in the wider context. First, what may appear to be marginal improvements to the outsider can be of great importance to the poorest, especially in a situation of marked economic decline. In other words, even if the NGO managed through its intervention to prevent the poorest from sliding further into hardship (as was the case in several of the Ugandan projects) this could be treated as evidence of success. Second, it would be unrealistic to expect significant change to occur over a short space of time, especially since many NGO interventions are short-term in nature. Third, some of those assisted were the 'borderline' poor, who experienced seasonal spells of poverty. For this group, even small increases in seasonal incomes were sufficient to prevent them from going without food. Likewise, the creation of additional periods of employment during the off-peak months also helped to reduce vulnerability.

In four of the projects, however, the poorest did gain in terms of increased incomes and outputs: these were the CASA Phase III programme in India, the ActionAid credit programme in Bangladesh, and the Simukai collective co-operative and the Campfire project in Zimbabwe. In the CASA and ActionAid projects, the NGOs worked hard to ensure that the poorest were well represented in beneficiary groups. Small loans were directed towards productive activities selected in consultation with the intended beneficiaries, where the poorest could utilise effectively the limited amounts of money loaned to them. In the Simukai co-operative, many of the members were unskilled, uneducated and assetless ex-combatants, and therefore among the poorest, but the numbers that benefited were small. In the Campfire project the poorest gained because all those in the designated area were involved in the project and wealth disparities were not great.

In other projects, the poorest gained from a localised 'trickle-down' effect, even if they were not actively participating in the project. Small farmers receiving credit from RDT in India increased the area that they cultivated, raised the proportion of cash crops and started to cultivate several crops over the year; all of these generated an increase in employment opportunities for the poorest. Employment expansion of this type was also evident from the UWFCT and ActionAid projects in Uganda from small businesses set up by individuals who received credit and skills training.

Besides their ability to reach the poorest, NGOs are also assumed to be effective in working with disadvantaged women, in that they typically set up special programmes to cater to their needs and play a role in highlighting problems that women often face. Contrary to expectations, there was little evidence to suggest that the projects as a whole greatly improved women's economic and social status, or effectively challenged prevailing patterns of discrimination. Men tended to dominate leadership positions in both the grassroots organisations and the NGOs, unless there was a specific attempt to involve women. Of the 16 case study projects only one, the Uganda Women's Finance and Credit Trust, was exclusively designed for women, even though some of the other projects had non-economic programme components for women. However, such findings need to be put in perspective, since it would be unrealistic to expect rapid change in gender relations over a short period.

In only six of the 16 projects did women benefit to any significant degree in terms of their participation and direct material benefits. In some cases, the attraction of additional household earnings outweighed traditional restrictions on women's mobility. Yet even in those projects where efforts were made to involve women and improve their well-being, there was a tendency to emphasise traditional occupations, where economic returns and market potential were low. Examples of projects where NGOs helped women identify new sources of income included tree cultivation and backyard nurseries in the Caritas Social Forestry programme in Bangladesh, and tailoring and dairying in the CASA programme in India. In such cases, there was evidence to suggest that increased income for women resulted in wider benefits for the household, such as improved food intake for children and higher expenditures on health and education. Moreover, increases in income also enhanced the self-confidence and independence of poorer women.

Cost-effectiveness

There is a pervasive assumption that NGO interventions are low-cost by virtue of their small size, low overheads and presumed effectiveness in terms of the benefits achieved. Although NGO project costs were often low, this was generally a reflection of their small size. Travel, subsistence and staff costs were certainly lower than for government and official aid agencies. Yet when it came to comparing NGO and government projects, the cost per beneficiary was either broadly equivalent or even higher in the case of NGO projects. The main reason for the higher costs is that the NGO projects were more staff- and resource-intensive; the corollary is that targeting the poor is a costly exercise which requires large numbers of staff on the ground.

In the case of NGO administered credit programmes the transaction costs can be very high in relation to the numbers and size of loans disbursed. When NGOs access credit from the official banking system a proportion of the transaction costs will be passed on, so the costs to the NGO will be lower, although this approach may not be more cost-effective if the full transaction costs (ie including those incurred by government and the banking system) are taken into account.

Although the quantitative data was insufficient to permit precise calculations of costs and benefits, it was possible to form some judgements for most of the projects. The 16 projects fell into three clusters: in five projects the costs clearly outweighed the benefits; in five others the objectives were achieved but at high cost in terms of staff and resources. For the remaining six projects it was difficult to arrive at a firm judgement, although for most of these (with the exception of the two projects which did not appear to have achieved their objectives) the benefits at least exceeded the direct costs of administration and staffing.

These findings suggest that there is a trade-off between costs, benefits and the desired level of targeting. Finer targeting has clear cost implications, for the reasons given above, and efforts to reach the very poorest are likely to result in declining marginal returns since such groups have a limited capacity to generate significant increases in income or output as they generally lack the land and assets to do so.

One final point to note in this regard is that costs were expected to diminish over time for those projects which were judged to have the potential to be sustained. The start-up costs of poverty-alleviating projects were invariably high, since there was a great deal of preparatory work involved in identifying and consulting with the potential beneficiaries, and in securing the support of local authorities and political leaders. The expectation in several of the projects was that over time a large proportion of the administrative tasks performed by the NGO would be taken on by local people. Moreover, in sustainable projects it was assumed that there would be no need for the NGO to continue playing a monitoring role since this would be undertaken by local grassroots organisations. There was evidence to support this line of reasoning from some of the projects where the NGO had already withdrawn, although it was difficult to estimate how far the costs had simply been transferred to local groups and were no longer visible, and the extent to which costs had genuinely declined over the lifetime of the project.

Sustainability

The expectation that project costs were expected to diminish over time in sustainable projects leads us on to consider the various factors that are conducive to sustainability.

As mentioned earlier, the question of sustainability may be approached from several angles. Financial sustainability is clearly of fundamental importance for credit and income-generation programmes. For a project to be financially sustainable it has to able to cover its direct costs and generate sufficient income to make it worthwhile for the poor to persist with it. This depends not only on the profitability of individual economic activities but also on factors such as local patterns of demand, marketing opportunities, the availability of inputs, government pricing policy (for the purchase of foodgrains) and national economic trends. In the case study projects many economic activities simply foundered once the NGO withdrew its direct support since these types of considerations were not properly addressed at the outset.

However, few of the 16 projects demonstrated the potential to be financially self-sustaining over the longer term. Relatively few could be expected to carry on without continued donor support or some form of ongoing subsidy. Yet there were several projects which were expected to be financially self-sustaining in the short term. These shared a number of common features: the beneficiaries were strongly committed to the objectives of the project; there were a range of tangible benefits; and the NGO was able to find ways of covering recurrent costs, either through user fees or by charging a premium on services. In contrast, projects which displayed little potential to become sustainable were not participatory, the intended beneficiaries were only weakly committed and the administrative costs were high.

These considerations highlight the importance of the wider environment into which NGO projects are inserted. Their impact is contingent on a range of local, national and even international factors. Few of the NGOs studied appeared to take full account of environmental constraints in limiting project potential. In addition to the economic factors listed above, many of the projects were located in resource-poor environments where the climate is unpredictable, the soils were of poor quality and the physical infrastructure (roads, power and communications) was undeveloped.

Sometimes natural disasters severely undermined project impact. Severe flooding in Bangladesh destroyed fish ponds in the GUP project and a tornado devastated housing and crops in the GKT project area. In coastal Andhra Pradesh a cyclone resulted in widespread destruction and the loss of livestock, assets and crops in the CASA and ASM projects. Clearly, environmental constraints, especially in the form of natural disasters, limit the potential for scaling-up NGO interventions by replication or expansion in a sustainable manner in resource-poor and vulnerable areas. The implication of this is a much more extended involvement on the part of NGOs in such areas and a larger commitment of resources. Before moving on to consider some of the scaling-up issues that emerge from these case studies, we briefly consider what appear to be the key factors in those projects displaying clear evidence of success.

Factors underlying successful interventions

Successful project interventions were found to be related to a number of different variables, none of which in isolation was sufficient to achieve project objectives. Three in particular stand out: genuine participation, strong and effective management, and skilled and committed staff. In addition to these factors, a favourable social and economic environment was found to be conducive to project success; it was far easier for projects to succeed in their objectives when the local economy was expanding, resources were plentiful and local elites were broadly supportive of their objectives. There was also evidence that those projects which had been prepared and designed more carefully were among the more successful performers.

The case studies confirmed the importance of beneficiary participation in the planning, design and implementation of projects. Projects were more likely to succeed where their objectives corresponded to the priorities of the poor, and where the intended beneficiaries were regularly consulted and involved in decision making at all stages of the project cycle. Although there was some evidence of success in projects lacking in participation, the benefits derived were unlikely to be sustained over the longer term without more direct involvement. Most of the NGOs placed a high premium on the formation of new groups or the strengthening of existing groups as a means of raising awareness, fostering participation and empowering the poor, although they were not always integral to successful interventions.

The projects highlighted the importance of a strong and competent leadership, skilled in management and possessing an overall vision of project goals. Strong leaders were able to maintain channels of communication with government officials, enabling them to lever additional resources or circumvent potential problems. At the same time, excessive centralisation of decision making in some projects undermined staff commitment and limited the potential impact of the intervention. Similarly, NGOs which failed to delegate effectively depended heavily on the leadership of particular individuals, rendering them vulnerable to sudden changes of direction or the departure of such leaders. On the whole, strong leadership was a more common trait than effective management, and many of the NGOs displayed management weaknesses.

A third factor underlying project success was staffing. The calibre of project staff, their sense of commitment to overall project objectives and degree of empathy with the intended beneficiaries all contributed to the more successful outcomes. Well-trained and educated staff motivated by a reasonable level of remuneration and decent working conditions played a critical role in this regard.

Attempts at scaling-up

A number of the NGOs examined in the course of the research had made some attempt to scale-up their projects and programmes, most commonly through working with government and expanding their activities by means of growth, replication and vertical integration. One (KDFSF) was actively engaged in lobbying and campaigning to complement its development work, and another (CASA) was seeking to scale-up its activities by promoting the formation of a federation of grassroots organisations to take over responsibility for managing the programmes. While such initiatives were not the prime focus of the research, some of the experiences of the NGOs in their attempts at scaling-up are relevant to the wider concerns of this book.

Working with government

At least three of the projects had established close working relationships with local government; CASA in India, and the Campfire project and Silveira House in Zimbabwe. CASA's approach was to access subsidised credit from the local banking system for income-generation schemes. Since the subsidies were allocated by local government, CASA had to develop close contacts with the relevant officials. The organisation was able to cultivate these contacts on the basis of the reputation that it had established for effective development work in the area. When a continued flow of subsidized credit was assured, this strategy proved very successful, and the administrative costs were low. However, it was also vulnerable to changes in government policy. In the late 1980s when the government decided that subsidies would be allocated on a strict geographical basis it became increasingly difficult for CASA to access subsidised loans for beneficiaries in the villages in which it was operating. Consequently it was forced to introduce subsidies of its own to keep up the momentum of the programme. CASA also suffered when government staff who were sympathetic to its programmes were transferred as new contacts had to be established, sometimes with officials who were less well-disposed to the organisation. It is also possible that a strategy which relies on levering subsidised credit increases competition for scarce resources which could prove inimical to effective coalition-building among NGOs.

In the case of the Campfire project in Zimbabwe the aim was to assist local communities in managing wildlife resources and to derive a share of the benefits from commercial hunting operations. The success of the programme depended to some extent on the relationship between the local community and the district council over the sharing of revenues derived from fees paid by safari operators. In practice the relationship was rather weak and there were frequent wrangles over the allocation of these revenues, but since the district council had managerial responsibility for the safari operations, some basic understanding over the revenue-sharing principle was essential to the continuity of the project. The possibility of the local community assuming direct responsibility for safari operations was under consideration but it did not yet possess sufficient managerial and technical capacity to enable it to do so.

A rather different approach was adopted by Silveira House, which introduced one of the first credit schemes for small farmers living in the communal areas prior to independence. Credit was successfully provided on a small scale to farmers' groups over a number of years for seeds and fertilisers to raise productivity and promote a shift to cash-crop production. After independence the groups were transferred to a newly established government credit scheme modelled on the Silveira House approach, and serious difficulties were encountered. The amount of credit made available to farmers expanded too fast and commercial rates of interests were levied, with the result that many of the groups collapsed under a heavy and unsustainable burden of debt.

These three examples suggest that working with government can further the aims of specific development interventions, but that it can also prove problematic, and even act as an impediment to success. Clearly the potential for working with government varies across countries and regions and is often a function of the individual predispositions of key government officials. As such it represents one among a number of strategies for scaling-up which may offer dividends when the government is politically accountable and reasonably well-disposed to the activities of NGOs. What may be appropriate in one context may not be appropriate in all instances, especially where the government is repressive or where it neglects its development functions.

Expanding existing operations

Several of the NGOs had sought to scale-up their existing operations by replicating the project in a neighbouring area or in different parts of the country. Some tacked on additional sectoral activities to existing programmes, whereas others favoured a process of vertical integration to extend existing programmes into complementary areas of activity. CASA's approach, for example, was multiplicative, concentrating its resources on a small number of villages, initiating a series of phased development activities (community organisation, village uplift, credit and income-generation), handing over responsibility to the local grassroots organisation and moving on to adjacent villages after a few years. In contrast, the Rural Development Trust sought to increase the impact of its programmes by enlarging the area in which it was operating in order to reach larger numbers of people. Other NGOs also opted for a strategy of geographical spread. Caritas Bangladesh, for example, expanded its Social Forestry programme to 21 districts of the country, based on an approach first launched on a pilot basis in a limited number of areas.

Several NGOs replicated approaches which were initially pioneered by another organisation. ActionAid modelled its rural credit programme on that developed by the Grameen Bank. The Campfire project in Zimbabwe has acted as a model for similar programmes centred on economic wildlife management and game farming in other parts of the country with the support of bilateral donors. Neighbouring countries have also been influenced by the Campfire approach and similar projects are under consideration in Zambia, Tanzania, Kenya, Namibia and Botswana.

Finally, in the Indian state of Tamil Nadu, a pioneering approach to fish marketing in one or two villages in the late 1960s formed the basis for a model which has been adopted by artisanal fishing communities all along the coastline, in some cases without any external encouragement (see Chambers, chapter 3 on 'self-spreading'). The apex body representing local grassroots organisations (KDFSF) has lobbied government to introduce subsidies on outboard motors and kerosene to make mechanisation more accessible to the fishermen, but so far with little success. It has also mobilised fishermen to lobby the state government to ban trawler fishing during the peak months and has made some headway in the face of concerted opposition from trawler owners.

In the case of those NGOs which were actively pursuing a strategy of scaling-up there was a tendency to follow the path of expansion and simple replication, and in several cases of working with government, rather than that of advocacy and promoting local-level initiatives. One possible reason for this is that NGOs which focused their energies on programme implementation steered clear from what was perceived to be a more confrontational or activist approach to avoid prejudicing their relationships with government. This line of reasoning would suggest that lobbying and active engagement in policy debate is easier for NGOs which are unencumbered by project activities although examples from elsewhere seem to indicate that the two are not necessarily incompatible (Clark 1992; Randal 1992). Alternatively, it may be the case that once an NGO has created a basic level of awareness and material security among the poor it may be in a better position to promote local grassroots organisations which are more autonomous and capable of determining their own priorities and agendas.

Increasing the potential for effective scaling-up

The 1990s are likely to see a further expansion of NGOs, both in terms of numbers and influence, fuelled in large measure by a continued increase in official funding. NGOs are responding by increasing the number and the size of their interventions, both of which are premised on good performance. Two, more general, implications of this trend are first that a donor approach to scaling-up of funding greater numbers of local NGOs has meant a *scaling-down* in the size of projects, and second that poor coordination, both between NGOs and between NGOs and government, limits the potential impact of NGO interventions.

The previous section highlighted some of the ways that some NGOs have approached the question of scaling-up through collaboration with government and various forms of expansion and replication. The challenge for NGOs is to maintain, and even improve, the quality of their interventions while at the same time scaling-up the impact of such interventions. Yet there are a number of limitations on the potential of NGOs to scale up the impact of their projects and programmes, many of which are institutional in nature. These can be partly addressed through a process of building up the institutional capacity of NGOs, thereby enabling them to consider a range of complementary interventions that may be appropriate for tackling the problem of persistent poverty, within the boundaries set by the broader political context in which they operate.

The 16 case-study projects indicate that there are at least six areas where NGOs could potentially augment their institutional capacity with a view to strengthening the prospects for a more effective approach to scaling-up impact since enhanced programme quality is an indispensable precondition for increasing the size and quantity of interventions. First, more time could be spent on project identification, to assess the likely distributional impact of specific types of interventions, and to determine whether the physical and economic environment is conducive to sustained poverty-alleviation. For instance, if the approach involves levering subsidised credit from the official banking system on a large scale the potential for doing so will hinge on the economic viability of the proposed investments which in turn will depend on local patterns of supply and demand.

Second, staff and management requirements should be systematically assessed at the outset of a project, to determine the local availability of qualified staff and the need for training. Ambitious attempts to expand or replicate successful projects can founder on the paucity of appropriately trained personnel who are experienced in community development. Third, some assessment of the likely costs and benefits of different types of interventions should be attempted before any programme is initiated. Few NGOs fully anticipate the costs of administering complex development programmes which seek to involve the community in design-making and target the intended benefits on the very poorest. Such programmes are costly to implement, even on a small scale, and attempts to scale-up by expansion without allowing for a commensurate increase in costs, at least in the short term, could dilute their impact. Fourth, NGOs intending to initiate new programmes should attempt to identify what development activities are being sponsored by government and other NGOs in the immediate vicinity to improve co-ordination, increase their potential leverage and facilitate the exchange of information. This would help to counter the characteristic tendency, in some areas of dense NGO activity towards competition and duplication and could upgrade the prospects for more effective scaling-up in its own right. Fifth, it is essential that projects are properly monitored, so that staff and the intended beneficiaries are aware of the progress that is being made and are able to tackle problems that arise during the course of implementation with a view to enhancing the utilisation of scarce resources (Roche 1992). Finally, closer attention needs to be focused on the methods and circumstances of withdrawal in order to maximise the prospects for sustainability. This is especially relevant for those NGOs which seek to replicate a successful approach in another area using the same level of staffing and resources, since a lack of local capacity for project management will simply result in a no-growth situation where there is no cumulative impact.

All these factors point to the need for institutional capacity building, especially to enhance the aptitude of indigenous NGOs, though training, greater flexibility of funding, and improving research and analytical skills. Unless NGOs are effective in their project interventions at the local level, scaling-up may simply mean attempting to replicate and extend approaches which are less than optimal, without the ability to implement and manage more complex interventions. It is for this reason that a strategic approach to scaling-up NGO impact must be complemented by a strategic approach to enhancing their organisational capacity for implementing effective poverty-alleviation projects.

3

Spreading and self-improving: a strategy for scaling-up

Robert Chambers

Introduction

In their introduction to this book, Edwards and Hulme distinguish strategies which are 'additive' – implying an increase in the size of an organisation and programme, 'multiplicative' – where impact is achieved through deliberate influence, training, and networking among other organisations, and 'diffusive' – where spread is informal and spontaneous. They further distinguish four strategies for scaling-up or having a wider impact. These are:

1. working with government
2. organisational growth
3. linking the grassroots with lobbying and advocacy
4. advocacy in the North

This chapter explores a fifth, methodological, strategy for wider impact, which crosscuts the others: generating, spreading and improving approaches and methods. This fifth strategy can be both multiplicative and diffusive: spread of an approach or method can be multiplicative through deliberate training or networking; or it can be diffusive, occurring informally and spontaneously; or it can be both. In this chapter 'self-spreading' refers to spread which occurs without formal training or the creation of formal networks. 'Self-improving' is used to describe approaches and methods which have improvement built into them, so that they should, from their very nature, get better and better the more they are used.

Some NGOs have already made impacts in this fifth manner. However, this may not often have been part of a deliberate strategy. Nor are the generation and spread of approaches and methods always included in evaluations of organisations or programmes. There seems to be here a neglected aspect of NGO impact, both actual and potential.

This fifth strategy will be explored through two examples of methodological innovation which have spread: rapid rural appraisal (RRA); and participatory rural appraisal (PRA). This will lead to an assessment of the potential for approaches which are self-spreading and self-improving, and finally, some wider lessons.

RRA and PRA

Rapid rural appraisal (RRA) emerged in the late 1970s as a set of approaches and methods of enquiry about rural life and conditions which tried to offset the anti-poverty biases of 'rural development tourism' (the brief rural visit by the urban-based professional) and to avoid the many defects of large questionnaire surveys (for which see eg Moris 1970; Campbell, Shrestha and Stone 1979; Gill forthcoming). RRA stressed and continues to stress cost-effective trade-offs between quantity, accuracy, relevance and timeliness of information (Carruthers and Chambers 1981). Methods and concerns included semi-structured interviewing, and the management of team interactions. In the 1980s, agro-ecosystem analysis (Gypmantasiri et al 1980; Conway 1985) contributed another powerful stream of methods including sketch mapping, transects, and diagramming. RRA came of age and acquired respectability, not least through the international conference held at the pioneering University of Khon Kaen in Thailand in 1985 and the evidence, methods and theory presented there (KKU 1987). RRA was seen as a flexible and cost-effective approach to learning, with a repertoire of methods. Training people in these methods was seen as a precondition for spread.

Participatory rural appraisal (PRA) is a continuing outgrowth from RRA. In the latter 1980s, and in parallel, the word 'participatory' was applied to RRA both in India through the work of the Aga Khan Rural Support Programme with the International Institute for Environment and Development, London (McCracken 1988), and in Kenya through the work of the Kenya Government's National Environment Secretariat with Clark University, USA (PID and NES 1989). Quite quickly, the term Participatory Rural Appraisal was adopted and spread, especially in South Asia (Mascarenhas et al 1991). Whereas RRA is extractive, with outsiders appropriating and processing the information, PRA is participatory, with ownership and analysis coming to be more by rural people themselves, who map, model, diagram, rank, score, observe, interview, analyse and plan.

To date, the experience with PRA in India, Nepal and Sri Lanka has been that rural people are better at observation, interviewing, mapping, modelling, diagramming, ranking, scoring, analysis and planning than outsiders have believed. There can be little doubt now that we have witnessed a discovery, that rural people have capabilities which earlier were little expressed and unsuspected by most outsiders.

Outsiders' ignorance for so long of rural people's capabilities has to be explained, and has implications for spread. The strongest working explanation is that outsiders (whether in Government departments, NGOs or universities) have almost universally believed their knowledge to be superior, and so have consistently behaved in ways which have devalued the knowledge of rural people. In the field, most outsiders find it difficult to keep quiet, to avoid interrupting people, to abstain from criticism and to refrain from putting forward their own ideas. Anil Shah, of the Aga Khan Rural Support Programme (India), has invented 'shoulder tapping' (Shah 1991) to correct this – a contract among outsiders that they will tap the shoulder of any colleague who criticises, asks a leading question, or puts forward his or her own ideas. The experience has been that for local people confidently and capably to express their own knowledge, to conduct their own analysis, and to assert their own priorities, outsiders have to step off their pedestals, sit down, 'hand over the stick', listen, and learn, in ways which conflict with much professional conditioning and self-esteem. Personal change for the outsider can, thus, for PRA at least, be a precondition for successful spread of the approach.

Modes of spread

In their spread, RRA and PRA have had common features. Both began as heresies. Both rejected conventional professional norms and behaviour, and developed and shared new methods. Both have been espoused and developed by independent-minded people. Both have faced opposition from professional establishments. Their modes of spread, too, have spanned a common range, though with differences of emphasis.

Spread through training

One difference of emphasis is in training. The contrast can be overdrawn; but RRA has tended to be taught didactically while PRA in its South Asian form has tended to be learnt experientially. With some caricature, the two training approaches can be polarised as follows:

	Didactic (more RRA)	Experiential (more PRA)
Aim	Teach methods	Change behaviour and attitudes
Duration	Longer (weeks)	Shorter (days)
Style	Classroom, then practice	Practice, then reflection
Source of learning	Manuals, lectures	Trials, experiences
Location	More in the classroom	More in the field
Learning experience	Intermittent Intellectual	Continuous Experiential
Good performance seen to be through	Stepwise and correct application of rules	Flexible choice, adaptation and improvisation of methods

The more didactic mode has been represented by formal training with manuals. RRA and PRA have been codified and embodied in handbooks (eg Meals for Millions 1988; PID and NES 1989). Training courses have been conducted with these as a basis. The tendency has been for such training to require weeks, to stress the correct learning and performance of methods and sequences, and for those trained to have a sense that the time was not long enough. The six weeks of one training course in Thailand was considered too short. The outcomes of formal training have, perhaps, been mixed. Methods have surely been learnt. But sometimes trainees have experienced difficulty in implementing what they have learnt, once they have returned to their home environments.

The more experiential mode has been prevalent in South Asia. Training has quite often been brief, lasting only three to five days, but with outsiders camping in a village and interacting intensively with the villagers. In the Indian Government, one of the leading trainers, Somesh Kumar, would spend less than a day on briefing about PRA before sending people into the field for three days and nights, followed by a day's debriefing (Kumar 1991). The emphasis was on behaviour and attitudes rather than methods. The effectiveness of this approach was indicated by an experiment he carried out (personal communication). In one training exercise, after initial orientation on behaviour and attitudes, one group was given only a sketchy idea of methods and sent straight out; another group was first given a stricter briefing on do's and don'ts for the methods before starting in the field. It was the first group, with less training, which did better. Knowledge of rules and procedures helped less and may have hindered; open, learning and self-aware attitudes and behaviour helped more.

Spread through individuals

Spread has taken place through individual fieldworkers who pick up ideas, hear about possibilities, who have experiential training, or who simply start, learn by doing and help others to learn. Spread here can be through self-selecting individuals. In a five-day training conducted in Bihar in mid-1990, of some 20 participants about five rejected the approach, about ten were interested and enthusiastic but probably did not introduce it in their organisations, and about five took it up, introduced it, and spread it. Ravi Jayakaran of KGVK and Kamal Kar of Seva Bharati are two who immediately introduced PRA in the NGOs which they headed, and who have since been providing training for NGO and Government staff alike; while Anup Sarkar of the Xavier Institute of Social Service, Ranchi, introduced PRA as the approach and methods for the fieldwork of all students. Among the participants in the training experience, thus, the short, intense experience had limited effect with a majority, but through a minority, a large and self-sustaining spread.

Self-spreading: success and sharing

Spread also occurs through ideas passing through informal channels such as networks, publications, and word of mouth. This can be termed self-spreading. With RRA and especially PRA, two factors have contributed to self-spreading.

The first is practical. RRA and PRA, unless abused, usually work. For outsiders they can be fascinating; and PRA is also often fun. For villagers PRA can also be enabling and empowering. There are many problems, especially in Government, but good experiences have been common among those NGOs that have tried it. Exaggeration must be avoided. But there is justification for describing good PRA as both popular and powerful. As with other innovations, they spread if people want them.

The second factor, with PRA in South Asia, is that sharing has been part of the culture from the start. MYRADA, a large NGO based in Bangalore but working in a dozen or more districts, adopted and developed PRA, and spread it among other NGOs and Government by inviting and welcoming people to its field training exercises. These often entailed camping in villages for several days and nights, a total experience which had its own impact on participants. Other NGOs in parallel and in collaboration did likewise, among them, in alphabetical order: ActionAid, Bangalore; Activists for Social Alternatives, Trichi; the Aga Khan Rural Support Programme, Gujarat; Krishi Gram Vikas Kendra, Ranchi; Seva Bharati in West Bengal; SPEECH, Madurai; and Youth for Action, Hyderabad.

Spreading and self-improving

The examples of RRA and PRA can also shed light on quality control and assurance with spread. Much spread is degenerative. In this mode, as some RRA has spread, it has been done less well. The term 'rapid' has been used to justify rushing and sloppiness. Misleading findings have resulted. Johan Pottier's exposure (1991) of hurried farmer interviews conducted in Northern Zambia warns of such error. Theo van Steijn's review (1991) of RRAs conducted by NGOs in the Philippines similarly points to quite widespread practices of low quality. In this mode, the label and the language of RRA have been used to legitimise bad work. Quite often, as RRA has spread, it has got worse. The normal reflex to degenerative spread is quality control from the centre, through manuals, setting standards, and training.

A contrasting mode of spread is self-improving. Some PRA, as it has been spreading and evolving in India, Nepal, Sri Lanka, Kenya (Pretty 1991) Vietnam and elsewhere, can illustrate this. To understand this, we have to see PRA as an approach and philosophy, a set of attitudes and behaviours. These include critical self-awareness, 'handing over the stick' (passing the initiative to villagers), 'they can do it' (having confidence that villagers can map, model, rank, score and so on), 'embracing error' (welcoming and sharing mistakes as opportunities for learning), and 'use your own best judgement at all times' (stressing personal responsibility). If these are part of the 'genes' of PRA as it spreads, then wherever it is adopted, practice should get better and better. Good performance comes not from quality control, from an external centre, to prevent degeneration, but from quality assurance through internal monitors, to achieve improvement.

This mode of spread might at first sight look like wishful evangelism. Missionaries who try to spread Buddhism, Christianity, Hinduism, or Islam are, after all, concerned with changing personal beliefs and behaviour. But basing analysis on the example of PRA, the self-improving mode of spread differs from the missionary mode in four respects:

- **Empiricism**. It is experiential, not metaphysical. It is based on what is found to work, not deduced from theory or drawn from dogma. Any theory is induced from practice.
- **Diversity**. It is not concerned with uniformity. It invites and accepts rejection, and welcomes and embraces diversity of response. This could be dismissed as a covert strategy, like a paradoxical psychotherapy, to induce adoption. But it is more than that. Diversity in development has a positive value. It is good that we are different, and fitting that we have different ideas and different methods and that different things are done in different places by different people.
- **Uncertainty**. It embraces uncertainty. We know that we do not know. We are dealing with conditions and processes which are unforeseeable. In such conditions, reductionist, deductive, preset solutions rarely work well. Open-ended participatory improvisation, drawing on a repertoire of methods, works better.
- **Responsibility**. It places responsibility on the individual. In this respect, it resonates with successful practice in American business management. The one-sentence manual of the large retailer Nordstrom (Peters 1987:378), also adopted by an Indian NGO (Krishi Gram Vikas Kendra), is 'Use your own best judgement at all times'. Even in some spiritual contexts, a paradigm of personal choice and responsibility may be emerging, as with the question 'If you were given the task of devising your own religion, what would it be like?' (Forsyth 1991:264,277). In this paradigm, authority and responsibility reside neither in a

bible or manual, nor in a sequence of ritual observances or procedures, but in personal judgement and choice.

Quality assurance is, then, sought through empiricism, diversity, uncertainty and responsibility, which hang together as paradigm, perhaps even as ideology[1] Self improving strategies of spread fit this paradigm through their dynamic culture of adapting, improvising, and creativity.

Wider applications

The potential benefits from good changes which spread and self-improve seem large. The question is now how widely applicable the lessons from RRA and PRA are as examples of methodological innovations which have spread. And should spreading and self-improving strategies be more consciously pursued by more NGOs? Is there a even a specialised role here for 'niche NGOs', one pioneering example being already the Sustainable Agriculture Programme of the International Institute for Environment and Development in the spread of RRA and PRA, but with scope for many others?

In searching for answers to these questions, two forms of spread of methodological change can be identified.

Through approaches and methods

The first form is through new approaches and methods, and ideas about them. Many ideas are self-spreading. Ideas and knowledge of experiences know few boundaries and can travel fast. Sometimes, as with participatory mapping (Mascarenhas and Kumar 1991), all some people need is to hear an idea about something to do, or to see a few slides, and then go off and invent their own form of it. Other approaches and methods of NGOs sometimes spread fast and well. The system of community health workers which spread worldwide following the Alma Ata conference originated in NGO experiments. Another case is the poor people's savings and credit groups of the Grameen Bank in Bangladesh, an improbable innovation which has spread internationally, helped by the knowledge that it has already worked elsewhere. Another is the idea of farmers as extension agents, popularised by World Neighbours (Bunch 1985).

This points to methodological innovation and the sharing of innovations as NGO activities which can have a very wide impact indeed. An NGO which develops an approach and method which then spreads can count that spread among the benefits from its work. A small NGO can, in such a manner, have a good impact vastly out of proportion to its size, especially if it shares open-handedly and builds in self-improvement. Indeed, where small NGOs have successful innovations, they should consider changing their strategies to stress dissemination.

Through people

The second form of spread is through people. Some NGOs more than others socialise their staff to become disseminators and self-starters – people who will go off and work in and influence other organisations or start their own NGOs. For the

---

[1] For a forceful statement, see the last chapter, 'More diversity for more certainty', in *Development in Practice* (Porter et al 1991:197–213).

parent NGO this may look like failure as staff leave. But the other organisations or new NGOs can then in turn be generators and spreaders of approaches and methods, and socialisers of others. NGO A and NGO B might be similar in size and activities, but A might develop and send out staff who acted in these ways while B retained its staff. NGO A might appear to do less well in the field than B, but its impact could be immeasurably greater.

This points to staff development, to personal changes in people who work in NGOs, and to personal mobility. A practical issue is how training of NGO staff, as conducted already by the Centre for Partnership in Development, Oslo, and as proposed by INTRAC (the International NGO Training and Research Centre) in the UK, can contribute to spread of change through people.

The two forms of spread – through approaches, methods and ideas, and through people – are linked. The next challenge is to make self-improvement a part of spread. Whether ideas or practices are self-improving depends not only on their nature, but also on who adopts them, with what commitment, and with what attitudes. Religions seek self-improvement by linking evangelism with confession, repentance, penance and prayer. But PRA, and other innovations from the NGO sector, are not a religion. Instead, the PRA experience suggests a secular answer: to stress self-critical awareness, learning by doing, embracing error, and sharing ideas and experience.

A growing potential

Short of some big human disaster, the scope and potential for spreading and self-improving approaches and methods should grow in the 1990s. First, the institutional cultures of NGOs are changing. Some NGOs remain narrowly bounded, possessive and territorial. Such NGOs are less likely to share, spread, adopt and improve, than those which are open and undefended. But with the trend towards openness and sharing, such institutional cultures are becoming less common and less marked. Contemporary Christian NGOs of different persuasions, for example, show less competitive antagonism than their more missionary forerunners. Over the past few decades, the ideologies of development espoused by NGOs have quite often become more democratic, decentralised and tolerant. To the extent this is so, then self-spreading and self-improving strategies should do better in the future than in the past. Sparks spread fires where there is tinder; and there is more tinder now.

Second, changes in government organisations (though less marked) are quite widely in the same direction, especially with key individuals who are sympathetic. Other strategies for scaling up link in here. Government organisations are notoriously resistant to change, being typically hierarchical, given to top-down target-setting, quite often corrupt, and frequently misled about programme performance by false positive feedback. But there are scattered indications of change, and reasons to expect it: increased collaboration at the field level between NGOs and government; more training of government staff by NGOs; more high-level recognition in democratic governments of a need to change; and in India, to be specific, requests from government organisations for training in PRA, and its use in the fieldwork of probationers of the elite Indian Administrative Service. In the 1990s many government organisations may well be increasingly open to adopting approaches and methods pioneered by NGOs.

The third factor is communication. To spread fires, sparks need not only tinder but also to be carried by a wind. If NGOs generate the sparks of new approaches and methods, communications are the mounting wind which carries them. Communications are speeding up, penetrating, and persuading more and more. Despite contrary oaooo with local dealing, disaster and dislocation, this penetration and linking is occurring in more and more places. It is a commonplace already to speak of the global village; and the 1990s are likely to see a world of human experience which shrinks and is shared yet more. The innumerable NGO networks and network letters, the floods of photocopies, the pervasive reach of radio, television and now video, and the spread of telephone and fax – all these have augmented communication and sharing and can be expected to do so more and more. At the same time, many who work in NGOs are becoming better qualified and more professional, and more able and likely to use wider sources of information. A good idea can now spread faster and better than before. Informal international networks are easier to create and use. *RRA Notes*, informally and quickly produced by the International Institute for Environment and Development, spreads innovations in a matter of months. Through even less formal communication, an innovation in South India has been applied within a few weeks in Sierra Leone. Video is another powerful example: 'Participatory Research with Women Farmers' released by the International Crops Research Institute for the Semi-Arid Tropics presents a new approach to agricultural research which in less than two years been widely seen all over the world, both in its original and in copies which have been made. Quicker and more effective communications have brought NGO innovators closer to each other and to other people and organisations than ever before.

If these judgements and conjectures are correct, the potential of the fifth strategy – of new approaches and methods which spread and self-improve – has increased and is increasing. That potential could and should receive more attention. To realise it requires innovation as normal practice, critical self-awareness as personal attitude, and sharing as institutional culture. The question now is how many of those who work in NGOs and government organisations have the vision, will and creativity to recognise this and to make innovation, spread and self-improvement part of their way of life.

Part II
Working with government

4

NGO–government interaction in agricultural technology development

Anthony J Bebbington and John Farrington

This chapter draws preliminary findings from a study[1] across Africa, Asia and Latin America of the potential for closer links between NGOs and government agricultural technology development and dissemination services in the development and dissemination of agriculture-related[2] technologies and management practices. While at a practical level concerned with the functions that the respective organisations might jointly or separately undertake, the study also sought to locate potential actions in the wider context in order to prevent attempts to generalise 'success stories' into inappropriate contexts. The central methodology of the study was to generate a substantial number of case studies (over 70) prepared in collaboration with the NGO or government practitioners who had been involved in them. These were supplemented by country or area-based overviews of wider NGO–state relations.

This chapter starts by placing the study in the context of other statements regarding GO–NGO collaboration. It then reviews the characteristics of the NGOs whose experience was documented in the Overseas Development Institute (ODI) study, briefly reviews examples of their success and failure in agricultural technology development, and then examines in what ways GOs and NGOs can help to strengthen each other's effectiveness in enhancing livelihoods for the rural poor.

Introduction

Over recent years many have argued that agricultural and rural development strategies would benefit from increased collaboration between government and non-governmental development organisations, hereafter called GOs and NGOs

---

[1] Conducted from the ODI Agricultural Research and Extension Network and published in four volumes by Routledge (Farrington, Bebbington and Wellard, 1993; Farrington and Lewis (eds), 1993; Wellard and Copestake (eds), Bebbington et al. (eds), 1993).

[2] Agriculture is defined broadly to include annual and perennial crops, livestock and farm-related trees.

respectively (Carroll forthcoming; de Janvry et al. 1989; Farrington and Biggs 1990; Jordan 1989; Korten 1987). Donors, in particular, have begun to call for more NGO involvement in programmes that have traditionally been implemented through the public sector (World Bank 1991a, b; Farnworth 1991; IDB 1991).

These advocates of closer NGO–GO collaboration have, however, underemphasised:

- the wide range of interaction that currently exists;
- the limitations on efforts to work together;
- the preconditions for successful collaboration (in particular, the informal contacts necessary to build up mutual trust);
- the limitations as well as the successes of NGO action;
- the extent to which certain functions will remain more cost-effectively performed by the public sector than by NGOs. Analysis of how GOs might work with NGOs must be accompanied by continuing attention to ways of improving public sector management, an area in which structural adjustment reforms have not had the success expected (Nunberg 1988; Ribe et al. 1990).

It is also important to note that these calls for collaboration come from different points across the ideological spectrum, including NGO activists such as Clark (1991) and Jordan (1989), radical economists (de Janvry et al. 1989), and multilateral institutions. This may be cause for celebration; but it is also cause for circumspection. It suggests that different actors are seeking differing outcomes of such collaboration, and have divergent views on *how much* responsibility the state ought to continue to assume, and *which* subsidies to *which* social groups ought to survive.

This study sought to address the 'blind spots' of these statements, and to make the divergence between views more explicit. In particular it drew attention to the tension between those casting NGOs in roles which are predominantly functional (eg in service delivery) and those (including many of the more reflective NGOs themselves) who see NGOs' most valuable contribution in influencing the wider policies or strategies of development, in developing approaches towards livelihood enhancement for the poor which GOs might emulate, and in the design and monitoring of projects, rather than merely in their implementation. One difficulty seems to be that even where these multiple roles of NGOs are recognised, in reality it appears much easier to draw them into project implementation than into advisory or design work – 57 per cent of cases fell into the former category, and 32 per cent into the latter, according to a recent breakdown of World Bank projects (World Bank 1989).

Features of the NGOs studied

Our concern is mainly with the stronger of the South-based NGOs that provide services either directly to the rural poor or to grassroots membership organisations, although examples are also drawn from some North-based NGOs, and from some of their offices located in the South which operate with varying degrees of autonomy. Most of the NGOs considered pursue livelihood enhancement in a participatory fashion and in the context of wider value-driven objectives including group formation and conscientisation. However, a wide range of NGO philosophies and approaches exists, including those which are somewhat 'top-down' (eg

Bharatiya Agro-Industries Foundation – see Satish and Farrington 1990) and those which have become narrowly tied to government contracts for service delivery (see Aguirre and Namdar-Irani 1992).

The origins of NGOs vary widely, and are likely to have a strong bearing on the type and extent of potential NGO-GO collaboration. Some were formed in opposition to governments which discriminated against the rural poor[3], others as a reaction to government support for, or indifference to, prevailing patterns of corruption, patronage or authoritarianism.

Many NGOs were formed by left-leaning professionals formerly employed in universities or in the public sector. Their intellectual calibre has generally been high, but they were often socially and ethnically distinct from the rural poor. In the early stages of their formation, almost all were characterised by small-size, institutional flexibility, horizontal structure and short lines of communication. Many have found these characteristics conducive to a quick response to eventualities and a work ethic able to generate sustainable processes and impacts, and so have sought to retain them well beyond the initial establishment period. But the smallness and the political origins and orientation of NGOs are also their 'Achilles' heel' since:

- NGO projects rarely address wider-scale structural factors that underlie rural poverty;
- NGOs have limited capacities for agricultural technology development and dissemination[4];
- the activities of different NGOs remain unco-ordinated, and information exchange is poor especially among small NGOs.

These strengths and weaknesses of NGOs, and their implications for NGO–GO relations, are discussed in more detail below, and illustrated by examples from Africa, Asia and Latin America.

Successes and failures of NGO technology development

Public sector agricultural technology development is conventionally analysed by 'stage', ie from basic agricultural technology development through strategic, applied and adaptive, with some consideration of agricultural technology development–dissemination linkages. Application of this approach to NGOs would not be particularly illuminating, since practically all NGO agricultural technology development is problem- or 'issue'-based and NGOs tend to draw on several stages simultaneously in an 'action-oriented' mode.

Here we prefer to consider five main areas in which NGOs have been innovative and relatively successful.

---

[3] This opposition has covered a range of forms. For instance, Ghandian NGOs in India lie at the less confrontational end of the spectrum, in contrast with, say, those NGOs in the Philippines that have campaigned for land reform.
[4] But note that the Mennonite Central Committee has conducted several pieces of long-term research during its 17 years of experimental work in Bangladesh (Buckland and Graham 1990).

Diagnostic and farming systems agricultural technology development methods

Conventional public sector approaches to agricultural technology development have difficulty in coping with the wide range of agro-ecological and socio-economic conditions characteristic of the complex, diverse and risk-prone areas in which many of the rural poor live (Chambers et al., eds 1989; Richards 1985). In such areas, agricultural technology development must not merely be on-farm and farmer-managed, but participatory in order to draw on local knowledge and to meet farmers' needs, opportunities, constraints and aspirations. The approaches introduced in GOs have frequently been expensive and time consuming, and often not participatory (Biggs 1989). Some NGOs, on the other hand, have been innovative in developing more parsimonious approaches.

- In Kenya, the Diagnosis and Design methodology practised and diffused by ICRAF grew out of the development of methods by CARE and Mazingira in the early 1980s to elicit rapid farmer assessment of tree species (Buck forthcoming).
- In Chile, NGOs were responsible for the elaboration of farming systems perspectives, and their subsequent teaching to other institutions (Aguirre and Namdar-Irani 1992; Sotomayor 1991).
- In India, Myrada has been instrumental in developing participatory rural appraisal methods and training for both other NGOs and government staff (Fernandez 1991).

NGOs have also introduced systems approaches to agricultural technology development which go beyond conventional farming systems research (FSR). First, several have used food systems perspectives. For instance:

- In Chile, AGRARIA is experimenting with means of commercialising small farmer grain production, which a government department is now considering scaling-up (Aguirre and Namdar-Irani 1992).
- In Bangladesh, the Mennonite Central Committee conducted the varietal, processing and market agricultural technology development on which around 1000 hectares of soya production by farmers is now based (Buckland and Graham 1990).
- In the Gambia, production of sesame introduced by Catholic Relief Services reached 8000 hectares, owing in part to their simultaneous introduction of oil-extraction technology (Gilbert 1990).

In other cases, NGOs have successfully expanded systems perspectives beyond the farm boundary. For instance, in Bangladesh, Friends in Village Development have conducted much of the R&D into the rearing and management of the 350,000 improved ducks now kept on open-access areas of water in the Sylhet area (Nahas 1991). Female household members are the focus of this and numerous other NGO projects, but are rarely a priority for government agricultural development programmes.

NGOs have also been instrumental in introducing a social, organisational and management dimension into the testing and subsequent adoption of certain technologies, which government services typically find difficult to introduce. For instance:

- In India, Action for World Solidarity and a consortium of GROs in Andhra

Pradesh devised a strategy for integrated pest management of caterpillar (*Amsacta sp*) on castor together with government research institutes, and then helped to organise farmers to take certain action simultaneously in order to achieve maximum impact (Satish et al. 1991).

■ In The Gambia and Ethiopia, NGOs have helped farmers to organise local informal seed production in ways designed to avoid undesirable cross-pollination (Henderson and Singh 1990).

■ In Bangladesh, NGOs have helped to organise landless labourers to acquire and operate 'lumpy' irrigation technology (Mustafa et al. 1991), and have organised groups, mainly of women, to interact both among themselves and with government services in chicken rearing (Khan et al. 1991).

Innovations in technologies and management practices

While funding constraints make long-term agricultural technology development difficult for NGOs, several have done work which has had far-reaching implications. For example:

■ In India, the Bharatiya Agro-Industries Foundation pioneered research into frozen semen technology in India, and, through its 500 field programmes in six states, has been responsible for producing around 10 per cent of the country's cross-bred dairy herd.

■ Similarly, the Southern Mindanao Baptist Rural Life Centre (Philippines) has identified integrated methods of managing hillslopes using sloping agricultural land technologies (Watson 1991).

Most NGO research efforts are, however, at the adaptive end of the research spectrum. For instance:

■ In India, PRADAN has scaled-down technologies developed by government institutes for mushroom and raw silk production, and for leather processing so that they can be used by low-income households (Vasimalai 1991).

■ Under the Farmer Innovation and Technology Testing programme in The Gambia, eight NGOs collaborated with the Department of Agricultural Research for on-farm testing of new crop varieties (Gilbert 1990).

■ In East Africa, NGOs have been testing new crop varieties in Zambia (Copestake 1990) and in Zimbabwe (Ndiweni et al. 1991), and have been adapting tree management practices in Zimbabwe (Ndiweni et al. 1991) and Kenya (Mung'ala and Arum 1991).

Dissemination methods

In general NGOs have sought to develop participatory dissemination methods. Examples include:

■ In Thailand, the Appropriate Technology Association developed farmer-to-farmer methods of disseminating rice-fish farming technologies which have subsequently been adapted by the Department of Agriculture (Sollows et al. 1991).

■ In Ecuador, CESA has developed systems for farmer-managed seed multiplication and distribution (CESA 1991; Mastrocola 1991).

Training activities and methods

A number of NGOs train both members of other NGOs and of GOs in participatory methods (Fernandez 1991; Chakraborty et al. 1991; Berdegue 1990). A recently-emerging role for NGOs is that of intermediary. This is illustrated below.

■ In Gujarat, India, the Aga Khan Rural Support Project (AKRSP) identified village training needs through discussions with farmer groups (Shah and Mane 1991). Initially, AKRSP organised government provision of this training, but the courses were very formal in style and farmers' evaluations showed that they had learned little of practical value. In response, AKRSP developed an alternative training and dissemination methodology which it tested over several areas. Government staff were then brought in to observe, participate in and, finally, adopt the methodology.

■ The International Institute for Rural Reconstruction in the Philippines brought together resource people from NGOs and GOs at a one-week workshop, the objective of which was to produce a completed agroforestry resources training manual. The manual is now widely used (Killough and Miclat-Teves 1991).

Promoting farmer organisations

Many NGOs operate with a concept of participation that goes beyond a joint experiment or on-farm trials. For these NGOs, to strengthen participation means to work in strengthening peasant organisations and in popular education, enhancing the rural poor's capacities for self-management and negotiation with external institutions (Farrington and Bebbington 1991).

NGOs have therefore emphasised project methodologies and actions that contribute to strengthening the co-ordination between individual producers, and subsequently between communities. Seed and input distribution systems, small-scale irrigation and work with farmer groups in on-farm trials have thus become priority areas of action. In many cases such a combination of productive and organisational initiatives can increase the impact of the project and strengthen the organisation simultaneously. The ultimate aim is to establish financially and administratively self-sustaining organisations (CESA 1991), and although NGOs' contributions to the formation of farmer organisations have not always matched their rhetoric, most experience in linking agricultural development projects with organisational strengthening has been gained in the NGO sector.

The abilities and experiences of NGOs in each of these areas suggest contributions NGOs could make to wider public sector programmes. These are considered in later sections, but first it is important to recognise that NGOs also suffer from a variety of limitations.

NGO weaknesses

Careful examination of the case studies reveals numerous NGO weaknesses in the field of agricultural technology development. In particular:

■ their small size and limited resources limit NGO activity to the applied end of the agricultural technology development spectrum;
■ funding patterns tend to be short-term and donor pressure is towards 'action' and 'results', thus hampering work on issues requiring long-term R&D.

Kohl (1991) documents a case of NGO failure in technology introduction which illustrates such weaknesses. His survey of 40 NGOs reveals that few NGOs had conducted serious experimentation on protected horticultural systems (PHS) although many were promoting such systems; that the few conducting experimentation have not done so rigorously, that a 'folklore' of the supposed advantages of PHS has developed; that communication flows among NGOs regarding the outcome of PHS implementation has been inadequate, and that the rapid implementation of technologies easily visible from main roads has led to premature introduction of unproven designs and management systems, and to a neglect of farmers' objectives and constraints.

These weaknesses suggest several ways in which government programmes and initiatives could enhance NGO effectiveness.

High-quality public programmes oriented towards the needs of the rural poor

Whilst NGOs may grow in size and number to fill 'gaps' left by government, they will not to be able to substitute for *all* the services that might normally be expected from government in *all* areas. Their efforts are likely to be more focused and effective where government makes a clear policy commitment to remove economic distortions against the rural sector and provides the physical infrastructure (roads, telecommunications) and human capital formation (de Janvry et al. 1989) which NGOs cannot provide in more than a piecemeal fashion.

Easing access to quality resources and information controlled by the public sector

In a recent meeting[5], Asian NGOs expressed their need, first, to access the skills, facilities, genetic material, and specialist knowledge of government services and, second, to have opportunity to influence government policies and strategies at the design stage. Large NGOs acting in consortium have occasionally persuaded government to cater to their needs (see eg. Sethna and Shah 1991), but simply to garner information on government plans, let alone influence them, is generally beyond the resources of smaller NGOs. To address such obstacles, NGO desks have been created in some Philippine line departments in order to elicit NGOs' views on draft plans and to cater to NGO enquiries.

Promoting inter-institutional co-ordinating mechanisms

NGOs' small size contributes to poor co-ordination, competition and duplication (of effort and of failures)[6]. Smallness of scale and localism also hinders NGO influence on regional and structural issues that largely determine the viability and outcome of local actions (Bebbington 1991a). Ideally, NGOs could resolve these issues for themselves by setting up mechanisms for co-ordination among themselves, and between themselves and the state. Unfortunately, their record of doing so beyond areas of immediate concern is poor. National NGO apex organisations tend to be weak and too distant from field issues to have a credible impact, and area-based mechanisms are few. Government involvement in setting up

---

[5] Asia Regional Workshop on 'NGOs, renewable natural resources management and links with the public sector' held in Hyderabad, India, 16–20 September 1991.
[6] See the paper by Kohl (1991) for an extreme example of this problem.

such mechanisms can quickly become authoritarian, but cases do exist in which local government agencies have adopted sensitive approaches, and much can be learned from these. The agreement of NGOs concerned with agroforestry in South Nyanza District of Kenya to co-ordinate their action with local government offices is particularly noteworthy (Musyoka et al. 1991).

Fostering greater grassroots influence over NGOs

A recurrent and widely voiced criticism is that NGOs' rhetoric on participation exceeds reality[7]. NGOs are self-appointed, rather than elected bodies, and control institutional resources from within.

For the public sector, the principal implication of these observations is that NGOs should not be viewed as direct representatives of the rural poor. Thus in policy and programming discussions, government should invite organisations of the rural poor directly to the negotiating and planning table, as well as NGOs. This would, in turn, place pressure on NGOs to be more accountable to rural populations. A longer-term contribution from government would be to sustain educational programmes in rural areas. The institutionally and politically empowering effect of broad-based education could contribute greatly to increasing assertiveness and modern forms of self-organisation among the rural poor.

Potential lessons for GOs from NGOs

A number of the approaches used by NGOs which might, with advantage, be adopted by GOs emerge from the discussion in previous sections. Briefly, they are:

- participatory approaches to FSR; approaches which embrace *food* systems, not merely *farming* systems; approaches which treat on- and off-farm resource use in a holistic fashion;
- a scaling-down and de-mystifying of what were initially complex technologies in order to make them more accessible to the rural poor;
- innovative dissemination methods (eg farmer-to-farmer);
- the re-orientation of GO staff towards practical 'learn by doing' training techniques which address farmers' problems directly.

Perhaps NGOs' flexibility, work ethic and ability to respond rapidly to issues as they arise offer the most powerful lessons – lessons which go to the heart of how GOs are organised and managed *as institutions*. Farrington and Bebbington (1991) identify several factors which limit GOs' institutional capacity to conduct systems-based agricultural technology development and dissemination to meet farmers' needs:

- excessive centralisation of decision-making authority, the consequences of which are inflexible and inefficient management;
- inappropriate reward systems, generally based on scientific publications, which are likely to bias agricultural technology development effort away from farmers' needs and unlikely to offer adequate rewards to field-oriented agricultural technology developers;

---

[7] The criticism comes from organisations of the rural poor (Bebbington et al. 1991), from development consultants (Tendler 1982 cited in Clark 1991:58), and from multilaterals (World Bank 1989:25).

■ inflexible programming and budgeting procedures, which leave no 'unallocated' resources which might be used to respond to needs (whether of NGOs or of farmers directly) as they arise.

Careful observation of the working practices of NGOs would allow at least some steps towards alleviation of these public sector constraints, though it should be emphasised that the larger size of the public sector and its (at least nominally) stricter accounting and reporting procedures are unlikely ever to allow it the flexibility that NGOs enjoy.

A more profound change would be to take lessons from NGOs' institutional structure and incorporate them into GOs. This would mean decentralising authority within GOs, and increasing the flexibility and adaptiveness of local offices (cf Sollis 1991)[8]. It would also involve structuring local offices of GO programmes along the lines of NGOs' small, relatively informal field offices, while retaining the co-ordinating mechanisms made possible by the presence of the overlying institutional structure of the public sector.

A yet more radical institutional response would be to accept that the still limited accountability of NGOs to local populations is equally a shortcoming of the public sector (Fowler 1991; Fox 1990). If GOs are to criticise NGOs for not allowing real farmer participation in the design and monitoring of their projects, then GOs should also allow such participation in public programmes of agricultural development. This is not to argue that farmers should hire and fire GO staff, but that they should have a far more active role in guiding their work.

The likelihood, of course, is that this will rarely happen, partly because of GO resistance, and partly because representative organisations of the rural poor do not exist everywhere. So in the short term, the most that can be hoped for is that NGOs will be invited into these programmes as surrogate representatives of the concerns of the rural poor. Ultimately though, and sooner rather than later, it should be the poor themselves who are there, with NGOs advising as experienced specialists.

Further steps likely to have a fundamental impact on GOs' responsiveness to farmers' needs are discussed under potential areas for NGO–GO collaboration in the next section.

Potential areas for NGO–GO collaboration

It should be emphasised that collaboration here means *working together* in a mutually interdependent fashion. It implies more than simply 'linkage' or 'interaction', and so the areas in which it might be implemented are correspondingly fewer.

Nonetheless, such collaboration can be both short-term and longer-term and institutionalised. Training courses offer perhaps the easiest short-term and temporary forms of collaboration. We would expect such training to be in both directions, with NGOs offering courses to GOs in participatory methods, FSR etc, and GOs offering NGOs support with technical problems. As we have already noted, there has been considerable success in this type of collaboration in the field of agricultural technology development.

---

[8] Sollis (1991:19) argues: 'the key to converting a disabling state into an enabling one in terms of social service provision is identified in decentralisation policy'.

On-farm programmes seem to be perhaps the most promising area in which to initiate institutionalised GO–NGO collaboration. From an NGO viewpoint, a contact with such programmes could improve their access to GO technologies, provide them with stronger agricultural technology development support, and offer a channel for eventual NGO influence on experiment station agricultural technology development.

The potential gains to NGOs from such collaboration are complemented by those which GOs could obtain: due to the expense of on-farm research programmes they are often early casualties of resource cutbacks (Biggs, 1989) and so to spread the cost of them among different types of institutions offers more sustainable options. As an example of a GO response to this constraint, the former Director of Ecuador's On-Farm Research programme has proposed a collaboration with NGOs in which the GO provides technical assistance in the agricultural technology development, and facilitates NGO access to public-sector-generated technology, while NGOs provide local diagnostic knowledge, supervise on-farm trials, and conduct the bulk of the field adaptation, and on the basis of their experiences influence public sector agricultural technology development (Cardoso et al. 1991). Such collaboration could subsequently be the basis for the constitution of regional agricultural technology development planning committees, in which NGOs, farmers' organisations and the GO would all have voting power.

In the Santa Cruz area of Bolivia, a similar type of collaboration between the government research institute (CIAT) and NGOs has shown that a structured relationship can improve feedback between field conditions and the agricultural technology development process. Here, NGOs participate in periodic exercises for the planning of CIAT's agricultural technology development activities, and share responsibilities and ideas in on-farm trials.

Planning and programming of change in the agriculture sector is the responsibility of government at both local and national levels. To avoid duplication or incoherence among NGOs' and GOs' actions, this planning should be built on a dialogue between NGOs and (at least initially) local level GOs. This is best initiated by GOs, given their axial administrative role in local society, and could result in projects and programmes more adequately addressing the needs of the rural poor. However, in taking such initiatives, GOs and NGOs ought to be sensitive to each other's concerns and institutional contexts, and find room for manoeuvre within these. The goal would be to identify the most appropriate division of tasks for the characteristics of the area and of the institutions involved. Ultimately one might envisage the emergence of area-based and national consortia of GOs, NGOs and farmer organisations.

Such consortia would allow joint planning and co-ordination *within the room for manoeuvre* allowed by shared institutional goals.

However, as we noted at the outset, the obstacles to any such collaboration must be made explicit and addressed early on. Such arrangements will be a new experience for many NGOs and GOs whose relationships were previously based on conflict or supervision. Success will require a prior process of building mutual trust and breaking down institutional stereotypes. Here informal personal contacts have an important role to play.

Similarly, the disadvantages of collaboration must be acknowledged from the outset. Collaboration will challenge old institutional identities and autonomy, and will introduce new constraints as well as potentials. For all involved the trade-offs implied by collaboration must be made explicit.

Finally we would stress that in collaborating with larger government agencies and multilateral donors, NGOs can easily be pushed into a position in which they implement other institutions' programmes. While some NGOs may decide that this role suits them, others feel that it will both hinder and compromise their roles as methodological innovators and policy critics. If they refrain from direct collaboration, however, the challenge to these NGOs is to find other means of exposing GOs to their innovations and critics. The parallel challenge to GOs and donors is to avoid seeing NGOs as simple vehicles for programme implementation, and to find means of learning from their experiences, and incorporating these into programme and institutional design.

Conclusions

NGOs' experience in the development and dissemination of agriculture-related technologies and management practices for the rural poor is highly diverse and exhibits both success and failure. NGOs' actions are restricted by the limited overall size, unreliability and short-term nature of their funding, as also by the action-orientation of their funding agencies.

Their success is rooted in locally-adapted participatory and empowering approaches, in a strong problem orientation, and in a capacity to think beyond the narrow on-farm bounds of conventional FSR. Failures tend to result in part from the pressures exerted by funding agencies, but also by a reluctance to share and critically analyse the lessons of failure. Linkages and collaborations between GOs and NGOs offer one means of addressing these weaknesses and exploiting the strengths to greater effect.

Overall, the majority of the interactions between NGOs and GOs that we have observed have been initiated by NGOs. Given their small size, they have frequently incurred high transaction costs in taking these initiatives. In the next decade, the initiative is increasingly likely to lie with GOs. Donors and the public sector need to offer NGOs a range of options consistent with their own aspirations, whether (at one end of the spectrum) these lie in delivering services on behalf of government or (at the other) in the development of innovative approaches to the enhancement of rural livelihoods. Providing that their approaches are sensitive enough, there is plenty of scope for them to work with NGOs at field and policy level, and to incorporate into their own programmes and structures many of the lessons deriving from NGO experience.

NGO–government collaboration in Bangkok

Somthavil Klinmahorm and Kevin Ireland

Introduction

The case study that is presented here covers some six years of co-operation between Save The Children Fund-UK and Rajanukul Hospital for Mentally Retarded Children in Bangkok, Thailand. The example is one of a small project, with limited aims, adapting and exploiting opportunities as they presented themselves, gradually enlarging its objectives and increasing the potential impact of its work. The project was not designed with wider impact in mind and the framework that is presented for analysing the process of scaling-up follows a retrospective assessment of experience in this and other projects. However, the authors believe that this framework may have wider (although certainly not universal) applicability in relation to the involvement of NGOs in scaling-up their impact in relation to government services.

Scaling-up: a framework

One of the most frequent models employed by NGOs interested in scaling-up their impact is the 'pilot project'. In essence such a project seeks to provide an example of good practice, in the hope – if not the expectation – that this can be replicated, either by other NGOs or by government. The framework outlined here relates specifically to working with government.

Replicability is a key concept in relation to scaling-up through pilot projects. The initial model needs to provide a practical and appropriate basis for service development on a large scale. Without this the lessons that can be drawn from the pilot project may be too local and specific to have wider influence. The second key concept is *sustainability*, by which we mean the ability to maintain services in the longer run without significant external support. Clearly, there is little point in demonstrating that a model of intervention or service development can achieve results and can be replicated in other circumstances if those circumstances require continuing high levels of external support.

Our starting point, therefore, is that a pilot project which aims to influence government service provision must demonstrate both its replicability and its sustainability. We interpret this to mean that the project must, *from the outset*, be implemented by and entirely within government structures.

NGO-implemented pilot projects that aim to set an example for the government sector to follow can only ever remain just that – pilot projects. NGOs operate in a privileged environment of flexibility, with greater access to funds for innovation and fewer bureaucratic constraints. Neither true replicability nor sustainability can be demonstrated by pilot projects that are operated by NGOs and outside the constraints of government structures. With this in mind we suggest that there are three stages to the scaling-up process, and that the failure to appreciate the essential difference between stages two and three may be one of the causes of the frequent failure of NGOs to influence government systems and structures over the longer term

Stage 1: Pilot project(s)   One (possibly more) project, exploring a new approach to service provision. At this stage it operates within the government sector, but on an exceptional basis and with significant NGO support/input.

Stage 2: Small-scale integration   The initial pilot project has proved successful and is replicated. There is greater integration into existing government structures and budgets. However, integration is dependent upon local and essentially personal initiatives.

Stage 3: Assimilation   The local example is adopted as an appropriate model, and systems, structures and budgets are adapted accordingly. Policy is reformulated and – most importantly – practice changes.

The essential message of this framework is that stage three is not simply a larger scale version of stage two. Stage two is dependent upon local initiative and committed government officials working creatively within – and extending – their sphere of responsibility. However, the model has not been internalised within the organisation's policies or practices. Thus, the loss (perhaps through transfer or retirement) of one key official can mean that all gains evaporate, practices revert to previous norms, and policy is no longer questioned. A similar effect may be achieved by the withdrawal of external (NGO) support at this stage – the project has demonstrated its replicability, but not yet its sustainability.

In stage two the driving force are those officials who are willing to extend the boundaries of their immediate responsibilities for maintaining existing services. A conscious decision is required from these officials to do more than the minimum. This will often lead to opposition, possibly resentment, within the bureaucracy. New approaches involve change and change means disturbing the balance of power and authority. Those wishing to maintain the status quo generally do not need to take overt action to block the initiative, as the absence of co-operation and support alone allows bureaucratic resistance to drain its energy. Stage two is dependent, therefore, upon personal initiative and sustained positive action to promote change.

In stage three, however, the position is reversed, as the organisation redefines roles and responsibilities. New policies and practices have been adopted officially so they are no longer dependent upon personal initiative. Indeed, anyone wishing to oppose the new policy must now operate outside agreed responsibilities. At this point the organisational requirements for sustainability have been achieved.

We argue that stage three cannot be attained successfully simply by extending or repeating activities from stage two. An entirely different approach is required – one which targets the promotion of change in organisational policy and practice. The implication for NGOs is that scaling-up requires a reassessment and change of approach as stage two moves towards success. It is as if a barrier exists between stages two and three. Repetition alone cannot surmount this barrier. A new strategy is required – in effect it is a new 'project': one which draws on the philosophy and methods of lobbying and advocacy, rather than replicating a model of service delivery.

Moving from stage one to stage two is essentially 'additive' in Edwards and Hulme's terminology (this volume). As such, if the model is appropriate and successful, this move is primarily a question of resource availability. The successful move to stage three, however, is more than this: it must also be 'multiplicative' in extending influence and support, so that the new model may have the opportunity to influence the use of existing, not just additional, resources.

This model is represented diagrammatically in Figure 1.

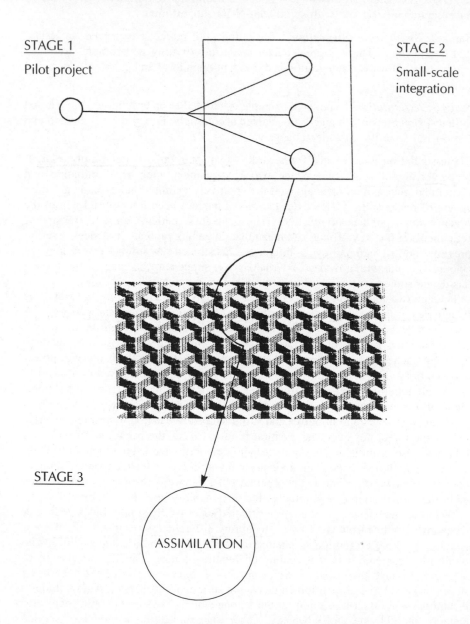

Figure 5:1 *Scaling-up: a framework*

The context

The project used in the case study that follows is concerned with providing support, development and educational opportunities to children who are mentally retarded. To appreciate the context of this project, it is worth recapping briefly some of the significant issues relating to disability and development that have become commonly accepted over the past few years.

In many ways, 1981 (the International Year of Disabled Persons) was a milestone, both in terms of drawing attention to the needs of disabled persons and as the precursor of the United Nations Decade of Disabled Persons (1983–1992). As part of this Decade, the UN General Assembly adopted a World Programme of Action Concerning Disabled Persons. Along with prevention of disability and rehabilitation, this Programme of Action stressed the need for equalisation of opportunities for disabled persons. It stressed, for example, that disabled persons should not be separated from their families and communities and stressed that the education of disabled persons should as far as possible take place in the general school system.

The World Programme of Action represents a significant marker in the wider acceptance that disabled persons have rights as individuals and that those rights require positive action to avoid discrimination, facilitate integration and acceptance within the community, and provide equal opportunities for personal development, support and employment.

The World Health Organisation (WHO) estimates that between seven and ten per cent of the population in developing countries is disabled (Helander et al 1989). UNESCO (Hegarty 1990) reports that there are some 200 million children in the world with a disability and that around 80 per cent of these live in developing countries. It further estimates that less than two per cent of these receive special services of any kind.

Such large numbers include people with a wide range of disabilities. In only a small minority of cases, however, would the disabilities be classified as severe. Nevertheless, opportunities and access to services are frequently restricted for all disabled persons, irrespective of the severity of disability or their ability to integrate (Hegarty 1990).   •

Disability in Thailand

While Thailand has made considerable economic advances within the past few years, there has been only a limited interest shown in responding to the needs of disabled persons in the country. The statistics that are available concerning the numbers of disabled persons are contradictory and often unrealistic. For instance, compared to the WHO estimate of seven to ten per cent of any population with a disability, the most recent official statistic quoted for Thailand gives a total of 385,560 disabled persons (NSO 1986). In a population of approximately 56 million, this would represent less than 0.7 per cent. Other, disability-specific, information may give a more accurate picture. The results of one recent survey suggest that around two per cent of the population may be classified as 'mentally retarded' (Dheandanoo 1991). This percentage would mean that there are probably around 240,000 mentally retarded children within the age range of 6–14 years and thus eligible for schooling. Against this level of need, it is estimated that only around 5,000, or less than two per cent, are attending school (Dheandanoo 1991).

The case study: Rajanukul Hospital and integrated education[1]

Save the Children Fund's co-operation with Rajunukul Hospital began in 1985. Rajanukul Hospital operates within the Ministry of Public Health and is the only hospital specialising in mental retardation in Thailand. It provides an outpatient clinic for around 40–60 people daily, plus inpatient/residential facilities for mentally retarded children from birth to age 18. There is an early intervention programme for the youngest children, a preschool, primary school and vocational training activities. Over 700 children reside at the hospital, mainly on a permanent basis. The primary criterion for admission to schooling in the hospital is that the children are 'trainable'. The hospital also has a Community Services Department, which is responsible for outreach work within the community.

The first contact between Rajanukul Hospital and SCF was made by a VSO volunteer, an experienced paediatrician and specialist in mental retardation, who was assisting the hospital to develop its outreach and community services. However, at this time the hospital itself was more concerned with the fact that it had a large and growing waiting list and could not meet the demand for residential places. Thus, when the hospital submitted a proposal to SCF for a pilot project, it was 'to help mentally retarded (children) and their parents who are waiting for hospital treatment, or who do not have the opportunity to get it'.

Of the seven objectives listed for this 'pilot project' the first two related to preparation of children waiting for hospital places. With the third objective an element of community orientation was introduced. Overall, however, the original concept appears to have been not so much to create an alternative to institutional care, but to help children prepare for it.

The original project was also very limited in size. A small room was obtained in a government community centre, located adjacent to the hospital. At most this could cater at any one time for ten children, plus staff. Within six months of opening in October 1985, nine children were registered and four attended regularly. A year later 26 children were registered, with ten attending daily, in rotation. The staff comprised two teachers and one care attendant.

After nearly two years the experience of the project was reviewed. SCF drew attention to the lack of involvement of parents and suggested that this should become a greater focus of attention. Using the project as a base for greater contacts and integration within the community was also recommended.

From around this time the objectives of the project began to broaden. A close personal relationship had been established between the SCF staff member responsible for the project and key personnel within the hospital's Community Services Department. At this level it was agreed that the future of the project lay in developing a community-based alternative to residential care.

It was also clear by this time that the existing facility was too small, and it was therefore proposed to find a new location. SCF agreed to fund building works, so that a larger centre could be created in vacant space under an adjoining public-

[1] The authors would like to express their appreciation to past and present officials in Rajanukul Hospital, the Bangkok Metropolitan Administration, and the Ministry of Education, who have co-operated over such an extended period. It must be stressed, however, that the views expressed in this paper are those of the authors alone, and should not be attributed to any of the government officials involved in the case study.

sector housing block. The owners, the National Housing Authority, had on a number of previous occasions given approval to infills of this kind for community purposes.

In developing the revised proposal SCF and the hospital reached agreement that the involvement of the parents would be increased and that the project would attempt to integrate more effectively with the local community. Unexpectedly, however, the National Housing Authority refused the hospital permission to build the centre.

Throughout the first three years the project did not move beyond stage one of the scaling-up process described above. Initially, in fact, it is difficult to see it as a pilot project in providing any wider lessons for service development. As it evolved, however, it did move towards presenting an alternative model. At this stage the issue of sustainability was discussed, but the project was still entirely dependent upon the external assistance provided by SCF. Curiously, it was the rejection of building permission by the BMA that marked the first steps along the way to stage two.

In July 1988 SCF co-sponsored Thailand's first National Seminar on Community-Based Rehabilitation. By drawing together most of the people in the country interested and involved in community-based initiatives for disabled persons, the seminar provided a stimulus to a number of interesting initiatives. One such initiative came from the Bangkok Metropolitan Administration (BMA). The BMA is the authority responsible for regional government in greater Bangkok, including certain aspects of primary education. Their representative at this seminar was interested in the project described by Rajanukul Hospital and the problem of finding suitable, larger accommodation. As a result, contact was made with a local primary school operated by the BMA (Vichuthit School) and approval given to use two of its rooms.

The project moved to Vichuthit School in February 1989. At first it operated within the school as an entirely separate entity, with the hospital providing staff and technical support. However, as part of the strategy to improve sustainability, the hospital negotiated successfully with the Ministry of Education (MOE) for the allocation of a special education teacher to the project. With the support of an interested teacher from within the school, integration of mentally retarded children into mainstream classes began, on a limited basis, with physical education, and has since spread to music and art. There is considerable preparation at each stage of integration, to make sure that children and teachers are adequately equipped.

The project is considered successful, both by the hospital and the school. The children within the project have better levels of adjustment and development than those residing within the hospital – even though the project caters for children with more severe disabilities. Indeed, in 1990 the project was selected by the Ministry of Public Health to receive an award as an outstanding project of that ministry.

During this period SCF held discussions with Rajanukul Hospital and the BMA about replicating the model and planning for the transfer of SCF's financial input to the government. With some financial assistance from SCF a similar unit was established in another BMA school, and a third was planned, both utilising special education teachers provided by the Ministry of Education.

The programme by now had moved to stage two of the scaling-up process. The initial project was being replicated and there was greater integration into existing government structures, budgets and services. However, it was still dependent upon the initiative and co-operation of key individuals – there was no fundamental change of practice or transfer of responsibilities within the education sector.

Over the past six to twelve months, Rajanukul Hospital and SCF have come up against the barrier that separates stages two and three in the scaling-up process. While national policy statements have been in favour of integrated education for mentally retarded children for many years, the reality has been that very limited opportunities exist[2]. This appears to derive more from attitudes and lack of knowledge of the extent of need than from resource constraints, although there also appears to be a certain confusion, if not conflict, between the three or more branches of the educational service that have responsibility for this area of work.

At this stage SCF has determined that it is inappropriate simply to support further isolated units within schools. We are now assisting Rajanukul Hospital in a campaign to change attitudes and to increase the awareness and acceptance of mentally retarded children. We anticipate the potential for further financial assistance, but this is more likely to be directed in support of a programme of implementation within one of the responsible educational authorities. We would seek to avoid financing any recurring staff costs, but can envisage providing help with training and technical support, in order to help develop the organisational structure necessary for implementation.

Lessons of experience

Pilot projects need to be operated within the government sector. Because of the particular advantages enjoyed by NGOs, pilot projects which aim to demonstrate a new model of service provision need to be operated within the government sector from the outset. Greater organisational constraints within government mean that only limited lessons of replicability can be learned from pilot projects implemented by NGOs. This is not to deny that such projects may have a useful 'demonstration effect'.

In this case study all operational responsibilities have been retained by the government sector – initially by Rajanukul Hospital and subsequently by the schools involved, in co-operation with the relevant administration. Thus, the process of developing the project from idea to implementation has required the identification and opening up of bureaucratic pathways that would not have been necessary if SCF itself had taken this responsibility.

Replicability does not indicate sustainability. Both replicability and sustainability are conditions which must be met before scaling-up can be achieved. However, the ability of the government sector to replicate a pilot project, particularly where this involves a continuing input from an external agency, does not of itself indicate sustainability. Pilot projects can be repeated many times, but still remain essentially outside the government's accepted responsibilities and practices, even when carried out by a government agency.

In this case study, the initial project has been repeated once successfully, and

---

[2] The first integrated learning programme for mentally retarded children was introduced in 1957 and the National Education Policy announced in 1977 indicated that special education 'may be arranged in specific institutions or integrated in ordinary schools, as deemed suitable.'

another is planned. The two existing projects have demonstrated the efficacy of the model when applied in a supportive environment, ie where the principal of the school concerned identifies with the objectives and provides the necessary space and assistance. Such successes are still dependent upon such personal initiatives, as there is no requirement for school principals to provide support, and a number have declined to do so. Indeed, a recent change of Principal at Vichuthit School raised questions about the future of the project, as the new incumbent was at first uncertain whether to continue support.

Sustainability involves both financial and organisational components. It is most common to see the question of sustainability linked to the continuing financial viability of a project or service. Whilst this will always remain important, there is a further element of sustainability which is vital when considering the possibility of scaling-up services within the government sector: the attainment of the necessary organisational and structural conditions.

In this case study we have been fortunate in having confidence (reinforced by the government officials concerned) that financial sustainability is not the major issue. The questions raised by this project concern the way in which resources are allocated within budgets, rather than the size of the budgets themselves. Achieving acceptance within government decision-making is a prerequisite to obtaining commitment to sustained funding for any new initiative.

Scaling-up is threatening. The scaling-up process involves change. Change involves disturbing the existing balance of power and authority. Opposition can therefore be expected once the process appears to have the potential to influence structures and responsibilities.

In the case study, for instance, once the Vichuthit School project started to demonstrate its success as an alternative to existing policies at Rajanukul Hospital, it became inevitable that opposition would arise within that institution. In particular, the new model raised fundamental questions about the hospital's residential school (remembering that the integrated project assists children with equal and, in a number of cases, more severe disabilities than are accepted into the hospital's own school). Problems were encountered in gaining the support of the Principal to refer suitable children from the residential school to the school in the community. Fortunately, under the clear lead of the Director of the hospital, these problems have been overcome.

A separate strategy is required for scaling-up. We believe that a barrier exists between the partial integration of successful pilot projects and the necessary internalisation and assimilation that represents scaling-up (stages two and three of our framework). Surmounting this barrier requires a new strategy, one based more on the 'multiplicative' than the 'additive' approach. Perhaps it is this fundamental change of style that provides such a barrier for many operational NGOs, which are more used to dealing with 'projects' than lobbying and advocacy.

In the case study, we are moving from supporting pilot projects to assisting in a campaign of attitudinal change and awareness-raising. This involves contacting a wide range of interested people outside of those immediately concerned with the project – academics, senior government officials and others. We have supported the production of a video of the Vichuthit School experience, which is aimed primarily at decision makers, senior administrators and opinion leaders, but which is also due to be screened on national TV. Both our project partners and ourselves have found that we are working in new ways, and are having to develop new skills, particularly in the area of lobbying and advocacy.

National policy statements do not necessarily reflect practice. In our experience in this and other projects, we have found that the policy framework at national level may be way ahead of actual practice within the government sector. In Thailand, for instance, there has been a policy in support of integrated education since 1957, but achievement since that time has been very limited, as the statistics quoted at the beginning of this chapter testify. Given the educational priorities of the period (principally to extend primary school enrolment rates throughout the country) this is neither surprising, nor necessarily a matter for criticism. The implication, however, is that it is not necessary to target changes in official policy in order to achieve the necessary improvements, but to analyse why existing policy has not been implemented in practice.

In part this may reflect constraints due to budgetary, staffing or other resource restrictions. As we have found, it may also be due to reasons related to structure, responsibility and power within the government sector and the resistance to change that is evident in such large organisations.

The role of individuals is vital. The development of a successful alternative model of service provision within the government sector requires the identification and support of officials who are willing to work with commitment beyond their normal responsibilities. Such individuals provide the necessary energy and ability to overcome bureaucratic inertia.

This lesson is demonstrated by comparing the progress made in the case study project with longer-term and more intensive support of other government departments. In these cases we have been supporting training and other activities to improve standards within child-care institutions and to help practitioners to follow stated government policy which avoids the institutionalisation of children. Regardless of the many statements of support received from individuals within the department concerned, real progress has been absent. In large part this has been because there has been no official with sufficient weight who has been willing to commit herself to acting for change within the department. This may reflect a realistic perception within that department that the time is not yet ripe for significant change.

The NGO as an agent of change. An NGO is usually a small player in relation to government services, and therefore plays a supportive but secondary role. However, the flexibility enjoyed by NGOs allows them a potential influence as an agent of change beyond the scale of resources applied. Both in the case study reported here and other positive involvements with the government sector in Thailand, officials have drawn attention to our ability to make contacts and facilitate initiatives outside of formal networks. This is particularly important when it comes to the type of lobbying and advocacy that is needed to achieve stage three of the scaling-up process. The ability to arrange for a video of the project for use as a campaign tool, is one obvious example, but our most significant contribution has probably been in networking with contacts, both within and outside the government.

Scaling-up: a long-term process. It does not seem helpful to us to view scaling-up as a product which can be targeted and obtained within a fixed period of time (especially the three or four years that often represents the time horizon of NGO interventions). It is a process which occurs over a longer and ill-defined period. NGOs seeking to assist in this process need to be willing to maintain their involvement over an extended period and to retain flexibility in the definition of their short and medium-term objectives.

In retrospect it has been particularly interesting to note that, while we have targeted integrated education for scaling-up in this project, the greatest impact has probably been on the health rather than the education sector. Six years ago Rajanukul Hospital was still fundamentally committed to an approach which favoured institutionalisation, but now it gives priority to community-based initiatives. The Community Services Department of the hospital has gained much in credibility and experience (including political and advocacy experience) in trying to extend the bounds of integrated education. With the support of SCF and the British Council two of the key staff within the hospital have visited community-based programmes in Britain and have returned committed to extend the hospital's activities in this area. Perhaps most significantly, long-term plans for a second hospital for mentally handicapped children in the north of the country are being reconsidered, with a view to minimising residential facilities and stressing a community-based service model, including integrated education. These results do not arise only from the case study presented here. This project has, however, provided a focus for the transmission of policy into practice and ideas into experience.

Conclusion

This case study is an example of a project that was initiated without any serious reference to scaling-up as an objective. In fact, this objective was introduced only after it became clear that it was both feasible and part of the agenda for SCF's partner. It was an opportunistic response, one which developed gradually and informally rather than being designed at the outset. If there was a single conclusion from this experience it would be that the issue of scaling-up is as much about the quality of relationships between NGO and government personnel, as it is about the technical efficacy of a service-delivery model. In the final analysis scaling-up can occur only when the appropriate people within government support it. International NGOs should see their role as supporting their partners within government to create the necessary conditions for this to happen, but they cannot create these conditions from the outside. To misquote John Clark's paper (in this volume), we cannot deliver, we must learn how to facilitate.

6

Multiplying micro-level inputs to government structures

James Mackie

Introduction

VSO is an agency that provides low-cost technical assistance to support the work of other development agencies. Typically individual volunteers ('VSOs') are placed within the staffing structure of an indigenous agency, be it a government department or a local NGO. Occasionally they may work for a development project run by an external agency. For VSO therefore, scaling-up is not usually about running the same project on grander lines. Rather it is about identifying a successful VSO posting and then working with the employer to see how it could be replicated on similar lines through their organisation.

This chapter presents an overview of VSO's experience in scaling-up. It attempts to draw some general lessons which should be of wider interest. In particular it seeks to illustrate the following main themes:

- Integrating development work into existing structures and systems and in particular government structures can pay rich rewards in terms of impact, replication and sustainability providing the conditions of integration are right. VSOs are placed within the structures of indigenous institutions. They are managed by these employers and not by VSO. Their work is part of the work of the institution that employs them. By keeping their conditions of employment and living situation as close as possible to those of their local colleagues we endeavour to further encourage their integration.

- NGOs are in many ways best suited to micro-level work. Scaling-up involves handling processes we are less familiar with and less able to conduct successfully; when we do achieve success, sustainability can then be a serious problem as we do not have the resources to maintain this greater degree of activity over a long period. Once we depart from the core area of VSO's work (the individual volunteer placement) we are on much less familiar ground, and our ability to get it right and achieve successes is correspondingly reduced.

- NGOs are more likely to be successful at scaling-up if they do so through the *planned multiplication of micro-level inputs* rather than through a process of designing and implementing macro-level projects. By this we do not mean replicating a particular post many times, but rather a process of enhancing each new post by studying earlier ones, identifying what conditions, structures and resources made them work well and doing our best to ensure that future posts of the same type are set up from the very start with these conditions.

This chapter contains six case-studies in which scaling-up has occurred or is being planned. These are grouped into three sets of two, each set representing a different strategy for increasing impact. The first set involves two major education programmes in Bhutan and Nigeria where VSO has over the past five years posted 40 and 100 volunteers respectively to work in government schools and introduce new teaching programmes. VSO has also contributed a limited amount of funding for specific inputs. The next two case studies are also in the education field but involve programmes where the field offices in Uganda and Kenya, building on their experience of existing VSO posts, have suggested to the Ministries concerned the establishment of identifiably separate 'projects' to be grafted on to the government structures. Having agreed these projects with the authorities, VSO has then taken on the task of organising and implementing the projects and of finding donors to pay for them. Both projects involve less than a dozen volunteers.

The third set involves two cases where VSO has made much smaller inputs to existing government services, yet the impact of this input has still been important. Both projects involve a key volunteer who, partly through circumstance and partly because of the sort of person they are, has acted as a catalyst in helping an existing government institution to scale-up and improve fairly rapidly a service it is already committed to providing in principle. One of these examples in The Gambia has involved a few other volunteer posts, the other in Nepal so far has not, but both are expecting a further limited number of volunteers in the year ahead.

Introducing new teaching programmes

The first two case studies are the 'New Approaches to Primary Education' or NAPE programme in Bhutan, and the 'Introductory Technology' or Introtech programme in Nigeria. In both cases VSO has undertaken to help the Ministry of Education to introduce a new teaching method and curriculum across the school system. Volunteers have all worked within existing school or Ministry structures and while the bulk of them are classroom teachers, some have also had curriculum development or teacher-training jobs. VSO is not involved in the management *per se* of either NAPE or Introtech, though our field staff and indeed some of the volunteers have been able to suggest changes or even sometimes influence decisions at the management level within the Ministry. Both the volunteers and the field staff have, however, had considerable impact at a methodological level and the resulting curricula bear the mark of their approaches and ideas. Both cases also provide a good example of what is meant by *multiplying micro-level inputs* in that the 'projects' are essentially a whole series of individual VSO placements.

While these factors are common to both programmes there are also some major differences, not the least of which is that we are much more confident of the long-term impact and sustainability of VSO's input to NAPE than to Introtech. Thus in Bhutan, while there is still considerable work to be done, it is possible to envisage a day where NAPE will have become well-established in all primary schools throughout the country and there will be enough Bhutanese teachers trained in the methodology able and willing to carry on the work. In Nigeria, even in the states in which VSO works, it still seems to us that little headway is being made towards Introtech becoming properly established and it is hard to see how most of the schools where VSO has placed Introtech volunteers would be able to continue the programme in any meaningful way were VSO to withdraw.

Thus while both cases involve multiple micro-level inputs by VSO the difference between them lies in the degree to which this was *consciously* planned and how well the scaling-up process was integrated into existing structures. The reasons for the projects' varying degree of success, in terms of prospects for replication and sustainability, lie precisely in this area.

In the case of NAPE the concept for the new teaching methodology arose out of a congruence of several factors: the ideas of one Bhutanese teacher recently returned from a training course in the UK where he had observed child-centered teaching methods, a report from a British Council education adviser, and the ideas of two teaching volunteers already in Bhutan, were particularly significant. However, there were also a number of circumstantial conditions, some of them political, which meant that the Bhutanese Ministry of Education were receptive to a new approach to primary education. More important is to note that while VSO was involved at the initial conceptual stage, the concept was by no means VSO's alone but was well-rooted in the government's own structures. Moreover, the decision to scale-up was clearly a Ministry decision based on their own interests and priorities, although they would have been aware that VSO were interested in being involved.

NAPE has encountered difficulties along the way but clear government 'ownership' of the project and VSO's close integration into their structures have meant that these have been overcome. Thus at one stage the project faltered in response to a public perception that NAPE was becoming too dominated by foreigners, but a positive UNICEF evaluation renewed the government's commitment. For VSO the speed and extent to which the Ministry wanted to scale-up also caused problems in terms of recruitment. This was resolved partly by VSO London undertaking special recruitment initiatives and partly by close co-operation with the Ministry to devise different jobs which increased the use made of VSOs already working in NAPE in their second and third years.

With Introtech, VSO was not part of the decision to include Introductory Technology in school curricula. This was taken at the Federal government level. However, when schools had to start teaching the course, VSO quickly became involved as we already worked in the schools. The potential for VSO to scale-up and help a large number of schools to introduce this new subject (for which they had no trained teachers) was also quickly apparent. Thereafter the decision to go ahead and actually post Introtech volunteers in large numbers was essentially taken by VSO. Obviously we could only do so in response to actual requests from the schools and, while these were forthcoming, there was never any formal central agreement between VSO and the education authorities at either the State or Federal levels that VSO should scale-up and set up a major Introtech teaching programme.

Subsequently this lack of Nigerian 'ownership' of VSO's scaling-up efforts meant that whenever VSO wanted to suggest improvements to our involvement (eg with in-service teacher training seminars, funding for materials and equipment or even to teaching methodology), there was no single authority overseeing and managing Introtech with whom we could deal. This was exacerbated by discontinuities caused by government staff turnover. Thus while VSO sees itself as participating in a single large-scale programme, we are effectively dealing with the Nigerian authorities on a case-by-case basis at the individual school level. Inevitably this makes it difficult to achieve the sorts of adjustments to job content, qualifications requirements, teaching methodology and curricula which would make the scaling-up process easier.

Despite these differences both NAPE and Introtech can be seen as effective and successful at the micro level. In the schools in which they work the VSOs can make a definite and positive contribution. They are able to teach school children, help their local colleagues with new ideas on teaching methodology and skills, and the most able among them can do extremely worthwhile and rewarding jobs. However, differences start to appear when we look at the macro-level impact of the two projects. With NAPE in Bhutan there appears to be a high degree of impact and very good prospects of sustainability, but this is much less the case with Introtech in Nigeria. Clearly the conditions surrounding the scaling-up process in Bhutan have a lot to do with this: the access VSO has to a central co-ordinating agency, this agency's own commitment to scaling-up which feeds through into a greater degree of planning and coordination, the fact that there are several external actors in the project making distinct and complementary inputs, and VSO's ability to influence the central planning process and at the same time work at the grassroots level (the individual school) all contribute to greater macro-level impact.

The conclusions one can draw therefore are that micro-level inputs are an important foundation for successful scaling-up: moreover, if the scaling-up process is unsuccessful at the macro level this does not necessarily prevent the project achieving at least some success at the micro level. However, if multiplying micro-level inputs can be achieved in a way in which integrates well into existing structures and can be consciously planned, macro-level impact can also be effective.

Creating new specialised services

The second set of case studies comprise a project in Uganda known as STEPU ('Science & Technical Education Production Unit') and another in Kenya called the 'Youth Training Support Programme' or YTSP. In both cases the projects were designed, established and are now being implemented by VSO. They are both in fields that VSO has worked in for a number of years and where we have close links with the Ministry involved. Both are therefore 'operational' projects where VSO has scaled-up its involvement in a sector that we are already familiar with by creating a new and more ambitious project which builds on our experience to make better use of the volunteers that we can recruit. Both projects employ VSOs but are conceived as free-standing projects and therefore do not conform to our model of *planned multiplication of micro-level inputs*. The volunteer jobs within them would not be possible without the superstructure of the project.

Establishing these two projects has taken VSO into unfamiliar territory. We have first had to design the projects, agreeing guidelines and details with the concerned Ministries as we proceeded but nevertheless essentially designing them ourselves. We have had to persuade official donors (the ODA Country Desk for STEPU and the EC Co-financing Scheme for YTSP) to finance them and lastly we have had to set up the management structures to implement them. This process has involved various pitfalls of which we might have been aware but had only limited experience. At times the projects have looked distinctly vulnerable, but while there are no doubt still hurdles ahead both are operating well and successes are being achieved. However, the remaining issue that we are still some way to resolving in both cases is sustainability and the proper integration of the two projects into existing government structures.

To draw lessons from this experience it is worth examining both projects in more detail. STEPU is a unit attached to the Ugandan Ministry of Education's National Curriculum Development Centre (NCDC). It consists of a small workshop and office at the NCDC headquarters and a mobile unit that travels to secondary schools round the country to repair and maintain school science and technology equipment, and to train teachers and technicians in the use and maintenance of this equipment so that they can improve their practical laboratory sessions with pupils. In addition STEPU seeks to identify equipment which could be easily designed and produced in Uganda either at STEPU itself or at a school so as to reduce dependence on imports.

The STEPU concept goes back some 15 years but it was not until late in 1987 that it was formally established by the Ministry. ODA funding for the establishment of the Mobile Maintenance and Training Unit, in many ways the key element of STEPU, then only started in March 1989. VSO has longstanding contacts with the Ministry and therefore became involved fairly early on at the conceptual and design stage. The VSO Field Office worked with Ministry staff on the initial groundwork and then wrote the funding proposal for the British Overseas Development Administration (ODA). VSO has also managed the ODA funding and handled the reporting requirements. One of the major problems encountered so far has been in the management of the project. After the approval of the ODA funds there was some delay in appointing two key project staff: the Uganda Project Coordinator and a VSO Business Adviser. In the interregnum, as VSO was handling the funds, the Field Office ended up having to manage the project, a role which we had not properly thought through and were, at the time, ill-prepared for. Our ability to get through this difficult period successfully was greatly enhanced by the excellent working relationship the field office had built up with the Ministry in the early stages of the project.

The second issue is longer-term sustainability, and this involves persuading a major multilateral or bilateral donor to support STEPU financially over a five- to ten-year period. Both the World Bank and UNESCO are interested and there is therefore a fair chance that a second scaling-up phase will occur, but one in which VSO can phase out its management involvement though continuing to support the project with volunteers as required. If this occurs the project could then become something of a text book example of the value of an NGO guiding a project to the point at which the concept has proved its worth and larger development agencies and/or government structures are prepared to take it over.

YTSP has a rather different history. The concept belonged to a much greater extent to VSO. VSOs have worked in Youth Polytechnics (YPs) throughout Kenya in fairly large numbers for several years. This experience had demonstrated to us the need to upgrade the quality and scope of courses offered by the YPs so as to increase the chances of graduates getting jobs. Our contacts with the Ministry were close. We realised they were also keenly interested in this issue and therefore proposed to them that VSO should raise funds to scale-up our involvement in the sector and help the government upgrade courses on a trial basis at a limited number of YPs. VSOs initial proposal concentrated on increasing volunteer posts, but the Ministry were keen to see a project which also involved a substantial element of upgrading of facilities and a much greater degree of capital expenditure. The proposal was therefore changed along these lines, making it considerably larger in financial terms than STEPU. Finance was sought and obtained from the European Community. The project has now been running for two years, during which time the construction work has been virtually completed and the first specialised YTSP courses started.

For YTSP VSO appointed an ex-YP volunteer as Project Coordinator. He reports to the Ministry and the VSO Field Director but on a day-to-day basis is effectively managed by the latter. This, coupled with the fact that VSO has arranged EC funding, means that we are closely involved in the management of the project. Dealing with the delays and other problems of implementation have therefore all been our concern. While this has given us a lot of freedom to run the project as we want, as time moves forward and the funding package nears its end the issue of government involvement has become more pressing. Possibly because we suggested the project and then took all the steps to implement it, we are at times unsure of the extent to which the Ministry feels any 'ownership', and whether they will be able and prepared to take it over in the long run.

Comparing the experience of STEPU and YTSP, question marks remain with both in terms of project management and longer-term sustainability/adoption by government. YTSP involves higher infrastructural construction costs than STEPU, and so these problems take on correspondingly greater significance. The first fairly obvious lesson for VSO is that the more an agency attempts to scale-up, the greater the departure from the micro-scale work that NGOs are used to, the more unfamiliar the management task becomes, and the less likely the agency is to have the systems, skills and experience required to achieve success.

However, the second lesson relates to integration: in STEPU the idea came originally from government, and while VSO played a major role in putting it into practice the project was established in government premises. Once the Coordinator was appointed he reported primarily to the Ministry rather than to VSO. From the start, and at various stages of the project, decisions were taken that ensured close integration with existing government structures. With YTSP, while VSO knew the government was interested in the issue, the project was proposed by VSO. Government influence on project design was important and they did provide land for the buildings at YPs they selected, but implementation was VSO's responsibility. Thus, while they take a keen interest in progress they do not manage the project on a day-to-day basis and the transfer from a VSO to a government project will therefore be that much more difficult.

Micro-level inputs with macro-level impact

The third set of projects consists of the 'School Farms and Garden Project' (SFGP) in The Gambia, and a 'Speech and Hearing Therapy Clinic' (SHTC) in Nepal. In both cases VSO's input is not large, but impact has been considerable. They are, at least in VSO's eyes, both projects which provide a strong vindication for VSO's traditional role of providing skilled technical assistance to indigenous projects. In both cases there is a key volunteer who has had a important influence on the way the project has developed. The projects are, however, entirely within government structures. VSO has had no involvement in their design or indeed implementation other than through the work of these volunteers. The success of the projects, and of the volunteers' involvement within them, has prompted VSO to scale-up in a modest way through placing further volunteers and by providing small grants (less than £10,000 in both cases) to assist specific aspects of the projects' work.

In The Gambia, the School Farms and Gardens Project (SFGP) started in 1986 when a group of about 20 schools started a pilot scheme with agricultural plots to encourage pupils to take a greater interest in farming and integrate agriculture as a subject into their curriculum. The scheme was coordinated centrally by the Ministry of Education and supported by both VSO and UNICEF. Two VSO horticulturalists worked on this pilot scheme from mid-1986 to early 1989. UNICEF provided some basic funding which was managed by the VSO field office. In 1989 a review of the SFGP took place and plans for expansion were drawn up. A third VSO who arrived in The Gambia in early 1989 was centrally involved in this review, but Ministry of Education, UNICEF and WFP officials and the VSO field office also participated in the discussions. Human-resource shortages in the Gambian government, poor integration of the SFGP into the formal education system, and delays were identified as major problems. The Ministry agreed to formalise the place held by the SFG in the school curriculum and to appoint a Programme Coordinator as well as four Field Coordinators to work with the VSOs. VSO agreed to increase the number of volunteers to four and provided some very modest amounts of funding for stationery and workshops. WFP and UNICEF provided the funding required to buy tools, dig wells and pay basic running costs. Workshops were held with headteachers, garden masters and agriculture teachers attending. Now, over 60 schools are involved in the project. Recently UNICEF has committed itself to provide longer-term funding and VSO has agreed to grant the funds to construct a small project office and demonstration garden.

VSO's input to the SFGP has therefore consisted of volunteers and a limited amount of funding. The main funders were international donors. However, perhaps VSO's greatest contribution to the success of the project has been the co-ordinating and 'brokerage' role that the volunteers and the field office have been able to play between all the parties involved. Thus the key to the success of VSO's involvement has been good integration in existing government structures and the effective use of the contacts that an external NGO development agency has with other larger actors (including central government institutions) to reinforce the work carried on at lower levels.

In Nepal VSO had one volunteer speech therapist working at the Speech and Hearing Therapy Clinic of Tribhuvan University Teaching Hospital from 1988 to mid-1991. The clinic, the first of its kind in Nepal, was established only one year earlier in 1987. Since mid-1990 the VSO and a Nepali colleague were able to do some very effective work preparing some of the first culturally appropriate speech-therapy materials in Nepali. The clinic is obviously keen to scale-up its work and over the past year or so has discussed with the VSO field office various funding proposals for training field workers and community-based rehabilitation projects. In the end a relatively small package involving £9,000 for further materials development for speech-therapy training work was agreed with VSO. This built directly on the work of the volunteer rather than involving VSO in more ambitious projects with which we had little experience. In addition, however, the volunteer was able to help the clinic raise other funds from UNICEF and Redd Barna to fund the more extensive CBR work. VSO is currently also recruiting a further two volunteers to work at the clinic.

VSO's main input to this project has been a single volunteer and some funding for specific work. But the volunteer has, in addition to her professional contribution to the clinic, been able to assist the process of scaling-up by brokering various inputs of funding and materials and helping with contacts with donors. The VSO field office, helped by the presence of a medically trained Field Director has for its part contributed to the discussions involved in refining the proposals for expansion in addition to the provision of modest funding. Once again, therefore, integration is the key, with the emphasis of VSO's assistance being on working within the structures of the indigenous institution (the clinic) and providing limited, targeted inputs to its work. With further volunteers due to be posted to the clinic in 1992, the process of gradual scaling-up of VSO's micro-level inputs is expected to continue.

Conclusions

Like other NGO development agencies, VSO has felt the need to scale-up those aspects of our work that have been most successful. The examples in this chapter describe a range of different ways in which VSO has approached this challenge. With the benefit of hindsight it would seem that the approach we have termed *planned multiplication of micro-level inputs* is the most obvious way to scale-up, but our experience has shown that it is easy to depart from this principle and embark on considerably more ambitious projects. While we are not arguing that NGOs should never embark on more ambitious schemes in their attempts to scale-up, it is clear that in doing so they need to recognise that such projects will impose demands in terms of resources and management that NGOs are not necessarily familiar with in their micro-level work. Using *the planned multiplication of micro-level inputs* as a strategy for scaling-up may help NGOs to avoid some of the worst pitfalls of such approaches.

One of the main issues that NGOs need to consider in scaling-up is sustainability. Micro-level inputs and projects by foreign NGOs will nearly always be more sustainable and replicable locally without external resources simply because they are small and have low resource requirements. As soon as scaling-up occurs, sustaining the project without external inputs becomes less easy. This chapter has stressed the value of integrating work into existing local structures as a key solution to this problem. Scaling-up by careful planning of an increased number of enhanced or improved micro-level inputs which fit closely into existing structures is much more likely to be successful in enhancing sustainability, than scaling-up through creating ambitious new projects outside existing local structures.

In addition to the longer-term goals of sustainability and replication, NGOs considering how to increase their impact also need to reflect on their own ability to manage the changes this will require. There is the obvious need to be able to provide the increased level of inputs required over a longer period of time. But there is also the less immediately obvious need to be able to manage work on a larger scale. VSO's experience shows that large projects require radically different management structures and systems. Learning lessons along the way, VSO has spent time and energy developing the management capabilities for the larger-scale projects we have undertaken. However, we are reluctant to move too far down this road, thereby possibly sacrificing tried and tested methods of delivering and managing micro-level inputs. Instead, we are now experimenting more actively with the *planned multipication of micro-level inputs* that this chapter recommends.

The FFHC Agricultural Programme in southern Ethiopia

Beverley Jones

Introduction

This chapter explores some of the issues which have arisen from Christian Aid's involvement in the Freedom From Hunger Campaign Agricultural Rehabilitation programme (FFHC/AD) which has been running since 1985 in the famine-affected areas of southern Ethiopia. Following the drought of the mid-1980s, a combination of NGO and FAO consultants, at the request of the Ethiopian government of the time, formulated a programme based on community-oriented, participatory methodology, designed to meet the short-term objectives of providing rehabilitation for drought-affected farming families, and of laying a basis for sustainable long-term development.

The FFHC/AD proceeded to raise funds from Northern NGOs for a project which would work through Service Cooperatives (SCs) and Peasants Associations (PAs), with the expertise of local Ministry of Agriculture (MoA) personnel, coordinated through an NGO-Liaison Office/Unit (NGO-LO/U) established within the Ministry.

As a case study, FFHC covers several strategies to achieve greater NGO impact: it involves working through government; it is facilitated by a UN agency – the Food and Agriculture Organisation (FAO); and it works with other NGO partners in the region. In terms of scaling-up, this chapter argues that, while FFHC shows features of 'additive' and 'multiplicative' strategies in that the programme has been steadily increasing in size, scope and influence through inputs, training and networking, the 'diffusive' strategy of 'self-spreading' (which should perhaps be a natural outcome of the participatory methodology of the programme) has remained an elusive goal (Edwards and Hulme; Chambers, in this volume). Coming after the major political and social upheavals which brought the Ethiopian People's Revolutionary Democratic Front (EPRDF) to power in May 1991, a recent evaluation of the programme also addressed the impact that this change has had and will have on a programme that has sought to work through government structures.

It needs to be stated that the way in which this large programme operates within the central and local governmental structures of Ethiopia, and its relationships with the Northern NGO community, have been difficult to ascertain. As the evaluation team discovered in 1991, it is not always easy to discern actual relationships or lines of management between the MoA, the NGO LO, FAO Rome, FAO and FFHC Ethiopia, the FFHC field staff and the farmers' organisations. Despite being established with the intention of being a bottom-up participatory model of agricultural rehabilitation and development, FFHC has fallen into many of the bureaucratic traps which beleaguer projects with such complex multi-disciplinary webs of participation and responsibility. It might not be too harsh to say that it has become a 'top-down' programme which elicits support by describing itself as 'bottom-up'.

Background

Already established in other parts of the world, FFHC/AD began in Ethiopia following the drought of the mid-1980s when discussions took place between the Ministry of Agriculture, OXFAM-UK and the Food and Agriculture Organisation of the United Nations, to establish how NGOs might co-operate more closely with the Ministry. An understanding of the context in which these proposals were formulated requires an acknowledgement of the political, social and economic situation which existed in Ethiopia at the time:

- Land reform had taken place in the late 1970s; the peasantry were now tied to the hated Producers' Co-operatives (PCs), which replaced the landlords as recipients of their produce through a quota system.
- Extremes of drought and famine demanded international action in devastated areas quickly, even if that meant compromise with the regime.
- What other options were possible at the time, given the nature of the Derg government, the controlled economy and a centralised local administration of Service Co-operatives (SCs) and Peasants Associations (PAs) grafted on to the former feudal state?

Fundamental to the FFHC programme is an acceptance of the local government system of Peasants Associations. These associations formed part of the Service Cooperatives which, in turn, reported to the local departments of the various ministries at 'Awraja' (district) and regional level. The unpopular Producers Cooperatives were scrapped following a speech by former-President Mengistu in March 1990. Although these associations were not indigenous local organisations, they were as 'grassroots' as they could possibly be at that time; furthermore, they did represent the first kind of local government that the peasantry had experienced.

There is a contradiction inherent in working for 'grassroots' development through the bureaucracy of the FAO. However, the factors in favour of this strategy at the time were that FAO is part of the United Nations, of which Ethiopia is a member; and that the FAO is stable even though a bureaucracy and has a credible profile with the MoA – although not apolitical, it does not appear to be tied to the policies of any one country. At the time then, it was the only means by which such a programme could have been started.

For many reasons, this is an exciting time to put FFHC 'under the microscope.' The rationale which seemed appropriate seven years ago needs to be reviewed in the light of events over the last year. Although as suggested above, changes had begun to take place in local government structures once Mengistu's speech of March 1990 had heralded a retreat from the controlled economy, few were prepared for the impact of Mengistu's rapid departure, the brief interim government and the entrance of the Tigrayan-backed Ethiopian Peoples Revolutionary Democratic Forces (EPRDF) in May 1991. Now re-formed as the Transitional Government of Ethiopia (TGE) preparing for elections in 1993, the new administration and its charter have laid the basis for a government of ministers chosen to reflect the diverse ethnic make-up of the country. Regional boundaries have been provisionally re-drawn closer to those which existed before the 1974 Revolution which brought Mengistu to power, based on ethnic and linguistic groupings which would seem initially to favour the priorities of the Tigrayans more readily than other nationalities.

Whatever the intentions of the EPRDF, the charter theoretically provides each region with the opportunity to develop its own form of local government, suited to the ethnic groups of the area. While this may be feasible in Tigray which was cut off from the rest of Ethiopia for many years, the option is not an easy one for other regions to implement. This is particularly true of the southern regions where no one ethnic group is large enough to forge a regional identity. They have therefore been lumped together on the assumption that a line drawn around them will enable them to develop their own administration. Readjustment from a highly centralised and oppressive system of government is proving to be a slow and painful process. As a spokesperson from one of the FFHC-supported Service Cooperatives in Gofa pointed out during the evaluation mission:

> We used to have to dance for Haile Selassie; then we had to dance for the Derg. We don't even know the name of this new government – and we don't think we'll bother to learn it. By the time we do, it will have changed. (Evaluation Mission Report 1991)

At least two points are being made here: firstly, that the peasantry in southern Ethiopia do not identify with the new government any more than the previous two, which were also dominated by Ethiopians from the north. Secondly, the transitional nature of the government implies that there can be no guarantee of continuity or consistency for central or local government structures at this stage; all might change in two years' time.

Nevertheless, the new government, in the development of its economic policy and revision of central and local government structures, indicates that there will be substantial changes in state approaches to development. Ato Gebru Wolde (1992) of the NGO-Liaison Office outlines potential trends as follows:

> Top priority will be given to the reconstruction of areas, specially those ravaged by civil conflicts and drought. This means that regions eg. Tigray, Gondar and Wello which were off limits until recently will be of important concern to Government for development activities.

> Government will strongly promote participatory development throughout the country through decentralised administration. This will encourage local development programmes to be planned and implemented at the grass-roots level.

> Monopoly of power by one political party is replaced by political pluralism in which various groups and nationalities would participate in the development process.

Key questions

The challenge for the FFHC programme and the recent Evaluation Mission – which included Ethiopian MoA and project staff, NGO donors, independent consultants and FAO staff – was to review a programme designed to scale-up the impact of

NGO funds by working through MoA departments and local government in order to rehabilitate drought-prone peasant communities, and to consider how it should adapt to changed and changing circumstances. Was it wise, in terms of sustainability for example, to support a programme which depended on a system of local community organisation which had been imposed by an unpopular central government? Following the fall of the Derg, a number of FFHC-supported SCs were looted or badly damaged by their own members. This suggests that there was not a strong sense of ownership felt by the members, despite the inputs they received from the project.

For the donors, it is important to decide to what extent the large input of money into FFHC has helped the programme to achieve its stated objectives, and whether these objectives remain appropriate to the needs of drought-prone farming communities. Has the funding of several external structures, such as the FFHC/Rome and Addis office to facilitate the programme in the field, really been worthwhile? In the absence of the Derg, are they still necessary? The answer to this question depends on the future shape of central and regional government and the extent to which the increasing problems of security in the south and east of the country can be controlled.

There are two further considerations: to what extent has the targeting of resources and MoA services towards selected SCs had the effect of scaling *down* the impact of the MoA in other equally needy areas? What difference is there between the ideals of participatory development and the reality of community participation in project formulation and implementation? Finally, has the identification and implementation of one solution to the problem of vulnerability to drought exacerbated problems for others, or created a new set of problems, requiring new solutions?

Programme formulation and objectives

The FFHC/AD was originally established in the mid-1980s to facilitate the funding, planning and implementation of projects via a new NGO Liaison Unit in the Ministry of Agriculture, and to disseminate the concept of participatory development. By the end of 1986 these objectives had become more detailed. The project's long-term aims were to assist peasants in drought-prone areas to strengthen their organisational, productive and managerial capacity for food production and self-reliance; support peasant organisations; strengthen partnership between Northern NGOs and organisations of the rural poor in Ethiopia; and strengthen the capacity of the technical staff of the MoA to apply participatory planning and an integrated approach to rural development.

In the short term, this meant providing agricultural inputs, increasing crop yields, improving water supplies and small-scale irrigation schemes, reversing the deterioration of the environment through reafforestation, soil and water conservation, training, and support to the staff of the MOA. It was decided to add a separate set of objectives to ensure that women benefitted from the project.

Participatory methods

A key feature of the NGO-LO and the FFHC/AD programme is the adherence – in principle at least – to a participatory approach to decision-making in the development and implementation of programmes. This is a form of scaling-up by enabling, ideally, community-wide involvement in the process of development. To this end, the objectives of the NGO-LO were included in the revised outline of the FFHC programme. As the *Guidelines for MoA/NGO Collaboration* revised and reissued in late 1990 point out:

> The theory of participation is very difficult to put into practice...While many individuals and organisations discuss the merits of participation, few agree on a standard definition (Ministry of Agriculture 1990).

Gebru Wolde (1992) reinforces this point thus:

> The nature of participation dictates that the NGO/MoA offer more than just a lukewarm endorsement of the approach. The tenets of participation should permeate all aspects of the project, from the initial stages of project planning through to the phase out of project activities. The effectiveness of participation will depend upon the commitment and consistency with which it is implemented.

FFHC recognises a potential tension between the needs expressed by members of the community, and what may be perceived as needs for the wider community by outsiders. They do not appear to recognise that there will be conflicting needs within the various communities between generations, between genders, and between wealthier and less well-off members.

> During the project identification process, one must first concentrate on the communities' priorities, gain their confidence and then address some of the problems which may have been overlooked by the community but which relate to important problems such as conservation of the environment ... It is of paramount importance that the community be facilitated at an appropriate point in time to develop awareness of such issues. Only in this way will they uphold conservation measures as their own priority and include them as major components (Ministry of Agriculture 1990).

Gebru Wolde (1992) identifies the selection criteria which should be considered:

- the urgency of the farmers' needs;
- the risk or severity of environmental deterioration;
- the potential for increasing sustainable food production;
- less accessible areas;
- the strength of the community and its readiness to participate and benefit from the project.

There is a danger here of 'trying to have it both ways': on the one hand, appearing to adopt a fully participatory methodology, while on the other attempting to introduce external priorities in such a way that they appear to be 'owned' by the local community. This was a particular problem identified by the Evaluation Missions in 1988 and 1991, and illustrates a contradiction in the selection criteria listed above: farmers never expressed soil and water conservation as a priority for themselves or the community, although they recognised that the loss of trees and land erosion was making it difficult to reduce their vulnerability to drought. Further examples of the same issue include:

- the emphasis which farmers place on oxen and credit for oxen, even though food

for oxen and land may be of greater importance in terms of sustainability.
- The introduction of gender issues by NGOs and the former Project Coordinator into the objectives of the programme.
- The farmers' understandable preference for interest-free credit from the FFHC programme rather than the more sustainable source of credit from local banks at market rates.
- Encouraging reluctant men to participate in family planning by attaching family-planning education to discussions on popular credit schemes.

The phrase 'positive push' was coined by various members of the Evaluation Mission in 1991; this referred to attempts made by the project staff in other NGOs to push participating communities in directions which were considered 'for their benefit' even if the community itself had not recognised the benefits on offer. This might involve incentives (such as food-for-work), mild threats (such as withdrawal of inputs), or peer pressure (such as community members being denied credit until their neighbours had repaid).

Such measures may be effective but they do have implications for the power relationships between donor, project staff and community which bring into question the nature of participation as it relates to the normative statements contained in the Guidelines for MoA/NGO collaboration.

Problems encountered over time

What kind of a programme has FFHC become since its inception in 1986? Is it or has it ever been a bottom-up model of participatory development? Has it become a top-heavy bureaucracy centralised twice over in Addis Abbaba and Rome, at great distance geographically and developmentally from its intended beneficiaries? If it is the former, then the intention to scale-up the impact of NGO funds by strengthening relationships between the various external agencies and ministry departments would seem to be justified. Farming families will have been the key players in the planning and implementation of their own development, and their points of view will have had an impact on all aspects of the programme.

However, it is probably fairer to say that the actual mode of planning and implementation followed a top-down approach once the programme was underway. Has there really been full participation of *all* members of the farming community? Has the programme stagnated because the farming families' priorities can never move beyond the micro-issues of day-to-day struggle for survival in under-resourced, drought-prone areas? Is the participatory methodology currently practised within FFHC really suitable for a scaled-up programme run through non-participatory government structures?

By taking a closer look at the relationships which exist between the various components of the programme, and the impact that the programme has had on farming families, farmers' organisations and MoA field workers, we can examine the implications of scaling-up through government structures. The analysis will seem negative in many ways. This is not to say that the programme as a whole is a failure, although it is a recognition of the particular difficulties faced by any kind of development initiative in the Horn of Africa today. The Evaluation Mission was met time and time again with positive comments and evidence of improvement in the lives of farming families within the FFHC-supported SCs.

The target community

As has already been suggested by the looting which followed the recent change of government, it is difficult to assess the extent to which the SCs and PAs feel that they 'own' the rehabilitation and development process which is underway in FFHC-supported SCs. This is partly because of the ambivalence shown towards local government structures which were linked to an oppressive central government and which did not correspond to indigenous affiliations of people within the community. Realistically, however, NGOs would have found it difficult to find alternative community structures to support in the mid-1980s. In the case of the revolving credit fund, the programme has found that there is a greater chance of repayment if funds revolve within the smaller Peasants Associations than the Service Cooperatives. This is endorsed by another NGO in the area which by-passes the SCs altogether in setting up Cereal Banks in selected PAs.

The Evaluation Mission was told that in southern Ethiopian farming communities no one is a 'rich' farmer. However, the FFHC credit scheme still tends to encourage better-off individuals to take risks rather than establishing a system which enables the poorest farmers to obtain oxen. There seemed little evidence that increasing the wealth of individual farmers had had a beneficial 'trickle-down' effect for the poorer farmers. For individuals without land (or other means of income such as trading), the project offers little.

Where there is a clearly-defined indigenous social system in operation (such as the Borana Pastoralists' practice of providing livestock to one another when in need), the FFHC programme has found it difficult to adapt its revolving credit scheme or find other ways of assisting the community.

Women

Despite the programme's stated aim of focusing on the role of women in the economy, there is little evidence that, beyond the practical needs of grinding mills and small livestock, and a degree of increased participation by some women in formal meetings, the programme has built up a database of information on women as originally intended. This is partly because participation has tended to be narrowly defined – using formal structures such as group meetings where, even if women are interviewed on their own, they are reluctant to express opinions which differ from those of their men. Project staff, in most cases male, have tended to assume that this means that men and women are in complete agreement about the priorities of the project. The less public lives and needs of women require a less formal approach to ascertain whether or not this is the case. It was clear, for example, that those women who had received formal education were far more likely to take on and benefit from credit schemes for purchasing small livestock.

Ministry of Agriculture: Development Agents and Awarja staff

The work of Development Agents from the MOA who operate the 'training and visit' extension system has been facilitated by the provision of motor bikes in many areas. However, Development Agents are rarely from the local community, do not speak the local language and are usually urban-educated. They may lack commitment to work in SCs and PAs although this is by no means generally true. The programme has not yet moved into the area of training local members of the farming community to fulfil agricultural development roles, something which is vital if the project is to scale-up by multiplying its influence.

The same might also be said for the MoA Awraja (district) staff who have also been supported through the project with, for example, the provision of vetinerary medicines and transport for use in selected SCs. Naturally, this is very popular with Awraja MoA staff, who also have quite close contact with FFHC project staff. They consider this to be morale-boosting in many ways. In fact, unlike other NGO programmes which work with the MoA or set up parallel systems alongside ministries, many MoA staff expressed the view that they regard FFHC as 'our own programme because it enables us to carry out the job we are trained to do.' This is a recognition of the positive relationship that the project field staff have fostered with the various MoA staff.

However, for those SCs which fall outside the programme (and, of course, the majority of them do), there is a feeling of resentment that the MoA is working in some areas but not in theirs, even though they felt that they were equally badly off when the sites were selected. As one SC spokesman pointed out, 'There are two governments: one for the people over there who have the project, and none for us. We are in the dark – it is light over there.' FFHC, in scaling-up impact in some areas, has highlighted the absence of MoA services in others. However, some might argue that disgruntled SCs serve as a catalyst, putting pressure on central government to improve service delivery in all areas. While FFHC has followed the lead of the regional MoA in the selection of project sites, it is clear that some of the logistical difficulties of working in remote SCs have worked against the NGO-LO objectives of working in less accessible and more deprived areas.

Inevitably, Awraja MoA staff feel that with greater resources from the FFHC programme they could do an even better job. They do not believe that additional resources will come from central government and are fairly sure that were NGO funds given directly to central government, they and the local communities would never feel the effect of the money.

Impact of project inputs: credit and training

The programme is now running into its sixth year. Oxen numbers have increased, although it is difficult to assess the impact that this has had on crop yields. Repayment of loans has generally been poor – although better among women who had purchased goats and sheep. The grinding mills provided to SCs have clearly made a qualitative difference to the lives of women and are a good source of income for the SC (although mills are operated and managed by men). Some of the training – particularly in account-keeping, midwifery and for the health post – is considered useful. But all other forms of training for men and women did not appear to have made an impact on the daily lives of the community, or their ability to earn extra income. Indeed for women, the project created expectations (in hygiene and food preparation) that they had neither the time nor the resources to fulfil. It had even created guilt amongst women who felt ashamed to appear in dirty clothes, though the fault here lies as much with the health curriculum of the MoA as with the project itself.

Water

The water development programme within FFHC has had its ups and downs. Covering too wide an area, and with insufficient resources, it has been unable to mobilise the local community to undertake community water development – except in a few areas. On the other hand, the profile of the two former highly-qualified water engineers led to expectations from local farming families for large-scale irrigation and reservoirs which cannot be met within the budget of FFHC, nor by the capacity of the water team, especially as the contracts of the water engineers have come to an end. As a result, other NGOs have implemented some of the proposals and groups have been employed with local foremen on piece-rate work, which rather undermines the participation of the community in its own water programme. In this respect, scaling-up by adding on more areas and activities to the programme has proved over-ambitious. It would have been better to maintain the water programme at a small, village-maintained scale which might have been replicable, even 'self-spreading', had expectations not been so high and community participation so low.

Working with other NGOs

The Project field staff have been slow to take up the opportunity of working with or alongside other NGOs in the area. FFHC does not have the means to expand beyond its current brief – although it may decide to reallocate some of its funds. However, with greater coordination between NGOs, it would be possible for the scope of the programme to be deepened through co-operation with other operational NGOs who have been working, for instance, on cereal banks, disability, women's self-help projects, income generation, and so on

Management

Another area of difficulty has been the line of management between FFHC/Rome, FFHC/Addis Ababa and FAO/Addis Ababa, and the FFHC field office in southern Ethiopia. This has been particularly noticeable in the area of staff appointments, and in the lack of direct contact between the Addis office and the field. It has also proved difficult for field staff to spend prolonged periods in the local communities when their own families live in Addis Ababa.

NGO funders have also had little direct contact with field staff because all reports and accounts are processed in Rome – so that informal communication and rapid response both ways is rarely possible. Occasionally there are also unexpected delays in the approval mechanism for new project sites in Rome – which can have serious consequences for the field staff who have, in good faith, set up an agreement with an SC. The longer the delay, the greater the decline in motivation among farmers.

A further factor which has become increasingly important in the last six months is the level of insecurity in the area of the project. This has made travel between Addis and the region hazardous and has caused the postponement of the participatory workshop. It has made the distribution of inputs to SCs difficult and delayed follow-up by project and MoA staff. This is bound to have had an effect on SC and PA participation, compounding the period of uncertainty which came in the wake of the change of government.

Conclusions

Notwithstanding the above reservations, the general findings of the 1991 Evaluation Mission were that from the point of view of the farming communities and MoA staff, the project is achieving progress towards its stated goals, at least in the short term. However, the project's approach to development has become stereotyped, and the process of participation in planning and implementation has not yet reached full participation or self-reliance. When farming families were asked if they were any closer to self-reliance, they all replied that if the project were to withdraw now, they would quickly slip back into the same situation in which the project staff found them.

In this respect, the programme fits comfortably into the additive category for scaling-up NGO impact in that it has focused on equipment and credit inputs over an increasing number of SCs, and on expanding MoA capacity in these areas. However, the cost of maintaining the central structures required to expand in this way in the face of uncertain funding and the absence of community financial responsibility, has meant that the programme faces the prospect of an abrupt halt to this process of enlargement. *Phasing-out* has not been built into the project's plans. The short-term benefits of the programme are not sustainable and, in many ways, contravene the NGO Liaison Office guidelines concerning size, scale, sustainability and community ownership.

In terms of scaling-up through 'multiplicative' strategies, FFHC, in itself a globally-franchisable institution, has sought to replicate projects across the region's Service Cooperatives. One result of this has been a standardised approach which has become too inflexible to take into account the needs and resources specific to a particular area or community. This is one consequence of being overstretched by scaling-up the size of the programme.

Learning processes may be replicable, but this takes time to evolve; development 'packages' rarely are. There are no short cuts and yet the programme has sought to plan projects and replicate them within a year or two. This is partly a result of the short time-frame and high expectations of donors which put project staff under pressure to demonstrate quick results. In practice 'community need identification and community attitudes and aspirations crystallise over time and in the course of activities which demand the participation of the whole community' (Sandford 1992).

Participatory methodology was part of the rationale for scaling-up involvement in the rehabilitation and development programme. However, the interventionist nature of FFHC – always referred to as 'FAO' by farmers and MoA staff – as an external benefactor raining interest-free credit, grinding mills and motorbikes on to local communities, has probably undermined a community sense of ownership or control over what should be regarded as their own programme. Furthermore, competition over goods and services from FFHC has divided communities with shared needs, perhaps preventing them from reaching collective solutions to their own problems.

The issue central to the reduction of vulnerability to drought and famine must lie in the root causes of drought and food insecurity. Soil and water conservation, animal feed and population pressure are crucial areas for action – and yet the programme has not even been able to begin to address these key factors. It would be wrong to assume that the communities themselves are unaware of these problems. However, they cannot regard them as priorities when they are preoccupied with day-to-day survival. 'Communities have an innate understanding of resource degradation and are often anxious to conserve if ways can be found to alleviate the pressures that drive them to present destructive land use' (Sandford 1992).

For FFHC, there is a need for a new stimulus and impetus which might be provided by a focus on conservation-based land use systems, in particular on exploring incentives through which farmers can extend their time horizons from thinking about next season's crop production to safeguarding food and energy requirements of future generations (Evaluation Mission 1991).

Sustainability in rehabilitation and development initiatives comes when these activities grow out of needs experienced by those most vulnerable to the effects of resource depletion. The expansion of peasant farmers' time horizons in a development programme suggests a scaling-up operation of a different kind altogether – one that is rooted in the unique needs and resources of each community rather than a package which is replicated across the region. Only when communities are convinced of the long-term effectiveness of community-based (rather than externally-induced) actions might other communities choose also to adopt them. This kind of 'diffusive' scaling-up strategy is unlikely to occur within FFHC-targeted communities. However, in the new, decentralised Ethiopian context, it may be a model for the future. Such a model would probably mean the sacrifice of additive and multiplicative strategies in order to allow a diffusive strategy to develop at grassroots level.

8

Scaling-up via legal reform in Uganda

John Parry-Williams

Introduction

This chapter argues that NGOs can increase the impact of their work by supporting appropriate legislative reform by governments in developing countries. How this form of co-operation evolves, and whether it is effective, will vary with circumstances in the country concerned.

Since 1987, Save the Children Fund-UK (SCF) in Uganda has played an advisory role to the Ministry responsible for social welfare in the preparation of two pieces of legislation concerning children, one of which is currently in the process of implementation. This chapter highlights the positive factors that enabled the reform process to develop, the constraints that have had to be negotiated or overcome, and the strengths and weaknesses of legal reform as a strategy for increasing impact.

The two examples of legal reform used in this chapter are the 'Babies and Children's Homes Rules' (hereinafter referred to as 'the Rules', and gazetted as Statutory Instruments in August 1991), and the 'Report of the Child Law Review Committee' (or CLRC), which was presented to the Minister responsible in March 1992. The Rules set down the standards of care expected by government from organisations (including NGOs) which run children's homes, the procedures for obtaining approval to operate, and the regulatory system which maintains and improves standards over time. They grew out of a shared concern about standards of care among the Ministry responsible for children's welfare, the National Council of Voluntary Social Services, the Child Care Agencies Forum (representing children's homes) and the SCF Social Work Department. The Rules were compiled by all these groups, as well as representatives from different departments within the Ministry of Health (including those responsible for child and maternal health, and the Public Health Inspectorate). The Minister of Relief and Social Rehabilitation chaired a committee which vetted the proposals. The Ministry and SCF were then involved in the final drafting with the Ministry of Justice.

The CLRC was inaugurated on 21 June 1990 by the Minister of Relief and Social Rehabilitation under Justice Musoke. The terms of reference 'for the Committee established to review current juvenile legislation and recommend changes' included as an objective to 'propose appropriate legislation which shall be beneficial to children who are disadvantaged and/or in conflict with the law'. Probably the most important current piece of legislation concerning child care and child offenders in Uganda is the Approved Schools Act, based on the England and Wales Children and Young Persons Act (1933) and enacted in 1951. Other relevant legislation includes the Reformatory School Act (which came into force in 1930), the Adoption Act (1943) and the Affiliation Act of 1946. The CLRC has drafted proposals to reform the law in the areas of child care, child offenders, parentage, custody, and maintenance, replacing the Acts mentioned above with a comprehensive Children Act. In addition, the CLRC made recommendations, but did not draw up legislative proposals, on the following: child labour, succession, the decriminalisation of offences and the age of marriage.

Factors encouraging legislative reform

The Ugandan experience shows that even a relatively straightforward piece of legislative reform such as a Statutory Instrument takes at least 18 months from initiation to formal approval. In the case of the Report of the CLRC, it was submitted 21 months after its inauguration, and it may well take a further 12 months before it becomes law. Given these long timescales, political stability and continuity is essential to successful legal reform. In 1989, when the preparatory thinking for these reforms took place, the National Resistance Movement (NRM) government had been in power for four years, and the National Assembly agreed that the government should stay in power for another five years from January 1990. This extension in the government's term of office means that there are unlikely to be major changes in political direction which might sabotage the work of the CLRC and the implementation of its proposals.

Another basic prerequisite for legal reform is institutional support – in this case the Department of Social Welfare had a policy that emphasised the needs of children and of preventive and developmental strategies to enhance their rights. Given stability and an appropriate institutional framework, the most critical factor behind the development of legal reform in this case was the commitment and leadership of government. The Minister of Relief and Social Rehabilitation chaired the Committee that reviewed the new Rules, and also established the CLRC. The role of the Minister has been and will continue to be pivotal to the success of the reform proposals. In addition, the President, Minister of Justice, and Solicitor-General have all supported the reform process. In 1988 President Museveni commented that: 'the bulk of Uganda's laws were transplanted from Britain's wholesale without much consideration for our social and cultural set up ... Uganda still retains the bulk of such laws although in the country in which they originated, they have long been replaced' (New Vision 1988).

He also stated: 'as important as the need for human rights, even more important is the need to recognise and protect the special rights of children who are the most vulnerable members of our society' (UNICEF 1988). More specifically, the Minister of Justice said he 'had no kind or good word to say about the Law of Uganda in relation to the child' and reform was 'long overdue' (Mulenga 1988). Such statements (particularly from the President) have provided vital encourage-ment and endorsement to the CLRC's efforts.

In Uganda in the 1970s there were two attempts to reform the laws concerning children which never reached the National Assembly, in part because of the civil and economic upheaval which took place between 1972 and 1986. There is therefore a historical dynamic in favour of legal reform in Uganda which had not been fulfilled, and which further emphasises the legitimacy of the CLRC's task. The present government has not simply exhorted the need for change, but (as a result of the World Summit for Children) has directed the Ministry of Finance and Planning to coordinate the writing of a 'National Plan of Action for Children'. Hence, the government's attitude towards improving the circumstances of children is very positive. It is also fortunate that there is a large degree of congruence between the CLRC proposals and government plans to decentralise the judicial system.

This strong national lead is supported at the international level by the UN Convention on the Rights of the Child, which has now been ratified by Uganda. In addition, the 'African Charter on the Rights and Welfare of the Child' drawn up by the Organisation of African Unity (OAU), gives a vital African dimension to children's rights and in some respects improves on the UN Convention. The OAU has declared the 1990s to be the 'Decade of the African Child'. In 1990, world leaders including Uganda signed the 'World Declaration on the Survival, Protection and Development of Children' and the 'Plan of Action' for implementing its proposals. The success of the England and Wales Children Act of 1989 was also helpful to the Committee, as was the experience of similar (though unsuccessful) legislative proposals in Papua New Guinea. International attention to children's rights has provided a very positive framework within which to reform the laws concerning children in Uganda.

Legal reform also requires the support of all the main actors involved: practitioners, administrators, academics and independent professionals. The CLRC drew its membership from all these groups and from all regions of the country. The question of gender balance was not seen as a priority at first, but was corrected with the enlargement of the Committee from 14 to 20 members (12 men and eight women) and the appointment of two female researchers. In retrospect, gender balance should have been a more important criterion in the composition of the Committee. Without the input of the female members, the Committee would probably have produced discriminatory proposals which would have failed to protect the best interests of children.

The widening of the Committee's membership ensured a greater degree of ownership of the proposals by all concerned, though with hindsight a major omission was the failure to include a senior member of the Ministry of Local Government. Apart from the Ministry responsible for children's affairs, the most important governmental input came from the legal draftsperson in the Ministry of Justice. The Committee was fortunate that the person who had been involved in drafting the Rules was also deputed to draft the CLRC proposals. Another positive factor was the involvement of outside social work and legal consultants, who exposed the Committee to different ideas and emphasised the importance of information collection and research. The Committee had appointed a social work and legal researcher, and for a short time a research anthropologist. Research on 'Children in Court' and 'Children and Resistance Committees and Courts' was of fundamental importance to the deliberations of the Committee. For example, it was learnt that, over a period of two years, only 20 per cent of children in nine major courts were granted bail.

Consultation with opinion leaders in Kampala and other districts, and with representatives from all levels of the Resistance Committees (RCs), the administrative structure of the NRM, was also important. It showed that there was widespread support for the ideas of the CLRC and in some cases gave further emphasis and authority to its conclusions.

Another area stressed by the consultants was publicity. A Public Relations Officer was appointed, and many articles on children, child abuse, child labour, corporal punishment, child rights, and institutionalisation have been published.

Sensitising public opinion in this way has been and continues to be of benefit to the reform process.

Against this background, SCF has had an important supporting role in the development of the Committee and its work. Since 1987 SCF's Social Work Department has worked closely with government to build up trust and confidence, and became the major funder of the CLRC, also providing a representative to give professional advice on a continuous basis.

Difficulties and constraints in legal reform

Legal reform is a slow process. Despite Uganda's political stability, there is a high degree of unpredictability in day-to-day events. For example, in April 1992 a sudden 73 per cent cut in Ministry budgets was announced. Keeping a high-level committee together for two years is not easy. The Secretary to the Committee left half way through for further study, and other members were away for fairly long periods. The Minister who inaugurated the Committee was replaced half-way through, as was the Minister of Justice.

Uganda is also undergoing a period of considerable economic and political change due to 'structural adjustment' and decentralisation. This process will continue with the ratification of a new constitution and the reform of other outdated or inappropriate laws. There is a danger that new laws may run counter to the proposals of the CLRC. Poor communication between Ministries increases this danger, and is a further reason for the broad-based membership of the Committee and the need for frequent publicity.

Entrenched attitudes and vested interests are major constraints to reform. Legal reform alters the 'status-quo' in society and changes the balance of power, and thus is likely to produce conflict. The patrilineal structure of Ugandan society has resulted in a patriarchal power system. The raising of the rights and status of children, which is closely linked with raising the status of women, undermines the vested interests of men. This challenge to the position of men in society, and therefore to the male members of the Committee, surfaced numerous times. In addition, international agreements in defence of children's rights are largely Western constructs and are open to criticism from supporters of an Afro-centric approach to social issues. The Committee's acceptance of a set of basic principles concerning the rights of children soon after its inauguration was the most important factor in resolving these conflicts.

The question of how customary law and practice should be accommodated in legal reform was frequently asked. In some ways the Committee has ducked this question, since there is no way that national law can take into account all the different customary laws and practices without becoming a meaningless jumble of ideas. Some scholars doubt whether customary law is in fact custom in the sense of traditions handed down from pre-colonial society. Chanock and others see customary law as a matter of politics rather than tradition (Chanock 1989). Although customary practices vary from place to place, some are common to all ethnic groups in Uganda, particularly the role of the extended family as an insurance against difficulty and a support network. The resilience of the extended family, which is often said to be collapsing and is certainly more limited in scope in urban areas, is still very much in evidence as a social safety net, especially in rural communities. Even in a district like Rakai, which is one of the areas of rural

Uganda worst affected by the impact of HIV/AIDS, the extended family has absorbed all but a few of the high number of 'orphans' under the age of eighteen (Dunn 1992). In Uganda, the village is still the basic unit for a large proportion of decision-making.

The sheer magnitude of the task of improving child protection and providing the means to fulfil this task were questions that occupied the mind of the Committee. The Probation and Social Welfare Department did not reach every district, let alone have a presence at county or sub-county levels (except in a few areas which have special projects like Rakai). Even with an integrated approach to child protection using all the district government agencies and with Probation and Social Welfare staff fully implementing a community welfare role, most children are unlikely to feel any sustained impact from new legislation to protect their rights. Therefore, the CLRC decided that the only way to build in better protection for children was to institutionalise this responsibility within the community, and that meant primarily at the village level. The CLRC proposed that one of the nine members of the Resistance Committee at each level from village through to district should have a special responsibility for children's affairs and interests. This has been approved by the National Executive Committee of the National Resistance Movement but has yet to be implemented.

The CLRC proposed that if the Chairperson or Secretary (member responsible) for children in the Resistance Committee cannot resolve something informally, then the RC Court should be given the responsibility to mediate where the rights of a child are being infringed or where a child needs care and protection – for example, in matters of succession, maintenance, child abuse, failure to immunise, educate, provide necessities of life, to give assistance to the disabled or where a child is beyond control. The Committee also proposed to give the RC Court the power to hear less serious criminal offences, something many were doing already (albeit illegally). Thus, the new laws concerning children proposed by the CLRC are to be implemented by two different judicial systems: the elected representatives of the community at the village, parish and sub-county level; and the state-appointed magistrates at the proposed District 'Family and Children Court'. The first of these systems, at the RC 1 level, would be the court of first instance, with the state-appointed magistrates providing a system of appeal.

Considerable time was spent by the CLRC in debating different models of social work but it was often the members of the Ministry responsible for children who had the greatest difficulty in discarding long-held beliefs. Changing attitudes and obtaining a consensus was extremely time-consuming.

The Committee was also aware that its proposals had to be affordable, and would be likely to fail if they necessitated increasing the numbers of salaried professionals, a court-building programme, or the establishment of a sophisticated infrastructure for individual casework. Therefore, the CLRC placed responsibility for children at the lowest level possible within the administrative structure of government, providing local solutions to local problems and building on traditional, informal methods of resolving conflicts. Sanctions at the village level were primarily those of restitution, compensation and fines (rather than incarceration). Caning of children is common but was not condoned by the CLRC.

At first, there was considerable opposition from lawyers on the Committee to increasing the power of RC courts, especially at village level, because of lack of training and because the same people would have both executive and judicial powers. However, the gross violation of children's rights by district magistrates courts (with, for example, an 80 per cent remand-in-custody rate and inappropriate sentencing), coupled with the distance of these courts from the child's home, outweighed the objections of the lawyers in the Committee's mind.

The Committee did not fully appreciate the financial constraints within which the Department of Probation and Social Welfare has to operate, particularly with regard to institutions (which eat up 75 per cent of the Department's recurrent budget). For example, the question of what is to be done with the five existing (and sub-standard) remand homes was not tackled. In general however the Committee was conscious of the need for the new system to be affordable to government, and drew up their proposals accordingly.

An area of considerable disagreement within the Committee concerned the limits to its legislative proposals. Some members felt strongly that the CLRC should include succession and child labour in its proposals, both being very contentious and difficult areas. In the end these questions were shelved because the Committee ran out of funds.

Constraints, concerns and opportunities in implementation

Although the following issues are drawn from the experience of the Children and Babies Homes Rules, it is likely that similar concerns will arise with the implementation of a Children Act, and on a much greater scale. In both cases, the driving force was a committee which developed shared values and an enthusiasm to succeed. But to be successful, *implementation* requires the transfer of these beliefs and energies to a multi-sectoral group which will have been only peripherally involved (if at all) in developing the original proposals. For example, regular inspection of children's homes requires District Probation and Social Welfare Officers, District Public Health Inspectors and District Medical Officers to accept new responsibilities. This is by no means a foregone conclusion, since local interests may have more influence over local officials than government regulations. *Acceptance* of reform is insufficient; vigilance and persuasiveness are then required if positive changes are to be consolidated, for the aim of the Rules is not to antagonise but to improve current systems.

Training and familiarisation meetings for District Probation and Social Welfare Officers, and for the staff of children's homes, are a pre-requisite for implementing the new Rules. It is vital to win over these staff to the philosophy which underpins the Rules. Fortunately, a 'Child Care Open Learning Programme' was devised prior to the reforms to offer staff an opportunity to upgrade their child-care skills (Sparrow 1992).

The training implications of a Children Act will be considerable, especially for the 30,000 village Resistance Committees. Because the proposals aim to change the status of children (and therefore women), and because men will be the main implementors of the proposed new law, there is a vital need for re-appraisal and re-thinking about basic values and attitudes. The successful implementation of the Act will require major attitudinal changes; the legal refinements are of secondary importance, especially since the CLRC stresses informal settlement of disputes as the priority at the village level. Therefore, a vital question is how to link the new proposals with 'self-improving' and 'self-spreading' methods as proposed by Robert Chambers in this volume.

In addition training will be required for magistrates, the judiciary, police, probation and social welfare officers, district administrators and other relevant government officials and NGOs. There will be an extensive need for publicity and educational material for different levels of understanding and in different languages. People must also have the practical means to undertake their new responsibilities. In Uganda, SCF has provided most District Probation and Social Welfare Officers with motorbikes, with fuel coming from the Ministry, but even this has been provided only infrequently.

In April 1992 all motorbikes were grounded as a result of the 73 per cent cut in Ministry budgets, which is likely to last for five months (up to the next financial year). Many government officers also lack adequate accommodation, stationery and other resources. New methods of funding will have to be considered by NGOs and other donors if they wish district probation and social welfare officers to continue to have a role in implementing reform for the better protection of children.

To achieve consistency in the implementation of the Rules the Ministry has appointed an Inspector of NGO Homes. At present, standards of care vary considerably from one home to another. Difficult decisions have to be made, and in some cases standards fall so far short of those expected that closure is inevitable if there are no resources to improve the situation. One of the ironies of this is that many government homes fall well below the standards set by the government's own Rules.

Despite the Ministry and Cabinet having agreed to enforce the new Rules, there have been forces both within and outside government whose actions and/or words have worked counter to their spirit. Part of the problem seems to be that children's homes are one of the easier ways through which NGOs can raise money from external donors, on the grounds of assisting children orphaned by war or AIDS, and other disadvantaged and vulnerable children. For donors, institutions offer a straightforward way of providing capital funding with something very visible to show for their investment. Donors must acquire a more sophisticated understanding of children's development issues, especially the importance of local self-reliance and sustainability.

The Rules pose an economic and political threat to all those whose motives for being involved in children's homes are other than the *best interests* of the child. For NGOs (indigenous and international), children's homes are an easy way of acquiring funds, a considerable proportion of which may be syphoned off for personal use. Some NGOs may also be diametrically opposed to government interference. However, some (primarily indigenous) NGOs, *have* voluntarily changed their manner of working, electing to close down and organise educational sponsorship and home support in the community, or transforming themselves into boarding schools rather than residential homes.

Successful implementation will depend ultimately on the availability of adequate personnel and finance. With increasing cut-backs in the civil service and ministry budgets, it seems unlikely that government alone has the capacity to implement new legislation.

A final question concerns the formation of a pressure group to advocate on behalf of legal reform once the CLRC had completed its task by submitting its report. To address this problem, a Chapter of the African Network for the Prevention and Protection against Child Abuse and Neglect (ANPPCAN) is being established in Uganda to advocate for the Rights of the Child. As an African NGO which attracts members from all the relevant disciplines and all walks of life, this should be a strong and authoritative body which can press for the proposed reforms to be adopted in the National Assembly.

Conclusion

If the law is neglecting to protect children then it needs to be changed. Legal reform brings about a better framework within which responsibilities can be clarified and mechanisms established to give children the best protection possible within prevailing socio-economic constraints. In countries such as Uganda where well over half the population is aged under 18, the scale of difficulties facing children is immense, and the number of children in especially difficult circumstances is registered in millions. The question for NGOs is how to use their funds to make the greatest possible impact for the benefit of their target groups. For SCF, effective legal reform which helps to make a reality of children's rights must be a high priority.

If the CLRC's proposals become law, more child-related problems will be dealt with in the locality in which the child lives. Clear responsibilities will be placed on elected village officials to ensure that children's rights to immunisation, education, fair treatment, and health care are respected. Serious offences by children and serious child-care matters will be heard in the District Family and Children Court, and not in the High Court. The law will limit the time a child may be remanded in custody, and set limits to the time by which a case must be heard, maximum sentences and the duration for supervision or care orders.

The proposals place the prime responsibility for the upbringing of children on their parents. In child-care matters, courts should not make orders unless the child is suffering or likely to suffer significant harm. The new law will allow parents to apply for maintenance at any time up until a child is 18. Parental custody of a child will be decided on the 'welfare principle' ie custody will be granted to the parent with whom it is in the best interests of the child to be with.

If NGOs are to increase the impact of their work through legal reform, it is helpful (and perhaps essential) that they become accepted and trusted partners of government. They will also need to have the expertise to assist in the reform process, particularly in identifying the underlying principles which will guide the reforms when the time comes to make specific proposals. Without this expertise, financial support may be wasted. In addition, involvement in legal reform is likely to require that financing continues into the implementation and evaluation phases of the process. To be successful, reform requires a long-term commitment and broad-based support. With the high failure rate in legal reform it is best not to 'put all one's eggs into one basket', and this means tackling a number of complementary issues of concern at the same time.

NGOs that become involved in developing policy and legislative reforms may receive a hostile reaction from other NGOs, and from those in and out of government whose freedom of action may be limited by new proposals. Even if NGOs do all they can to ensure that their role remains advisory only, their funding role means that they are often accused of having undue influence. This is a tightrope that any NGO will have to face in scaling-up its impact by using this approach. Therefore, it is important that the NGO's advisory role is made very visible, and that decision-making authority with regard to policy and legal reform is clearly seen to rest with government.

Despite the current positive international climate concerning children's rights, it is clear that there are a great many factors which need to be carefully considered before deciding to assist government in the process of legal reform. There may be other, more effective strategies for achieving the same objectives, and it is important to know whether, for example, a simple 'statutory instrument' (which is easier to effect) might not be sufficient. However, in much of Anglophone Africa the laws relating to children are outdated and inappropriate. Although the experience of the CLRC and the Babies and Children's Homes Rules in Uganda is still very young, they do suggest that legal reform may be one of the most effective approaches of all to scaling-up for agencies concerned with long-term change.

9
Bigger and better?
Scaling-up strategies pursued by BRAC 1972–1991
Mick Howes and M G Sattar

The Bangladesh Rural Advancement Committee (BRAC) is one of the largest Southern NGOs. It employs some 4,500 people, has an annual operational budget in the region of US$23 million, and operates a number of large-scale multi-sectoral programmes. This paper identifies the various scaling-up strategies which the organisation has used as it has grown, and shows how these have been combined to achieve diverse objectives. Most of what follows focuses on the core rural development activities, but briefer reference will also be made in the chapter to the nation-wide programmes with which BRAC has been associated. The account begins with an attempt to establish a typology of the scaling-up strategies which have been employed.

Concepts

Types of scaling-up

The first approach to scaling-up which BRAC has used may be described as simple replication. This is where a model is developed and refined on a pilot basis in a particular locality, and then promoted on a more extensive scale, without the intervention of other agencies.

BRAC has also sought to scale-up through intensification of effort within a particular locality, and/or in relation to a particular client group. This, in turn, may take a number of forms. One is vertical integration (Abed 1987) where an existing activity is strengthened by the establishment of forward or backward linkages (for example, by adding a processing capacity to an agricultural production programme). Another is horizontal integration, where a programme that begins with one or two components has other components added to it. A third might entail the substitution of a simple, small-scale activity, by something more complex.

Each of the four possibilities outlined thus far may be characterised as 'additive'. Once an initial learning period has been discounted, they are characterised by a state of affairs where any new benefits arising will entail an approximately proportional addition in the resources provided by the promoting organisation. These may be contrasted with 'multiplicative' strategies, where each additional input by the sponsor brings forth a more than proportional return.

These may be broken down further. Sustainable client-run institutions might be promoted within an initial locality, which once established might allow the organisation to withdraw partially or wholly, and then re-deploy the resources saved elsewhere. Multiplication of effect could also be achieved through the collaborative provision of services with government or some other external agency. Finally, under certain circumstances, it might prove possible to transfer a successful model to another organisation.

Each of these analytical building blocks will subsequently be used to illuminate specific aspects of the BRAC experience. In certain instances they will appear in relatively pure form, whilst in others, they will be combined. The analysis will attempt to establish the circumstances under which specific strategies or permutations, may or may not prove successful.

Learning curves

In seeking to understand how BRAC has scaled-up, it will also be useful to refer to a model developed by Korten and Klauss (1984) as a part of their work on the 'learning process approach'. This is especially relevant to the simple replication and multiplicative options discussed above (see Figure 9.1). The model identifies three stages, each of which poses a particular problem. The first is how to attain 'effectiveness', ie to determine how a particular task may best be performed. With this achieved, attention then moves to 'efficiency', ie how to reproduce the desired results at an acceptable cost. This invariably involves some limited erosion of effectiveness. The third stage involves replication or extension of scale. Paralleling the transition from stage one to stage two, this will entail an element of trade-off between the extent of replication, and the degree of efficiency retained.

The framework raises two questions which are central to an understanding of how BRAC has proceeded:

■ at what point is it appropriate to attempt to effect transitions from stage one to stage two, and from stage two to stage three?
■ how sharp a decline in the effectiveness and efficiency curves can be accepted in the critical scaling-up transition between stages two and three?

Scaling-up in the evolution of the core programme (1972–1991)

Figure 9.2 summarises the scaling-up strategies which have been used in the evolution of the core rural development activities, in the support services upon which the core has depended, and in the large programmes which will be considered later in the chapter. The history of the core and support functions subdivides into five distinct phases.

1. Relief and Community Development at Sulla (1972–75)
2. Targeting the Landless at Jamalpur and Manikganj (1976–79)
3. The Outreach and Rural Credit and Training approaches (1980–85)
4. The Rural Development Programme (1986–89)
5. The Rural Credit Project (1990–)

Each may now be considered in turn.

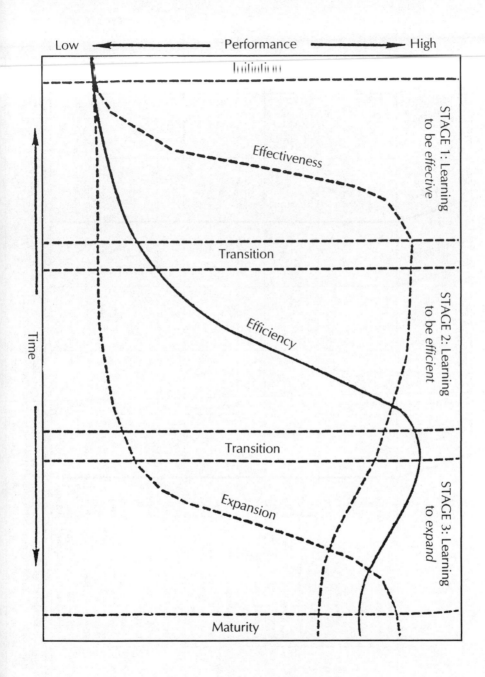

Figure 9.1: *Programme learning curves*
Source: Korten and Klauss (1984)

			Additive				Multiplicative		
			horizontal integration	simple replication	vertical integration	promoting larger enterprises	promoting sustainable institutions	co-operative production of services	model transfer
CORE RURAL PROGRAMMES	Relief and Community Development	1972–1975	X						
	Targeting the Landless	1976–1979	✓	✓					
	Outreach/Rural Credit & Training Programmes	1976–1979		✓			X		
	Rural Development Programme (phase I)	1986–1989		✓					
	Rural Credit Project	1990–1993		?		?	?		
SUPPORT PROGRAMMES*	Retailing Outlets (Aarong)	from 1978			✓				
	Rural Enterprise Programme	from 1985				?			
	Management Development Programme	from 1990							?
LARGE SCALE PROGRAMMES	Oral Extension Therapy Programme	1979–1990		✓					
	Child Survival Programme	from 1986						✓	✓
	Women's Health Development Programme	from 1990						?	?
	Non-formal Primary Education Programme	from 1985		✓					✓
	Income Generation for Vulnerable Group Development	from 1988						✓	✓

✓ Strategy successfully promoted
? Strategy currently being tested
X Strategy abandoned

* The Training and Research Centres (starting in 1976) and the Research and Evaluation Division (also starting in 1976) have contributed to scaling-up as well, but do not display the kinds of direct linkage with particular strategies which exist in relation to other programmes.

Figure 9.2:   *Types of scaling-up used by different programmes*

Relief and Community Development at Sulla (1972–75)

Relief and rehabilitation   The story starts early in 1972 in Sulla, a remote and, in many respects, rather atypical sub-district in the north-east of Bangladesh. Already disadvantaged in comparison to other parts of the country by its remoteness and ~~inaccessible physical environment, the absolute and relative historical~~ deprivation of the area was to be deepened further by its experience of the war of liberation from Pakistan, which culminated in 1971. Thousands of inhabitants had been forced to flee the war as refugees, and when the time came for them to return, they were confronted by a desperate situation.

Reasoning that Sulla's isolation would cut it off from most of the national and international efforts which were then being mounted, F H Abed, the founder of BRAC, who came originally from the area, and a group of close associates, decided to mount their own relief operation, under the banner of the Bangladesh Rehabilitation and Relief Assistance Committee.

In classic 'first generation' style (Korten 1990), tools were supplied, materials were made available for the reconstruction of houses and boats, and medical centres were established (Islam and Choudhury nd). A sum in excess of 3 million taka was raised and spent, and the basic process of rehabilitation was completed by the end of 1972.

The Community Development phase   At this point a decision was made to transform BRAC into a 'second generation' organisation, with longer-term objectives. Two hundred villages in Sulla were selected, and a community development programme was launched. At the same time, the name of the organistion was changed to the Bangladesh Rural Advancement Committee (the acronym BRAC being retained).

Almost from the outset, this new initiative assumed a number of characteristics which were subsequently to be incorporated into the model selected for replication. The approach pursued was multi-sectoral, with primary health care and non-formal primary education, alongside basic economic activities. Within the economic sector, following a brief and unsuccessful attempt to introduce tailoring, emphasis was given to the strengthening of traditionally established and small-scale production activities, such as drying fish and weaving fishing nets. Particular efforts were made to encourage the participation of women. Attempts were made to build institutions which would support the other activities being undertaken; with co-operatives being the medium favoured in the first instance. Heavy emphasis was placed upon training to upgrade the technical and organisational skills of the rural people involved. Similar provision was made to train staff, and a policy was adopted of only recruiting university graduates.

The wider significance of these initial measures will become apparent as the account unfolds. For the present, it is sufficient to note two key features. First, the multi-sectoral approach created a strong potential for horizontal integration from the outset. Second, by simultaneously developing expertise in a number of different areas, BRAC placed itself in a position to pursue a wide range of strategies at a later stage.

But while exhibiting these positive characteristics, the initial development effort was to prove, in important respects, flawed. The assumption of a community, where the needs of everybody could be addressed at the same time, and in essentially the same ways, overlooked marked internal social and economic differences. This led to a situation where the relatively wealthy were able to capture most of the benefits, and the poor were largely excluded. These socio-economic differences also rendered the intended co-operative structure largely ineffective, and in the absence of a viable institutional framework, the potential for horizontal integration remained unrealised.

Targeting the landless at Jamalpur and Manikganj (1976–79)

Programmatic evolution   In the light of the community development experience a decision was made that all programmes should henceforth be targeted on the landless poor, with special emphasis being given to women. It was further decided that the landless should be formed into groups, and that these would become the medium through which all subsequent activities would be introduced.

These changes were accompanied by the opening up of two new project areas in locations more typical of rural Bangladesh. The first was Jamalpur: the second, and more important, was Manikganj. It was here, working in 250 villages, over a four year period, that BRAC was to refine the model which was subsequently to be replicated on a wider scale.

Landless men and women were formed into groups, and then engaged in a process of functional education which was designed to raise consciousness and lay the foundations for eventual self-reliant development. Credit was provided, and together with the skills derived from an extended training programme, this established the foundation upon which a series of small-scale economic activities could then be built. Consistent with earlier practice, primary health care and non-formal primary education for children were also incorporated in the package.

While all of this was going on in Manikganj, Jamalpur was being developed as a laboratory for programmes targeted specifically on women, and as a location for training women staff. The Manikganj and Jamalpur initiatives, and the adoption of a similar approach in Sulla, helped to realise the potential for horizontal integration which had arisen from the early community development experiment. In Korten's terminology, this phase was, therefore, primarily about learning how to become effective and efficient. A degree of simple replication also began to take place, but this was confined, for the time being, to the three central locations.

Support services   The growth of activity in these three areas during the later part of the 1970s, was facilitated by the establishment of series of support services. Of these, the Training and Resources Centres (TARCs) were probably the most important. Building on the experience obtained during the community development phase, the TARCs helped to impart the technical and organisational skills required by newly established village groups. They also fulfilled the important longer-term function of training BRAC staff, and ensuring that an adequate supply of people with grassroots experience would be available to fill the growing number of managerial positions created as BRAC embarked upon the series of more ambitious scaling-up exercises which were to follow.

This period also saw the establishment of the Research and Evaluation Division (RED), which was given the task of examining BRAC's programmes, and of promoting understanding of the constraints and dynamics of rural development. This was to play an important role in helping to identify the prospects and weaknesses inherent in the various possibilities which were being explored, and helps to explain BRAC's reputation as a 'learning organisation' (Korten and Klauss 1984).

A further development saw the establishment of the first of a string of retail outlets to market the craft and textiles produced by the rural artisans which BRAC and other NGOs were assisting. These represented the initial exercise in scaling up through vertical integration, and were to be followed, at a later stage, by the establishment of cold storage facilities for potatoes.

The Outreach and Rural Credit and Training approaches (1980–85)

Competing paradigms By the end of the 1970s, the measure of success achieved in targeting the landless in the three project areas gave BRAC's managers the confidence to extend activities over a wider geographical area. But, at this point, a fundamental debate arose within the organisation as to how this was to be achieved.

One group held that the inclusion of a significant economic element in the approach was engendering dependency and undermining attempts at empowerment. According to this school of thought, the landless should have been encouraged to mobilise their own resources, to focus their efforts on wage bargaining, to pressurise government for the provision of services, and to organize themselves in order to resist the various forms of exploitation to which they were subject. Others, by contrast, felt that BRAC had no option but to provide credit to the poor, given the chronic shortages which they faced, and that there was no reason why this should not go hand in hand with the building of local institutions. In keeping with BRAC's ethos as a learning organisation, it was eventually agreed that both approaches should be tested independently, through two different programmes: Outreach, and Rural Credit and Training.

The Outreach Programme The Outreach Programme was established to test the limits of what the landless could achieve using their own resources and whatever else they could mobilise locally, or through the government system. These ideas were introduced first, and explored most extensively, in Sulla, but by 1984 they had been extended to 318 villages, concentrated in 11 *upazilas* (sub-districts).

The Sulla experiment began with intensive empowerment exercises which were designed to strengthen groups, and from 1981 onwards, BRAC started to run down the levels of economic support which had been provided earlier. As this was going on, a federation of landless groups was established with the intention that it should take over the role which BRAC had previously performed.

These moves were partially successful, most notably in the 1983 union parishad elections, where 15 of the 40 candidates from BRAC groups gained seats. Significant achievements were also recorded elsewhere. Many groups managed to secure government land for cultivation, to bargain for higher wages, and to secure access to a range of government programmes. In a number of instances, landless groups were able to establish funds through the mobilisation of savings.

These achievements proved, however, patchy and short-lived. The independent savings which the landless generated were never able to satisfy the demand for loans, and in the absence of a secure economic base, groups tended to degenerate into factionalism. Some survived longer than others, and women's groups tended to prove more resilient than men's, but almost everywhere it became apparent that the Outreach Programme could not be sustained. Some saw this as a failure to attain 'critical consciousness', and in a sense, this was correct. But it would perhaps be more to the point to argue that such advances in awareness and organisation as the landless were able to achieve were, in retrospect, never going to be sufficient to sustain them, without external support, in an environment where they were so economically and politically disadvantaged.

The Rural Credit and Training Programme   The Rural Credit and Training Programme (RCTP) was never conceived as a pure test of economic strategy, in the way that Outreach had sought to explore the institution building approach. Nevertheless, it gave much heavier emphasis to the economic dimension. Credit was initially provided shortly after group formation and with few conditions. It soon became apparent that the landless were simply viewing their membership in narrow instrumentalist terms, and that the approach was inconsistent with the building of viable institutions. Procedures were accordingly revised so that credit would only be supplied to members of groups which had met regularly for a year; had demonstrated a capacity to save; and had engaged in some form of collective activity. A further requirement was that no individuals would be eligible for loans who had not first completed a functional education course. It was this modified version, which made some concessions to the Outreach concept, which was finally selected for replication.

Lessons about scaling-up   Although it was utimately not chosen, the Outreach experience was perhaps the more instructive of the two alternatives so far as questions of scaling-up were concerned. The RCTP story was essentially one of continued model-testing – of learning, in Korten's terminology, how to be effective and efficient – accompanied by only a modest element of simple replication.

Outreach, on the other hand, whilst not directly perceived in such terms at the time, appears now as BRAC's first excursion into multiplicative scaling-up. If the approach had succeeded, and sustainable independent institutions of the landless had been established, this would have opened up the possibility of withdrawal, and ultimately the prospect of extended replication through the redeployment of resources elsewhere. As it was, the experiment had to be abandoned, and until very recently, no further attempt at this type of scaling-up has been made in any BRAC programme. Neither has the experience of groups engaging in local-level politics been repeated elsewhere, although the possibility of federating grassroots-level groups is now, once again, on the agenda.

The Rural Development Programme (1986–1989)

Initial consolidation   The next phase, from 1986–1989, saw a consolidation of the ideas developed in the early 1980s under the auspices of the Rural Development Programme (RDP). Geographical coverage expanded rapidly and, building on earlier models, it came to incorporate four major types of activities:

- institution-building (including functional education and training)
- credit operations (including the accumulation of savings)
- income and employment generation
- support service programmes.

The guiding objectives were to develop a viable organisation for the landless at the grassroots, to make them critically aware of their environment, and to initiate changes to improve the conditions in which they lived and worked. At the outset, emphasis was given to small-scale activities of a largely traditional nature, where loans were made to individuals, and could be repaid within a year. But as time passed, it was becoming apparent that this approach could only lead to marginal increases in the living standard of the landless.

The Rural Enterprise Project Against this background, a Rural Enterprise Project (REP) was launched as a new support service, which would experiment with different ideas, technologies and business enterprises, in order to identify new income generating opportunities. Most of the new possibilities identified for promotion under the programme (deep tubewells, power tillers, brick fields and shrimp culture) entailed a shift to a considerably larger scale of enterprise. In turn, this required more complex institutional arrangements, and the need for credit to be extended for longer periods.

REP was to be absorbed into the RDP in a subsequent re-organisation, but even before this happened, REP ideas were already beginning to be taken up, and to assume growing significance within the RDP. Thus, while the dominant characteristic of this phase remained simple replication of earlier models, scaling-up by increasing enterprise size came to establish itself as an important supporting theme.

The Rural Credit Project (1990–)

Two important events in 1990 were to usher in the fifth and most recent set of developments in the evolution of BRAC's core rural development programme. First, the RDP entered its second phase, with new areas being brought under the programme. Second, a new initiative known as the Rural Credit Project (RCP) was undertaken. This laid the foundation for a self-supporting credit institution, financing the employment and income-generating activities of the target group members. The RCP is designed to continue the RDP activities, but with a distinct structural identity. The intention is that groups will graduate to it after four years of conventional support under the RDP and that RDP resources can then be re-deployed in new areas.

If group sustainability can be achieved under the RCP, then BRAC will be able to start opening new RDP branches at an accelerated rate, without needing to increase the resources that it provides. By the end of 1990, almost 100,000 borrowers had made the transition to the RCP, while those registered under RDP had grown to more than 400,000. If things go according to plan, it is anticipated, that within a few years, the RCP will exceed the RDP in size.

Achieving multiplication

The prospects for scaling-up under the core programme

Can the institutional structures built up during the RDP survive the transition to RCP? Landless people's livelihoods may have been significantly enhanced, and their levels of consciousness raised, but if they still remain dependent upon the richer households for at least a part of their subsistence, will they be able to defend their interests when the main BRAC operation has moved on? A potential way of making this come about might be to revive the attempts from Sulla in the 1980s to build landless federations; starting perhaps at the union level, and then moving up to the *upazila*. This possibility is currently under review.

A second issue will concern the appropriate mix between larger and smaller enterprises as groups make the transition to RCP. The larger-scale initiatives, such as irrigation projects, hold out the opportunity of better returns, and hence should strengthen the prospects for longer group survival when adopted. They do, however, require greater inputs in the early stages, at a time when BRAC's objective is to organise the services it provides on a cost-recovery basis.

A third possibility is that the move to the RCP may be accompanied by a dilution of impact on selected target groups. Larger enterprises tend to fall mainly, if not exclusively, within traditional male territory, and might thus make it more difficult to retain the emphasis upon the promotion of women's livelihoods.

Over and above the gender implications of the RCP, it is also important to recognise that the 'landless' category is now becoming very large and internally stratified. There may soon be a case for distinctions to be drawn between the poor and the ultra-poor, which, if overlooked, could lead to the danger of replication only being achieved at the price of virtually excluding those who are in greatest need. To deal with the danger of the 'iron law of oligopoly', it might be necessary to introduce measures such as rotating leadership of groups.

The core programme in retrospect

These potential difficulties notwithstanding, it is clear that much has been achieved during the first twenty years of BRAC's core programme. The pattern of earlier success appears to be continuing with the RCP, under which 50 areas have already been incorporated since 1990. The major strength of the RDP, has been that replication on a major scale was only attempted after an extended process of experimentation with different approaches to horizontal integration had taken place. At first, and to some extent, this was a question of offering landless people the opportunity to engage in more than one economic activity, although this was exercised more frequently by male than by female members. The provision of health and education services alongside productive opportunities has proved a further source of strength for the female members.

Most important of all has been the horizontal linkage between institutional development and economic activities, supported by credit and training. The experiments conducted in phase three demonstrated that the economic advancement of the landless could not be secured unless basic skills had been internalised and collective institutions constructed to contain the potential for competition and conflict between group members. By the same token, institutions could not survive unless the basic material needs of participants were simultaneously addressed.

As Figure 9.2 confirms, the basic scaling-up formula has been for horizontal integration to provide the foundation for a subsequent process of simple replication. As the figure also shows, each of these elements, and the less important vertical integration, fall within the 'additive' category, where growth in impact is broadly proportional to growth in input. Behind the story which has been told, therefore, lies another, too complicated to relate here, of how BRAC as an organisation has expanded in line with its growing coverage. A further, more recent additive strategy, entailing the promotion of larger enterprises, is still at the model-testing stage, and cannot yet fully be addressed.

What the figure also makes clear, is that the core programmes have, until recently, attempted much less by way of multiplicative scaling-up. The early attempts to build sustainable institutions in Sulla, and elsewhere under the Outreach Programme, had to be abandoned after a relatively short period of experimentation, and it was only with the introduction of the RCP, that the possibility of sustainable institution building was revived.

Scaling-up under the large-scale programmes

The core programme, however, constitutes only part of the story. As it has been growing, BRAC has also been spinning off a number of large single-sector programmes which have been able to scale-up more rapidly, and which have employed a different set of options.

The first such initiative was the anti-diarrhoeal, Oral Therapy Extension Programme (OTEP). This was first developed and promoted around Sulla, and then subsequently extended, by simple replication, to approximately 12 million rural households. This gave BRAC's managers their first chance to operate at a national level. The success achieved dispelled fears that large-scale replication would lead to a dilution of quality, and created the confidence to go to scale in other programmes.

The next initiative, the Child Survival Programme, was mounted as OTEP continued. This built a number of other components, including child immunisations, and nutrition training, around the rehydration package. It was eventually promoted in about a third of the country, but rather than relying upon its own organisation, BRAC, in this case, achieved scale through the medium of co-operative production of services with government. The Women's Health Development Programme, begun in 1991, aims to promote a still wider package of measures, using similar methods (Lovell 1991).

Work in Non-formal Primary Education initially followed a similar path to OTEP. Two models were developed in the first instance. One offered schooling to children from poor families who were unlikely to enter the educational system. The other provided opportunities to older children who were unable to complete their primary education. Starting from a base of 22 experimental schools in 1985, a process of simple replication has now been used to expand this to 6,000 schools. At the same time, BRAC's example has encouraged a number of other NGOs to take up similar programmes transforming an additive into a multiplicative strategy, and representing BRAC's first use of the model transfer option.

More recently, still, BRAC has embarked upon a process of large-scale development of some of the economic activities with which it has been associated, through the Income Generation for Vulnerable Group Development Programme. Building again on procedures worked out in its core programme, this has involved the training of poultry workers as paravets to inoculate chickens. Vaccine and personnel are provided by the government, while BRAC supplies the necessary technical expertise; making this a second example of effective co-operative production of services with government. Developments in sericulture show similar arrangements evolving to a more complex level of interdependence.

The most recent advance of all has arisen with the establishment of a Management Development Unit. As a part of the support service structure this is designed primarily as a vehicle for the higher-level management training which is now required within BRAC. But provision has also been made for training of staff from other NGOs and, in certain instances, from the government itself. This opens up the possibility of a greater measure of impact through model transfer to other organisations in the future. The embryonic Rural Poor Programme, being implemented by the Bangladesh Rural Development Board, and deriving directly from a BRAC model, provides an early indication of what might be possible.

Comparative success in scaling-up

Taking the large-scale programmes as a whole, and contrasting them with the core approaches, a number of observations arise. First, we have seen that scaling-up successes in the core programme have been mainly of the additive type, with heavy emphasis being given to simple replication. Multiplicative approaches have proved more problematic, although the RCP now appears to be reversing this tendency.

The large-scale programmes have also used simple replication, but the dominant motif here has been multiplicative. Furthermore, these multiplicative strategies have led to clear successes, although they have been achieved through co-operative production of services and model replication rather than sustainable institution building. These successes have come about by extracting relatively small components from previously horizontally integrated packages, and then promoting them in an extensive fashion.

The types of components selected have also been significant, in so far as they have been those which benefit the landless, whilst not representing the kind of direct threat to more powerful interests within the rural areas that, for example, a conscientised group engaging in a large-scale economic activity, might be seen to constitute. The central lesson which others looking at the BRAC experience might learn from this is that the further scaling-up of the core, horizontally-integrated package is a more complex and potentially sensitive type of enterprise than the large programme initiatives, and one which inevitably imposes greater organisational demands.

This cautionary note should not, however, detract from a positive overall conclusion. BRAC's experiences, during its first 20 years, show quite clearly that the central features of innovative and cost-effective models do not have to be sacrificed in the search for wider replication. Where attention is given to building organisational capacities to support programme expansion, there is no inherent contradiction between quality and scale. Bigger can also be better.

10

The growth of the SANASA movement in Sri Lanka

P A Kiriwandeniya

Introduction

SANASA, the Sinhala acronym for Sri Lanka's Thrift and Credit Co-operative Societies, represents a rare success story among the many co-operative endeavours that it was once thought would be a major vehicle for rural development and poverty-alleviation in Asia. Its history dates back to 1906 and it is the oldest form of co-operative society in Sri Lanka. Approximately 17 per cent, or 1,000 out of the current 7,000 societies have been in existence for seventy years or more. These societies have managed to survive as indigenous, grassroot level organisations and have maintained their independent character despite bureaucratic and political intervention over the years.

Today the SANASA Movement is a national organisation which has remained true to democratic principles while other types of co-operatives have been co-opted and are controlled by politically or bureaucratically appointed boards of directors. All primary society members buy shares in SANASA and elect their own leadership. By-laws are determined by the general body of the primary SANASA society. District SANASA unions (representing 50 to 600 primary societies) form the second tier of the SANASA Movement. Each district union is governed by a board of directors elected annually by delegates from the primary societies. Delegates from the district unions in turn form the general body which elects the board of directors of a national body in the form of the Federation of Thrift and Credit Co-operative Societies (FTCCS). This organisational structure ensures accountability at each level of the structure while preserving the rights of the primary societies to exercise autonomy in managing their own institutions.

Evolution

Period of initial growth (1906–1940)

The Credit Co-operative Ordinances were passed by the colonial administration at the beginning of this century. They covered the formation and registration of credit co-operative societies and were a result of a report by a government appointed committee examining the feasibility of establishing rural agricultural banks. Under these ordinances, a mass formation and registration was able to begin. By 1940, the movement had grown to 1302 credit co-operative societies of both limited and unlimited liability designations.

As the system expanded, so did training in the co-operative ideal and methodology, providing the island with a cadre of rural leaders who understood rural organisation-formation, management and credit.

The decline (1940–1979)

During the Second World War, there was a phenomenal increase in the number of consumer co-operative societies in existence as a result of administration efforts to open up a network of retail outlets. This was to ensure the distribution of essential commodities at reasonable prices as wartime scarcities initially led to black marketeering by unscrupulous private traders and rises in prices that threatened the well-being of many people. Co-operative agricultural production and sales societies were also formed to extend credit to farmers and stimulate food production. The government continued with its high level of involvement in the co-operative sector after the war and in 1957 multi-purpose co-operative societies (MPCSs) were introduced serving as retailers, wholesalers, marketing agencies and providers of credit. In 1971 the multi-purpose co-operative societies were amalgamated into larger units which maintained branches across large geographical areas.

Due to these changes in the co-operative movement, the Thrift and Credit Co-operative Society (TCCS) system began to shrink after 1964. This was a result of a shift in its members' interest to the larger multi-purpose societies which had more funds for loans, did not emphasise saving, provided a wider range of services (eg government-subsidised agricultural loans, sale of consumables, sale of agricultural inputs). TCCS numbers decreased from 4026 credit co-operative societies in 1964 to just 1300 societies in 1978.

This decline brought along with it a host of problems including low morale among the remaining membership, loss of office bearers and members with adequate knowledge and skills to properly run the societies and increased incidences of mismanagement. Overall, though, thrift and credit societies retained a reputation as respectable and trustworthy but rather old-fashioned, village institutions, so slow and conservative that neither local politicians nor the local elite had much interest in taking control of them. The various governments of the period were similarly uninterested in SANASA, preferring instead to develop much grander structures that could be directly controlled, such as the multi-purpose co-operatives, which are now largely discredited.

The re-awakening (1977–79)

In 1977 a development activist with considerable experience in the voluntary sector, P A Kiriwandeniya, recognised SANASA's potential as a mechanism for achieving self-reliant and co-operative development amongst rural people. He observed that, despite thirty years of independence, villagers still suffered from low incomes and high levels of indebtedness. More than half of the people suffered from serious indebtedness, largely to non-institutional sources. The commercial banks, with their demands for security, implicit desire to maintain a large loan size and red tape, excluded most of the rural populace from taking loans.

Many believed that the rural poor had a fatalistic attitude – 'What can we do?' – and did not trust each other enough to take any joint action to improve their situation. Kiriwandeniya believed that with careful guidance the thrift and credit societies could change this. The societies were suited to the people's own (largely Buddhist) values, and participation in community activities has long been a feature of Sri Lankan culture. If societies could be encouraged to perform a broader development role it would be compatible with existing village activities and thus be acceptable.

The thrift and credit co-operatives also had the advantage that they had not fallen under the influence of political patronage and other abuses typical of the wider co-operative movement. This standing as a non-government, non-party political institution enhanced the societies' credibility as a genuine people's movement for rural development. The societies had also developed a strong institution spirit. From these roots it would be possible to develop a broader co-operative culture.

Finally, it must be observed that the societies were not relief or charitable institutions. They were focused on active self-help, initiative and human development. Although the capacity of society leaders to understand rural development problems was weak, and their capability to address those problems even weaker, the societies had the potential to become a viable institution for rural development.

In order to assist the societies to realise their potential it was necessary to analyse their history and their weaknesses and to design a strategy for the development of the movement based on that analysis. It was obvious that the existing societies were not business-oriented. Former co-operative leaders, quoting Buddhist principles, had encouraged a system which accepted deposits from members on low or zero interest rates. This ensured that savings in the societies remained low and so the funds available for loans remained very limited. The societies lacked management skills and, without support structures, individual societies were compelled to function in isolation. Small societies sometimes collapsed with borrowers falling into the hands of money lenders. Larger societies either retained their excess funds uninvested or deposited them with the commercial banks that took the resources out of rural areas. The societies had failed to become a vehicle for broader community development and had completely excluded the poor, youth, women and children from their activities.

So a revitalisation process began in the village of Walgama in Kegalle District. After some months of discussion and education programmes, awareness began to rise and the villagers gained greater respect for their own credit society along with more self-confidence and motivation. Once the people were aware that a credit society could be more than just a savings club they became open to the introduction of more business-like practices in the running of the society. Over the course of a year the society introduced a nameboard, office space, office hours, part-time and full-time workers, a deposit scheme for members and non-members and carried out a membership drive to attract a broader range of members, particularly women and youth.

At this experimental stage the basic model for the functioning of a primary society, which remains largely unchanged to this day, was laid down. To become a member of the society it was necessary to purchase at least one share worth Rs240, which could be paid for over 24 instalments of Rs10 each. The general body of the society established by-laws for loans (up to 10 times the value of the share holding), repayment arrangements and interest rates. The general body also established other conditions of membership; for example, compulsory attendance at no less than 50 per cent of meetings and good behaviour. The general body elected a committee of seven members (on an annual basis) while the committee elected its own president, vice president and secretary.

Underlying all of these changes was one simple principle: any development had to be undertaken from within the people's own resources and capabilities. Hence the office space was donated and the full-timers worked for Rs1 per day. Quickly people gained confidence in their own capacity to produce tangible results simply by using the resources they had in a more efficient way and with a longer-term vision of their community and its development.

Once these tangible changes in the business practices took place the whole village became more aware of the potential of the society to help them with their needs. For several decades the society had existed without name board or office. The community trusted the society but did not realise its potential. Now even non-members realised that the society was a place where they could deposit any small excess funds that they had. Gradually the society began to expand: it mobilised more savings; was able to increase the loan limit for members; and attracted more members. The society also introduced short term cash credits and became more and more relevant to people's needs.

Loans given at this time were largely for agriculture (42 per cent), housing repairs (30 per cent), small industry and trade (16 per cent) and consumer and other loans (12 per cent). Loans were usually small (Rs500–1000) with short repayment periods. In giving such loans the trust that could be placed in the borrower mattered a great deal; often no security could be offered other than that the person was known to the members, a service no commercial bank could match.

Repayment rates on the society's loans were high because the loan monies were mobilised within the community itself; mutual respect among the members guaranteed good behaviour. Loans were never written off. If a member could not repay, other members might contribute to repayment or the loan period would be extended.

The expansion phase (1980–85)

Following the success of the Walgama experiment a seminar was held for the whole of Kegalle District. From this seminar emerged the first TCCS District Union and the first serious attempt at institutionalisation. Prior to this time there were no district or national level organisations to coordinate activities. At the village level, individual credit society activities were limited to savings and credit. Meetings were held once a month, transactions were made, but there was little sense of belonging to an organisation. Few other organisational activities occurred and only limited time and effort was donated by the membership.

District union representation was soon recognised as critical for development of the movement. The benefits of education, training, inter-lending and other services and support were beyond the capabilities of individual societies. Within two years the advantages of co-operative education and coordination were widely accepted and five district unions as well as a national level federation had been formed.

Despite these rapid changes, there were still only 1,320 primary societies, five district unions and 26,556 members with total shares and savings of Rs111.2 million in 1980. The financial base was therefore too low for the movement to make any significant contribution to long-term rural development. Although a tertiary structure had been developed it was weak and the understanding of both leadership and members of the basic co-operative principles and practice were inadequate. The leaders lacked planning and management capabilities and did not have a vision of how they might contribute to rural development.

Drawing upon their own experiences in the development of the Walgama society, Kegalle and other district unions, the leadership of the movement developed a systematic process of securing and sustaining grassroots participation in the movement. This involved four processes: (i) motivating the people, (ii) mobilising human and financial resources, (iii) restructuring and developing the institution, (iv) ensuring long-term sustainability and impact. These are examined in turn.

Motivation emphasised using the primary society as a basis for analysing the socio-economic problems of the village, establishing in a very visible way, a data bank on village financial matters, forging much closer links between government extension staff and the primary society as the basis for upgrading the range and potential of investments, and introducing the concept of annual development plans.

Mobilisation focused on a removal of the barriers to entry which still existed. These involved changing the status of primary societies from unlimited to limited liability, encouraging the entry of women and children into the societies, and gradually replacing the old, conservative leadership. More attractive savings and lending policies were also introduced with interest rates on deposits and compulsory savings being set 2 per cent higher than those of commercial banks. Loans were made available for a wide variety of emergency, short-term and long-term purposes.

Institutional development included negotiation of a refinancing facility with the People's Bank and liberalisation of the co-operative laws to allow greater flexibility of operations. Within the movement, members and volunteers worked together to assist in the development of new primary and district unions. 'Paid' staff grew to almost 1,800 by 1985. Finally, SANASA was able to establish an inter-lending programme at district and federation level, thereby acquiring the ability to shift funds between areas and so vastly increase overall loan capacity. This inter-lending programme was established to operate at two levels. SANASA mobilises funds within the movement in the form of deposits, paying an interest of 12 to 14 per cent per annum (slightly higher than commercial rates). The Federation then on-lends this money to the district unions at 15 per cent. The district union mobilises funds at interest rates ranging from 11 to 13 per cent from the primary societies and at 15 per cent from the Federation to re-lend at 17 to 18 per cent to the primary societies. The primary societies which obtain funds from the district unions on-lend this money to their members at an average interest rate of 21 per cent. This is at or near commercial rates, well above the government subsidised rural credit rates but much lower than moneylender rates.

Sustainability was seen to be based upon the genuine participation of all the movement's members which, translated to village level, meant that SANASA must reflect the economic, social and cultural aspirations of all villagers, including the poorest. SANASA elected to emphasise the role of credit in expanding income generation and making better use of available resources. Careful planning became the cornerstone of SANASA's future with the first five-year plan emerging in 1985.

During the period 1981 to 1985 SANASA witnessed a great increase in all of its activities (Tables 10.1 and 10.2).

Growing pains (1985–1989)

SANASA's careful planning was thrown into turmoil when in 1985, SANASA was pressured by government to agree to act as a finance channel for the massive rural housing loan scheme which the National Housing Development Authority (NHDA) had launched with funding from USAID. This offered SANASA opportunities for a rapid increase in membership and loan volume. However, SANASA leaders had

Table 10.1:   *Growth in membership, societies and district unions 1981–1989*

Year	No of Primary Societies	No of District Unions	Members
1981	1,448	07	207,856
1982	1,570	11	169,201
1983	1,685	14	220,651
1984	2,166	16	241,615
1985	2,420	19	340,100
1986	4,387	24	470,200
1987	5,215	26	545,100
1988	5,885	26	568,320
1989	6,761	27	633,000
1990	6,821	27	675,000
1991	7,245	27	702,238

Table 10.2:   *Deposits and loans (1981–1989) Rs millions*

Year	Shares and savings	Loans disbursed
1981	113	68
1982	153	117
1983	172	220
1984	188	141
1985	220	188
1986	310	407
1987	352	408
1988	388	594
1989	418	601

very serious reservations that such involvement might divert the movement from its objectives and might jeopardise its carefully nurtured financial discipline.

As this new programme began to operate the leadership became aware that new societies were being formed simply so that the members could take advantage of the Million Housing Programme (MHP). Such new members had no commitment to credit discipline and to the self-reliant and co-operative principles underlying the activities of the movement. The default rate on housing loans began to increase during the late 1980s thereby blemishing what had otherwise been excellent repayment rates for credit co-operatives. However, repayments remained much higher than for loans disbursed by parastatal agencies and banks involved in MHP.

The movement's worst fears were realised in 1988 when USAID, frustrated with the low repayment rates being achieved through the National Housing Development Authority (NHDA), refused to re-finance the loan for the MHP. The government responded by writing off all outstanding housing loans for low income households in August 1988. This proved disastrous for credit discipline in SANASA and the movement is still grappling with the problems that were created. Although involvement in MHP has boosted membership and turnover (as indicated in Tables 10.1 and 10.2) SANASA has paid a high price for its agreement to work with government. In addition, much of the new membership is from middle-income groups and has diluted SANASA's poverty focus.

SANASA is now making great efforts to extend its services to poorer households and to recruit low-income members. By 1992, specially designed programmes, targetted on the poor, were being mounted with assistance from IFAD, CIDA and a range of other donors.

Conclusion

SANASA has made great strides since its reawakening in 1977. The Thrift and Credit Movement now stretches across rural Sri Lanka and has a membership and loans volume that exceeds those of government sponsored rural credit programmes. It suffered severely because of its collaboration with government in the MHP in the mid-1980s, but is now recovering. This fostered organisational growth but reduced the quality of impact. The plans for the early 1990s emphasise consolidation, rather than growth, although in the longer term the movement still pursues its objective of creating a financial institution that is self-sustaining and that meets the savings and credit needs of low-income families throughout the country. Although some evidence of the movement's ability to assist the poor exists, efforts are now in hand to more effectively monitor poverty alleviation impacts and to develop a greater capacity to provide 'credit for social justice'.

11

Growth and change in NGOs: concepts and comparative experience

David Billis and Joy MacKeith

Introduction

The rise in number, scale of operation and importance of NGOs in the development field has been accompanied by increasing interest in their organisation and management (Campbell 1987; Cernea 1988; Fowler 1990; Hodson 1992). This is not surprising since it is precisely their assumed organisational characteristics – flexibility, innovative ability, participatory approach and cost-effectiveness – that are so highly valued (Clark 1991). But there are additional important reasons for this increasing interest in management. First, there has been a growing dissatisfaction with the failures of the large official aid programmes and, in particular, a recognition that capital and technology alone cannot solve the problems of development. The result has been a refocusing of attention on institutional development in the South, and some writers have come to argue that effective institutions are a vital ingredient for sustainable development (Korten 1989; Brown 1990; Kajese 1987). Second, the rise in official and private funds flowing through northern NGOs has increased concern that organisations in receipt of these funds should be appropriately organised to ensure their maximum effectiveness (Chalker 1989; Dichter 1987).

However, despite this recognition of the 'organisational dimension' there is as yet little research on NGOs in the North and South. How are they structured? What kinds of organisational problems, dilemmas and constraints do they face? What management tools and concepts can be brought to bear on these issues? These questions are important at any time, but they take on extra significance during a period in which NGOs are challenged to scale-up their impact. Whether they choose to expand their operations, work with government, move into lobbying and advocacy, or put their energies into community mobilisation on the ground, increasing the level of impact is likely to mean organisational expansion. At the very least it will involve significant organisational change. Thus scaling-up is an organisational as well as a policy question. If it is to be achieved NGOs need to understand its organisational implications. But the growing literature on NGOs largely fails to examine the organisational dimension. Those writers who have looked at organisation and management have made a valuable contribution. However, much of their work has been based on personal experience and consultancy rather than systematic research. In this chapter we attempt to begin to fill this knowledge gap and explore the implications for the scaling-up debate. To do this we will draw on two sources. The first is a recent study of organisation and management within British NGOs. The second is the accumulated knowledge of fourteen years of study of voluntary organisations[1] in the UK by the Centre for Voluntary Organisation (CVO), a research and teaching centre based at the London School of Economics. The discussion will also be informed by the wider body of British and North American literature on the voluntary sector[2].

Before proceeding further, some words about the methodological approach underpinning the present study and the work of the CVO are important. The central feature of the approach is that it is a collaborative, problem-centred methodological approach, which seeks to develop theories of direct, practical use to managers by working with them in the resolution of current problems (Rowbottom 1977, Billis 1988). A key objective of the research programme undertaken by CVO is, therefore, to develop models which aid our understanding of the internal workings of voluntary organisations. Our conviction is that such an understanding is essential, both for individual agencies, and public policy makers, if they are to make informed decisions in pursuit of their goals. In accordance with this methodological approach the aim of the study which we draw on here is to identify several of the key organisational issues and dilemmas facing the larger NGOs operating in the UK. The first part of this chapter is devoted to outlining the findings of this study. In the second part we look at a model developed with voluntary organisations working in the UK, and examine its relevance for northern NGOs. In the final part we explore the implications of the study findings and the model for each of the scaling-up strategies outlined above.

Organisational challenges facing British NGOs

In order to investigate the organisational and management challenges facing British NGOs in the 1990s, 38 interviews were carried out with directors, senior managers, chairs and other governing body members in ten of Britain's largest development NGOs[3]. The overwhelming impression given by the interviewees was of thriving agencies successfully grasping the opportunities that the last decade had brought, and committed to their central missions. However there were also significant problems. Though a wide variety of challenges were described, seven key issues emerged.

Hierarchy versus democracy

One of the most frequently mentioned challenges was the conflict between staff and senior managers concerning the process by which decisions were made in the organisation. Typically, senior managers perceived themselves to be working within a hierarchy in which authority had been delegated to them by the governing body to make decisions regarding work falling within their area of responsibility. These they made taking into account as wide a range of considerations as possible, including the views of staff beneath them in the hierarchy. These subordinate staff, on the other hand, felt that the organisation should be organised in a democratic

---

[1] The term voluntary agency will be used to describe non-statutory, non-profit-making organisations that are primarily concerned with 'welfare work' in Europe, North America, and First World or developed countries.

[2] Some key texts in this growing body of literature are Powell (1987), Kramer (1981), Young (1985), James (1989), Van Til (1988) and Hodgkinson (1989).

[3] The results of the study are reported more fully elsewhere (Billis and MacKeith 1992). All interviews were carried out between October 1991 and March 1992.

manner, and that they should be full and equal participants in decisions affecting their areas of work. Though these views were not reflected in their agencies' organisational structures which were, in all cases, hierarchies, they were given credence by the agencies' self-proclaimed approach to development – an approach in which beneficiaries are seen as equal partners participating fully in the running of their projects. The argument of the subordinate staff was that the agencies should practise what they preached.

Raising money versus raising awareness

For half the agencies in the study tensions between fund-raising and other departments were described consistently as one of the main challenges facing the organisation. The dilemma facing these organisations is that the sorts of activities and images which they feel are most helpful and honest are very different from those which most inspire the public to make donations. The agencies believe in long-term projects which enhance the self-reliance of the recipients. The public, on the whole, prefer to help meet basic human needs in emergency situations. The agencies believe that positive images which depict their beneficiaries as competent, resourceful people are most accurate and respectful to their recipients. The public respond best to portrayals of desperation and helplessness. The result is tensions between fund-raisers, who are responsible for pricking the public conscience into making donations, and staff working in other parts of the organisation, who have more direct contact with the recipients of the funds and do not have fund-raising targets to meet.

Staff capacity and career development

The abilities of existing staff to cope with the increasing demands of a job, in which the responsibilities have grown enormously as the organisation has expanded, was an area of difficulty in a number of agencies. In those cases in which the post appeared to have developed more quickly than the incumbent, significant problems were experienced. The result was often that the development of the agency's work in this area was retarded.

In contrast, the lack of an NGO career structure and the small number of places at the top was also described as problematic in terms of the development of 'talented' staff. The result was a career bottleneck in the junior and middle management positions, with talented people quickly out-growing their jobs. The challenge for senior managers in this case was to find ways of creating the variety and opportunities which would keep their staff motivated in their existing posts.

Board capacity and governance

Interviewees in seven out of the ten agencies mentioned governance as an area in which their organisation needed to re-evaluate and make changes. Overwhelmingly, the issue that seemed most pressing was the question of the skills and expertise of governing body members to fulfil the tasks required of them. In one case the board lacked members with a good knowledge of work in the field. In another the board was made up exclusively of people whose strength was in this area, and as a result it was in need of members with other backgrounds. In some agencies it was not simply a question of the balance of skills but of the overall ability of members of the governing body to provide the kind of strategic guidance which interviewees felt their agencies needed.

Other issues relating to governance included the danger of the board becoming distanced from the staff, tensions between staff and board as a result of their different backgrounds and priorities, and large boards being too unwieldy in their operation.

Coordination and co-operation between departments

Some interviewees reported that coordination between different departments was a problem in their agencies. Different sections had different priorities which they pursued often with little reference to other parts of the organisation. This could result in organisational diffusion. In one agency the director described the organisation as resembling 'several smaller organisations loosely sheltering under the same umbrella'. This lack of coordination sometimes led to tensions between departments, and some interviewees expressed frustration that the work of their section was poorly understood within the agency and not afforded proper priority.

Managing at a distance

The difficulties associated with managing an operation which spans many countries and cultures was a question which concerned many agencies. In general the combination of mutual dependency and distance was seen to be a recipe for tensions between headquarters and field offices. There were also other problems in a number of agencies. In one organisation there was confusion about whether headquarters staff had authority over field staff or vice versa. In another the agency was experiencing difficulties in establishing which tasks should be carried out in the headquarters office and which were better done in the field. Some interviewees reported that keeping a good flow of information going was difficult. In particular the fact that field directors often met their immediate managers at headquarters as little as once a year or less was seen as a problem, as lack of information and contact could lead to mutual distrust.

Evaluating effectiveness

A fundamental challenge facing many of the agencies was the question of how the effectiveness of their work should be assessed. In the area of project work, interviewees reported difficulties in identifying reliable measures for evaluating the impact of interventions. Even with satisfactory measures of quality, wider global factors such as international terms of trade had such profound effects on the lives of the poor that it was almost impossible to establish whether local changes had resulted from NGO interventions or not. In many cases poverty increased as a project progressed. Was the project worthless, or was it stemming the decline, and is retarding decline a worthy NGO objective? In campaigning and development education work assessment was also problematic. Although campaigning work often has specific objectives, the goals can be so massive (for example major policy changes in multilateral agencies or multinational companies) that their achievement is a distant hope. Public education is even more diffuse. Some agencies took refuge in income levels as a straightforward and accessible measure of organisational success. Others rejected it but were at a loss for replacements.

The UK experience

In this part of the paper we explore whether there are conceptual tools and models which can help in tackling the problems discussed in part one and whether there are lessons that might be learnt from the experience of voluntary organisations in the UK. Any examination of two traditionally distinct fields raises an immediate question. To what extent are the fields comparable? Will ideas developed in one hold water when applied to the other, or are there important differences between them which will render them less helpful, or even useless? This is a complex question which we have considered in detail elsewhere (Billis and MacKeith 1992). Here it is sufficient for us to argue that, despite important differences in their organisation and work, development NGOs and voluntary organisations working in the UK have sufficient similarities to warrant comparison, and that both can be seen as part of the wider family of nonprofit organisations[4].

Our reasons for asserting this are threefold. First, voluntary organisations and development NGOs share a number of common features such as the centrality of mission and values, reliance on diverse sources and types of funding, and the existence of a voluntary governing body. Second, they share similar organisational challenges (Billis 1989; Billis and Harris 1991; MacKeith 1991). Third, voluntary organisations and NGOs also share a common public policy environment in which privatisation, and the off-loading of what were previously governmental responsibilities on to private groups, is a universal theme. Thus NGOs are increasingly being used by official institutions as channels for bilateral and multilateral aid, and voluntary organisations in the UK are also being looked to by government to expand their role in service provision (Department of Health 1989). Throughout Europe and North America similar trends have been reported (James 1989; Lipsky and Smith 1990).

These factors provide a sufficient basis to assume that NGOs and voluntary organisations may have something to learn from each other, and that concepts developed in the UK field may help shed light on the organisation of NGOs. To test this hypothesis we shall take the example of one theory which has proved useful in understanding a number of organisational problems in UK voluntary agencies.

Billis (1989) has outlined a model of the voluntary sector at the heart of which is the notion of three distinct conceptual 'worlds'. First there is the *personal world*. This is the world of relatives, friends and neighbours bound together by bonds of loyalty, affection and love. There are no formal roles, rules or boundaries to this world and social problems are resolved without recourse to contracts and without the aid of specialists or professionals, except in exceptional circumstances.

Second we have the *associational world*. In this arena groups of people draw a boundary between themselves and others in order to meet some problem or take action. There is an objective or mission, there is a name to the grouping and there is a membership with rights and duties. The rules of the game in this world are based on concepts such as voting and elections.

Finally there is the *bureaucratic world* – the world occupied by most public sector and commercial organisations. It comprises a system of paid staff who are organised into hierarchical roles. Managers are not elected by subordinates but are appointed by superiors and the system is bound together by concepts such as accountability and authority.

---

[4] Non-profit or non-profit organisation will be used as generic terms to refer to all non-statutory, non-profit-making organisations wherever they operate.

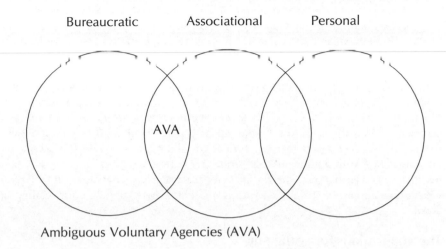

Bureaucratic   Associational   Personal

AVA

Ambiguous Voluntary Agencies (AVA)

Figure 11.1: *The personal, associational and bureaucratic worlds*

Although these three worlds can be described as distinct entities, there is an area of overlap or 'ambiguity' between them (Figure 11.1). Voluntary agencies are seen as lying in an ambiguous zone in which the bureaucratic and associational worlds overlap. Their history, voluntary governing body and ethos place them in the associational world, but, having taken on paid professional staff who occupy formal roles within a hierarchy, they also show many features of the bureaucratic organisation. This situation, in which two different sets of norms apply at the same time within the same organisation, leads to many of the characteristic problems of voluntary organisations. In particular, as the organisation grows, and possibly levels of public funding increase, the organisation is pulled increasingly into the bureaucratic world.

The theory can be elaborated by dividing the bureaucratic world into public and private sector bureaucracies. But even in its simple form (Figure 11.1) it helps to shed light on some of the tensions reported earlier. The conflict between hierarchical and democratic modes of decision-making, for example, can be understood as resulting from the tension between the bureaucratic world in which orders flow downwards, and the associational world in which decisions are taken jointly and each member has an equal say.

The tensions noted between field and headquarters offices may also be explained using this model. The headquarters office may be a fully fledged bureaucracy with clear lines of authority and accountability, while the field office, because of its mandate to work in a participative manner with the local population, may be operating under associational norms. In such a situation the two can be literally 'worlds apart', speaking a different language and appealing to different norms.

Similarly the framework may help us to understand problems of coordination and co-operation between departments. As an organisation grows and is pulled increasingly into the bureaucratic world, so the need for a clear structure and formal coordination systems increases. However in an agency which has only recently bureaucratised and has a 'foot in both camps', such mechanisms and structures may be only partly developed and thus interdepartmental issues remain unresolved.

So at least one theory developed to understand voluntary organisation problems in the UK has explanatory value in relation to some of the issues with which developmental NGOs must contend. There are other ideas and models which have been developed in response to the distinctive problems experienced within the voluntary sector. For example problems associated with governance have been extensively explored by Harris (1989, 1990) and a framework put forward by MacKeith (1992) may have explanatory value in relation to the tensions reported between fund-raising and projects staff. Clearly more detailed investigation of these issues will be necessary before any firm conclusions can be reached. Nevertheless this initial exploration indicates that further cross-fertilisation of ideas will be both fascinating and productive. Having made this first step, we now move on to explore what implications the results and ideas presented here have for the scaling-up debate.

The implications for scaling-up

Expanding operations and the problem of growth

Of the issues and challenges facing NGOs in the study reported earlier, at least four have one important aspect in common – they can be traced back to the rapid growth these NGOs have recently experienced.

The problems associated with staff capacity arose as a direct result of the rapid development of the organisation. Increased income and staffing levels required new levels of skills and competence that interviewees suggested not all employees could provide. Similarly, it appeared that the problems associated with governance and board capacity had arisen because the agency itself had grown and professionalised over recent years, leaving some governing body members behind. New board members were needed if the governing body was to be able to fulfil its policy-making role within the larger, more sophisticated organisation. Thirdly, the interdepartmental issues reported by interviewees were often linked to unplanned organisational growth. As new needs were identified and new money became available, new departments and sections would be created and 'bolted on' to existing structures. The implications for the work of other units might only become clear several months or years after the new section was created. The lack of coordinating mechanisms for dealing with such larger, more bureaucratic structures has already been noted. Finally, the tension between managers and other staff around decision-making processes can be seen as a result of organisational growth and the formalisation or bureaucratisation that accompanies it. Staff were accustomed to the sense of ownership and participation which is more easily achieved in a small or medium-sized organisation. When growth leads to the creation of new management lines and increases the distance between staff and key decision-makers, staff are likely to feel alienated, especially if this change takes place quickly.

It has already been argued that scaling-up, especially through expanding operations, is likely to involve organisational growth. The findings of the NGO study reported here indicate that the rapid growth many British NGOs have already experienced has lead to some substantial organisational problems. These difficulties are being tackled by NGOs in a variety of ways including restructuring, training (see Hodson, chapter 12), and initiatives to change organisational culture. Nevertheless, NGOs aiming to further increase their impact by means of expansion will be better able to do so successfully if they are aware of the organisational dimension to this policy decision, and are equipped to tackle the management challenges that lie ahead.

To meet these challenges NGO managers will need access to a range of concepts, models and ideas which will help shed light on the problems and point to ways of resolving them. They need theoretical tools which are relevant to their kinds of problems. We have suggested that a problem-oriented approach is a fruitful way of developing such tools, and that at least one model developed in this way with voluntary organisations in the UK seems to have significant explanatory potential.

This model not only sheds light on how some problems arise, and highlights the fact that growth involves qualitative as well as quantitative change. Unexpected issues arise because expansion has taken the organisation into the bureaucratic world. This is a world in which methods of working, approaches to funding, and relationships between personnel are all very different from those of the associational world in which the agency's roots lie. Thus growth and change within non-profit-making organisations is a highly complex process in which activities, mission, structure, governance and resources are knit together in a complex and mutually dependent web. Change in one aspect inevitably has knock-on effects on other aspects.

Other scaling-up strategies

With these points in mind let us now explore the possible implications of the analysis for other scaling-up strategies. We begin by considering community mobilisation which involves NGOs in stimulating and facilitating the operation of community-based organisations. Such organisations are part of the associational world described earlier. They are managed by members on behalf of members. They are groups of equals working co-operatively together towards shared goals. But, as we have already seen, NGOs themselves have become increasingly formalised, operating hierarchical systems within bureaucratic structures. Is it possible for an essentially bureaucratic organisation to work in an associational way in its front-line operations? At this stage we can only raise questions. We do not have answers. However it is interesting to note that a number of the NGOs studied are working towards 'decentralisation'. This is a process by which the agency devolves project management responsibilities to independent or semi-independent branches in the field. The northern NGO deals with only the policy, fund-raising and grant-making functions. It may be that this is an attempt to overcome problems arising from the direct management by 'bureaucratic' NGOs in the north of 'association' projects in the south.

Turning now to lobbying and advocacy as a means of scaling-up, the fact that tensions were found within UK NGOs between fund-raisers and development educationalists is very pertinent. Underneath this tension was felt to be a contradiction between the way in which many NGOs wish to respond to need in the Third World (by changing public attitudes, government policies and commercial practices) and the ways in which many of their funders wish them to respond (by taking immediate action to meet immediate needs). This raises the vital question of whether scaling up advocacy and lobbying is a realistic option for NGOs. If donors and government funders will not 'buy' this approach, how much room for manoeuvre do NGOs really have? This question is considered in this volume by Chris Dolan (Chapter 19). Similarly, attempts to scale-up through working with government may face significant organisational constraints.

Summary and conclusions

The core of our argument has been that scaling-up is an organisational as well as a policy question. The findings of the NGO study reported here support this case. The research reveals that rapid NGO growth appears to be a causal factor in the majority of the organisational problems facing British development NGOs in the early 1990s. Thus problems associated with staff capacity, board capacity, interdepartmental relations, and decision-making can all be directly attributed to rapid organisational growth. But it is not just operational expansion that has organisational consequences. We have drawn on a theory of non-profits developed with voluntary organisations in the UK to show that the community mobilisation strategy is also intimately linked to organisational questions. Furthermore it has been argued that advocacy and lobbying work are subject to internal organisational constraints.

By presenting the 'worlds' theory, we have attempted to demonstrate that the kind of organisational change that scaling-up must involve is a highly complex process. Appropriate concepts and theories must be developed to help manage this complexity. Equipped with these conceptual tools, NGOs will be in a better position to choose between scaling-up strategies, to design effective organisations to implement those strategies, and increase their real impact on the lives of the poor.

Small, medium or large? The rocky road to NGO growth

Roland Hodson

Introduction

Comprehensive analysis of the multifarious aspects of managing growth in non-governmental organisations is beyond the scope of this chapter which is an introduction to some of the main issues and considerations. This chapter was not written as the result of formal, systematic research but is the result of personal experience and informal discussions with staff in a variety of NGOs over 18 years.

NGOs have certain special characteristics which aggravate the already complex problems of managing rapid organisational growth. These characteristics include the strong sense of ownership of the organisation that staff develop and the associated attitudes that evolve. NGOs also suffer from a difficulty in achieving authoritative trustee-level decision-making.

The various stages of growth of an NGO may be viewed as a progression in the type of staff attracted to the organisation. Staff reactions to the stress of rapid growth and the difficulties of implementing changes in the management team's composition and structure necessitated by growth is a core management challenge. Transparent and highly participatory decision-making processes are probably a necessary response to the special characteristics of NGOs. The decentralisation of decision-making that must accompany growth may lead to greater difficulty in maintaining adequate accountability.

The case for growth

The management of growth in NGOs is undoubtedly difficult. But the case for growth, even rapid growth, remains strong. The record of organisations that did not cope well with growth or were diverted from their original mission by the pursuit of growth is well known. What is not often mentioned is the more numerous cases when NGOs have failed to pursue growth that would have been achievable. The failure to maximise growth results in leaving undone much that could contribute to greater justice in the world and the alleviation of human suffering. The internal resistance to growth, often arising out of a fear of diluting the purity of the mission or the culture of the organisation, should be recognized as a cause for concern within the NGO community. The documentation of the negative consequences of growth is necessary and useful. These stories serve as useful cautionary tales. But the NGO sector and poor people around the world would benefit from a wider recognition that failures are necessary and part of a wider learning process.

The spotlight on the failures should not unduly discourage NGOs from aggressively pursuing growth but should caution them to prepare to deal with the stress that growth will bring. In the medium term the harm done by the problems engendered by aggressively pursuing growth will be greatly outdone by the additional good achieved.

But not only is there a moral case for the aggressive pursuit of growth. The record of the sector shows the risks and negative aspects of growth are outweighed by the benefits. A classic example is the Grameen Bank. While the quality of its work may have suffered in some respects due to a remarkable pace of growth, who would argue that this cost has not been worth paying to achieve its remarkable outreach across Bangladesh? If the additional poor who have been served had been consulted, would they have argued for slower growth?

In Britain the concerns within OXFAM about the impact of rapid and sustained growth are well known but would any informed observer suggest that the larger OXFAM has not on balance been a greater force for good in the world, despite the internal tensions and associated management problems that growth has created?

Strategy and implementation

Within the NGO community there is considerable discussion concerning the relative merits of different strategies for scaling-up the impact of NGOs. Most practitioners are more interested in strategic issues than in the more prosaic questions of how to implement strategies through organisations. However a dispassionate analysis of NGO performance would probably reveal that failure to scale-up impact may more often be the result of organisational and management problems than faulty strategies. Strategies cannot be realistically discussed without simultaneously considering their organisational and management implications.

A significant body of literature is being developed, addressing the management of the non-profit or voluntary sector, particularly in North America and increasingly in the UK. However, there is still relatively little written specifically about management issues in development NGOs, as distinct from the rest of the domestic voluntary sector (Billis and MacKeith 1992). Although there has been a lack of interest in management issues in the past, most practitioners within the NGO sector now acknowledge that management issues demand careful consideration. Those NGOs that do experience rapid growth, which is often unforeseen, experience new and difficult management and organisational problems.

The organisational implications of growth are similar, whatever strategy a particular NGO may chose. Expanding work in advocacy, working with government, grassroots mobilisation, networking or expansion of operational programmes all involve linking greater numbers of people working towards a common goal. While some strategies and organisational structures can keep much of the organisational stress outside the defined boundary of the original NGO, achieving greater impact will still entail dealing successfully with the wider organisational implications.

For example choosing to work with government may mean that the NGO can restrict the number of staff it directly employs. However, the organisational and management problems of utilising greater numbers of people for greater impact will not be solved, just pushed into the government bureaucracy. Choosing to work through 'networking' may again help to keep down the number of staff within a particular NGO but the overall implications of growth on the wider 'network' will still apply.

Even attempts to scale-up impact through advocacy requires larger organisations. Amnesty International, a 100 per cent advocacy organisation, faced organisational problems as it attempted to increase its impact by employing more staff to investigate, publicise and campaign against human rights abuse. There is no escaping the organisational reality that any attempt to scale-up impact, whatever the strategy, has serious and difficult organisational implications.

Why have the management implications of organisational growth been often overlooked? There is an assumption that because of the nobility of the organisation's objectives, individual commitment will somehow ensure that management factors do not become an obstacle. Experience has shown this is not the case. Not focusing on the management implications is dangerous in any organisation experiencing rapid growth. The special characteristics of NGOs contribute to the exceptional problems they experience during rapid or sustained growth. These are discussed below.

Employee perceptions of ownership

Because of the nature of the work they do, NGOs attract individuals who have a high level of commitment to the objectives of the organisation. A majority of the individuals employed by NGOs believe, often with good justification, that in working for the organisation they are making a significant personal sacrifice both to their personal income (through accepting lower salaries than are available in the business, governmental and official sectors) and to their personal time through exceptionally long working hours and overall hard work.

This perception of personal sacrifice engenders a sense of ownership of the organisation among staff which is generally an organisational asset but which can be an impediment to the change necessary to manage growth. This phenomenon is not unique to NGOs but is perhaps particularly pronounced in NGOs and other charitable organisations. The concept of sacrificial work producing ownership has been called 'sweat equity' in the context of urban housing programmes, in the USA, and is also appropriate as a term within NGOs.

Suspicion of hierarchy

Associated with the concept of staff ownership is a suspicion of hierarchical organisational frameworks. A recent study of the UK NGO sector has highlighted concern about hierarchy as one of four main issues facing NGOs (Billis and Mackeith 1992). While this characteristic is not unique to NGOs, it is considerably more pronounced than in business or government organisations. In believing that the world can and should be more egalitarian and democratic, NGO employees want to see these characteristics functioning in their own organisation.

The suspicion of hierarchy is particularly acute when the North–South dimension is introduced into a management relationship. Tensions and conflicts are very difficult to avoid in any form of accountability of South to North. Experience shows that acute tensions develop both when the Southern entity is a genuine Southern NGO lead by Southern nationals or an overseas affiliate or office of a Northern NGO managed by a national of the Northern country.

Participatory decision-making

While the degree of suspicion of hierarchy will vary from organisation to organisation and from time to time, there is within NGOs a consistent demand for high levels of participation in decision-making. The aspiration for more democratic governance within organisations is one aspect of the concept of organisational development which is now a concern of many NGOs. This was evidenced vividly at the last general conference of the International Council of Voluntary Agencies (1989) and in the Billis and MacKeith study cited above.

Some organisations now consciously aspire to extensive democratic processes in internal decision-making. Democratic governance has at times been elevated to an objective in its own right, not as a means to be a more efficient and effective organisation. This characteristic can make it difficult to implement the tough decisions necessary to cope with growth and change.

One of the main reasons for the aspiration to democratic decision-making within NGOs is the view that the organisation should relate to its staff in a manner analogous to the way in which the organisation aspires to relate to its beneficiaries. This belief within NGOs is related to the view of the ownership of the organisation. If one thinks in terms of 'moral ownership' then ownership should be vested in the beneficiaries in whose name funds are being solicited, but the practical implications of doing this have not been successfully worked out in NGOs or other voluntary organisations. In practice, parties on all sides of an internal organisational conflict believe and argue that their point of view represents the real interests of the beneficiaries.

However, even staff who most believe in 'participatory development' are reluctant to get beneficiaries involved in issues such as staff salary levels or advertising campaigns. Certainly it would be very difficult to involve beneficiaries in decisions concerning resource allocation between countries or projects.

While the concept of ownership by beneficiaries is desirable but not feasible, the alternative, of ownership by donors is regarded as highly undesirable. Resisting what is perceived as the illegitimate and ill-informed expectations of donors is often the one point on which all NGO staff agree.

Equally, staff often do not accept the legitimacy of ownership by trustees for reasons discussed in the next section. This process of elimination further underlines the staff's belief, rooted in the 'sweat equity' concept, that they are the rightful owners of the organisation. If they are the owners, then surely they have the same rights to decision-making involving their organisation as those rights acknowledged to belong to beneficiaries in decisions affecting their communities.

Trustee ownership

Although staff may feel a strong sense of ownership of the organisation, ownership of NGOs in the legal sense is vested in a board of trustees. The trustees are usually a self-perpetuating group who, by virtue of their economic and social backgrounds, often have different perceptions of the world from those of the staff, the beneficiaries, and perhaps more surprisingly, the typical contributor. Under charity law in Britain and most other OECD countries, staff and beneficiaries are prohibited from serving as trustees.

This discontinuity between the legal owners and the major stake-holders (the staff, the beneficiaries and the donors) constitutes one of the major management problems within NGOs. The problems of trustee management in the domestic voluntary sector have been well documented by various writers. Charles Handy (1981) and Margaret Harris (1989 a and b) have led the way in the UK and Ralph Krammer (1981) and Tracy Connors (1980) in the USA. Most recently the Nathan Report (1990), produced by the National Council of Voluntary Organisations summarised some of the problems of trustee governance, going so far as to consider, but not recommend, the paying of trustees. It is not surprising that the problems documented in domestic voluntary organisations also appear in development NGOs.

While some trustees do not appreciate the unique characteristics of NGOs, more commonly they do realise that NGOs are very different types of organisations from those in which they work and therefore feel reluctant to exercise their authority. This can lead to a consistent deferring of trustee judgement to the staff consensus, or what they believe is that consensus.

Even when trustees have the will to impose their judgement they rarely have the time. By law trustees are volunteers and by custom are drawn from those who already hold major responsibilities and consequently have little time to study complex issues in depth or seek alternative expert advice. Although their responsibilities are equal to non-executive directors of public companies and although in some respects public reliance on trustees is higher, it is undoubtedly the case that on average they put in less time than they would with a non-executive directorship. The lack of relevant experience and expertise also makes it difficult for some trustees to contribute substantively.

This unwillingness or inability of trustees to substantially direct the organisation is generally welcomed by staff. Certainly I welcomed it during my years as a chief executive but it does lead to a further blurring of the roles of ownership and employment, bringing about potential conflicts of interest which the legal concept of trusteeship was designed to avoid. It is these special characteristics of NGOs that make the management of growth, difficult in any organisation, even more complex in their context.

Stages of growth

Although the numbers of staff and amounts of funds deployed are obviously key criteria, from the management dimension the nature of the staff employed is at least as important. In small and young organisations barriers to entry for staff are low. Typically, previous experience and proven professional competence are not prerequisites to getting jobs. The staff profile is young, inexperienced, committed and highly enthusiastic.

As the organisation grows, salary levels and job security also grow, making it possible to begin to recruit experienced and professional staff who were not previously available to the organisation. At this intermediate point there is a mixture of the original staff, who themselves are now more experienced and mature, and the new 'professional staff' who typically have higher academic qualifications and broader experience.

At a later stage, after the organisation has further grown in income and prestige, employment becomes relatively desirable and the organisation is able to choose from among a range of qualified and experienced applicants for each post. Different organisations go through these transitions at different rates and to different degrees.

There are exceptions. The British organisations WomanKind and Action on Disability and Development were founded with the benefit of large grants from corporate foundations and therefore started up in the intermediate if not the mature stage in terms of staff profile.

As NGOs get larger and begin to take on significant numbers of staff with experience of official and governmental organisations, the cultures of NGOs change substantially. Matters that were previously managed on the basis of trust and informal understandings of what was proper and acceptable are dealt with in a formal way. Personnel policies in particular are subject to this change but also affected are whole areas of operations previously taken for granted. While such formalisation is necessary and lays the foundations for further growth, there is a loss of flexibility and of the ethos of individual responsibility for which it is difficult to compensate. This process of formalisation and bureaucratisation has been extensively analysed in the literature of domestic voluntary organisations (Billis 1984b; Kramer 1981) but not for development NGOs.

The management of growth

Coping with growth requires either developing internally or recruiting externally (or a combination of the two) the management capability to deal with the enhanced scale of operation. It also entails developing an appropriate organisational structure to link the management team. Equally it is necessary to develop processes of participation in decision making that meet employee aspirations and maintain motivation. The challenge is to meet these aspirations for participation without eroding the levels of hierarchy necessary for effective operation in the external world.

Upgrading the management capability usually implies new talent. Unfortunately, the story-book scenario under which the original team continues to develop its management capability at a rate sufficient to cope with rapid growth rarely comes true. In the context of voluntary organisations Billis (1984a) has documented how the required management capability changes as the scale and scope of organisations grow and describes how different people develop their management ability at different rates. This provides a useful framework for anyone setting out to significantly expand an NGO.

Voluntary changes

Faced with increasing pressure and demands, some individual staff members resign voluntarily, allowing re-structuring and new recruitment. This is healthy and inevitable, although disruptive to the organisation in the short term and distressing for the individuals concerned. Great care must be taken in selection, initiation and integration of new key staff as each NGO is likely to have a strong culture that must be accommodated. However, because of the high levels of job satisfaction and the absence of alternative equally responsible positions, many individuals, even when their job has outgrown their capability, do not choose to leave voluntarily.

Resistance to growth

A common response to the stress of growth occurs when individuals and groups begin to resist further growth or argue for slower growth. The case for low or slower growth is often a compelling one, centred around preserving what these staff see as the unique advantages of the organisation. For some organisations this indeed may be the best plan. These internal debates about whether the organisation should continue to pursue rapid growth are some of the most critical periods in an organisation's development. The stress and tension engendered by rapid growth gives rise to serious internal concern and loss of morale. Often there is a community harking back to the way things were when the organisation was smaller and was perceived as a 'nicer place' to work.

There are undoubtedly certain qualities of small organisations that are attractive to staff, and often in coming to work for a small NGO individuals were expressing that preference. As they feel the small organisation qualities that attracted them in the first place slipping away, resistance is understandable.

Making the case for growth and keeping the organisation anxious to grasp new opportunities is a severe challenge for management. The need of beneficiaries does not always rank highest in the priorities of staff, particularly those who subconsciously are beginning to wonder if they will be able to continue to cope with their jobs if the scale of operations expand. Guiding an organisation through the internal debate about the appropriateness and pace of growth is one of the key tasks of senior management. If growth is resented and resisted, it is unlikely the organisation will cope well with the challenges that it will bring.

Involuntary changes

Those organisations that pursue rapid growth periodically face the most difficult aspect of managing growth: the involuntary transfer or dismissal of individuals in key positions who can no longer cope with the management demands of the positions they hold. Any chief executive or senior management team that addresses this situation will inevitably find it divisive and acrimonious. Personal loyalty to other individuals on the team, even when there may be a realisation of their inadequacies, is usually high within NGOs. Allied to this is the suspicion of hierarchy described earlier. Thus, there is a reaction in principle to the idea that a manager should be able to take decisions that impact so radically on the life of another individual.

Sometimes the individual who needs to be moved is someone to whom the organisation owes a great debt for past services, perhaps even someone without whose contribution the organisation might not have existed or survived. Rebuilding team spirit and morale after implementing such decisions is difficult and the trust and confidence that existed previously may never be restored. But if rapid growth and effective operation is to continue these considerations, however painful, must be overcome. Any senior management team that delays making these hard decisions compromises the organisation's effectiveness, often seriously.

Compromise solutions

Compromise solutions are common in these difficult situations. The staff may well recognise that there is a problem but will wish to avoid involuntary changes by creating supplementary posts that blur lines of accountability and engender overlapping job descriptions. This tactic may work for a period and may be better than an acrimonious fight but often serves to make the situation worse in the long term. Overheads are inflated and scarce resources that could finance client services are wasted. Decision-making is further slowed as more and more people become involved.

While no magic formula for dealing with these complex and difficult situations can be laid out, it is possible to highlight this issue as one of the key problems in the management of growth. The courage and skill to manage these very difficult personnel changes is perhaps the hardest part of managing growth.

The role of training

Training is often suggested as the solution to the problems outlined above. There can be little doubt that most NGOs do not provide adequate training opportunities for their staff and particularly their senior management. But sometimes the call for further training is simply an excuse to delay an unpleasant and difficult decision.

Small- and medium-size organisations must operate within tight management overheads and absorbing the cost of medium- and long-term training is often not cost-effective, even assuming that appropriate training is available and one had a reasonable assurance that the training would be effective (see Campbell 1987 for a discussion of training for NGOs). Undoubtedly with effective and timely training many individuals can continue their personal development and thereby make a further contribution to the organisation but the cost effectiveness of the expenditure to the organisation must be the major criterion. Because of their views about ownership, staff sometimes feel they have the right to training which objective analysis would find is not cost-effective. For example staff who enter the organisation in clerical roles but who aspire to be development professionals may believe that the explicit organisational principle of human development should apply to them. In this case the confusion over the roles of employee and owners is further extended by confusion between employee and beneficiary roles.

The changing nature of effective leadership

The leadership requirements of an NGO change as an organisation moves through different stages. A new organisation needs an idealistic and visionary leader who is often determined and single-minded. As the organisation matures the nature of the leadership task changes and it is no longer possible to rely on the vision of a single individual. As the number and seniority of the staff grows, it is desirable that the management style changes to a more consensual or committee-oriented approach. The nature of effective leadership changes to promoting consensus and being an effective spokesperson for that consensus to the trustees and the external world.

There are occasions, fortunately rare, when the organisational consensus loses touch with the external world and at those times of crisis the leadership requirement changes back to something similar to the single-minded visionary of the early days, able and willing to confront the organisational consensus and re-orient the organisation's perceptions and culture.

Participatory and decentralised decision-making processes

In addition to keeping the organisational structure and capability of the management team appropriate to the demands of the scale and scope of the organisation other fundamental changes are necessary as NGOs grow. Of particular importance are more decentralised and consensual forms of decision-making. This topic is too complex to be addressed in an introductory chapter such as this. However it is likely that after a certain level of growth a transparent and consensual decision-making process is essential for key policy matters (however expensive in time and resources this may be) in order for decisions to be seen by staff as legitimate. In addition to the measurable increased administrative costs, such a decision-making process is likely to result in decisions well within the boundaries of conventional wisdom. This is not always the best route for NGOs.

A common mechanism to promote consensual decision-making is to delegate important policy decisions to formal inter-departmental task forces. While this form of decision-making tends to dilute the authority of the hierarchical management structure, as important decisions are taken outside that framework, this cost can be minimised by ensuring that the task-force findings and recommendations are reviewed and endorsed by the management hierarchy before implementation. While senior management can influence the composition and terms of reference of such policy-making forums, in practice it is difficult for senior management to control the recommendations. The risk remains that major policies may be recommended about which the senior management team has severe reservations. This can lead to the type of internal tensions and under-performance that is sometimes observed in the sector.

Regular staff conferences and large-scale inter-departmental meetings are an essential feature of organisational life as more people become involved in key decisions. The expense in travel and time must be seen as an investment in staff commitment but must be carefully managed to ensure that it contributes to organisational performance.

Decentralisation of decision-making brings increased difficulty in ensuring adequate accountability to trustees and ultimately donors and beneficiaries, for the effective application of the funds managed. Overseas project teams are likely to be less concerned about conditions attached to funds than more centrally-based staff. Even headquarters staff, sympathetic to the motives of field staff, may connive at moves to divert funds from the purposes for which they were solicited.

As the solicitation of funds is usually done by different individuals and different departments in different countries from where the funds are spent, serious problems emerge. Retaining truthfulness and transparency with donors, while meeting the operational priorities of staff and partners overseas, is a fundamental problem. Sometimes NGOs deal with this tension by the deliberate use of ambiguous language and a willingness to look the other way, which is hard to reconcile with the ideals such organisations espouse. Joy MacKeith (1992) has produced an excellent study of this problem in one major UK NGO and set out a framework for helping to understand this problem.

However unjust the existing distribution of wealth and therefore the sources of development assistance may be, it remains the case that ownership and management of financial resources has a moral responsibility that cannot be totally delegated. There is no source of income for NGOs that does not have some explicit or implicit conditions attached and much of the funding for NGOs, rightly or wrongly, is highly conditional. If NGOs accept the funding, they take on the moral and often legal responsibility to meet those conditions. Staff overseas may not feel that they are genuinely contracted to accept those conditions and may feel a higher moral obligation to other priorities. This is understandable, but generates headquarters–field office tensions as to whether donor conditions or field considerations should determine resource use.

Conclusion

The management of rapid growth within NGOs is made exceptionally difficult by the special characteristics of this type of organisation. These include strong staff perceptions of organisational ownership and the obstacles to effective trustee decision-making. Staff resistance to growth sometimes emerges as a result of the stress of rapid change. The implementation of involuntary personnel and organisational changes while maintaining enthusiasm for expansion is perhaps the most difficult management challenge. Training is only a partial answer to such problems and must be limited to the extent to which it is genuinely cost-effective.

As organisations grow the nature of effective leadership tends to evolve, emphasising the skills of consensus-creation. A growth in participatory decision-making structures and decentralisation is needed as the number of staff grows and the composition of staff changes. Such a process must be carefully managed to ensure that the necessary level of hierarchy survives to manage the organisation effectively and maintain levels of accountability. But whatever the difficulties the moral case to maximise growth remains strong. The record of both NNGOs and SNGOs shows it can be done to the great benefit of the poor around the world.

Part IV
Linking the grassroots with lobbying and advocacy

13
The Philippine experience in scaling-up
Karina Constantino-David

Introduction: NGOs in the Philippines

Over the past decade, non-governmental organisations in the Philippines have not only grown in size and number – they have created a niche in public life. Government, business, academia, the church and ordinary citizens have recognised the importance of NGOs. National life is no longer defined solely by the traditional power-brokers, and NGOs are grudgingly acknowledged as critical components in Philippine development. Government records claim that there are more than 18,000 registered NGOs in the Philippines today, but this number is misleading, mainly because the term 'NGO' is used as a catch-all for all non-profit organisations that do not fall into the categories of government, schools, business, and political parties.

Among the 18,000 registered NGOs, about two thirds can be categorised as voluntary membership organisations, further subdivided into two groups: people's organisations (POs) and civic/professional associations. POs are grassroots membership organisations (unions, community associations, co-operatives, etc.) which function as primary groups, largely on a voluntary basis although as they expand in size and scope full-time secretariats usually emerge. On the other hand, civic and professional associations, while also voluntary membership organisations, are not restricted to a grassroots membership. The remaining third constitutes what are generally referred to in the Philippines as NGOs. These are intermediate agencies that operate with full-time staff and provide a wide range of programmes and services for people's organisations. They also divide into two groups: traditional NGOs or TANGOs (charitable, welfare and relief organisations), and those that are referred to as 'social development agencies'. The distinction between NGOs and POs is particularly important because, in the final analysis, it is people and their organisations who must make decisions about their own development.

Over the past five years, there has been a spectacular increase in the number of social development agencies in the Philippines as a result of an increase in foreign and local funding available, and the ferment that developed out of the struggle against the Marcos dictatorship, the victory of the people-power revolution and subsequent frustration over the failed promises of the new government. These

NGOs vary in size and reach, from small agencies with fewer than ten members to big NGOs (or 'BINGOs') with fifty or more. But not all of these are social development agencies. There are three major types of NGOs in the Philippines which hide under the cover of development but are really set up for economic and/ or political reasons. Because of the Filipino penchant for acronyms, they have been baptized as follows:

- GRINGOs (government-run, -inspired or -initiated NGOs), mostly formed as conduits for government and bilateral aid funds. They are viewed as extensions of government, having been set up by politicians or government functionaries. It is significant to note that most GRINGOs were created after 1987, at a time when it was becoming obvious that the Philippine government could not absorb the bilateral assistance that flowed into the country after the overthrow of the Marcos dictatorship. Many foreign governments expressly required that a portion of official development assistance be channelled through NGOs. In addition, the Philippine government formalised a policy allowing the contracting of NGOs to undertake part of their work. GRINGOs also became the main conduits for 'pork barrel' funds that were granted to a number of politicians.
- BONGOs (business-organised NGOs): although there are corporations that are involved in genuine social development activities, BONGOs refer to those that have been organised as tax dodges or as vehicles for quelling labour unrest and creating a benevolent image for the company by funding showpiece projects.
- COME 'N GOs (fly-by-night NGO entrepreneurs): these are paper organisations that never operated or operated only one project, and then disintegrated. There are also a growing number of NGOs who see funding as a lucrative opportunity, and can package large and expensive proposals for donors.

If all the above categories are excluded, approximately 2,000 agencies out of the 18,000 total will remain. These 2,000 make up the *development NGO community*. They are found all over the country operating through both salaried and voluntary staff, are largely dependent on donor agencies, and function as intermediaries that service the needs of people's organisations (POs). Development NGOs articulate and undertake concrete experiments to foster an alternative social order. They make no pretence to political neutrality: while development NGOs guard their autonomy jealously, most are (ideologically if not organisationally) related to existing political formations. This does *not* mean that development NGOs are a 'front' for political organisations – they insist on their own autonomy in the same way that they have guarded the autonomy of the people's organisations they support. Especially after 1986, many political activists made a conscious decision to use development NGOs to establish an institutional base for social change. This was due to a number of factors including: the emasculation of many POs because of a naive belief in the miraculous solutions that the ouster of the Marcos dictatorship was supposed to bring; the realisation that creating and sustaining POs is severely hampered by part-time, insecure work; moves toward conservatism by the Aquino Government; a generation that had devoted years to political protest and could no longer find fulfilment in traditional careers; and the avalanche of financial support that started to pour into the country for NGO work.

This chapter focuses on the development NGO community in the Philippines – and specifically the 1,500 NGOs that form the ten networks of the Caucus of Development NGO Networks, or CODE-NGO.

The key issues confronting Philippine development NGOs

Issues within the NGO community

The past five years have witnessed a growing concern for co-operation among development NGOs and networks, culminating in the formation of CODE-NGO. Despite these developments, a number of significant issues remain unresolved.

Flexibility versus impact   The basic strength of development NGOs has been their capacity to deal creatively with situations because of their small size. However, this also means that activities are localised and, even when successful, affect a limited population. Because of this, many development NGOs were treated as 'small-time players' in the national drama that posed no real alternative to the status quo. In addition, they could be accommodated within the prevailing order because they commanded no real power, even in terms of numbers. Flexibility and creativity are often undermined by the lack of a capacity to influence policy. The commitment of development NGOs to the empowerment of the poor stands in stark contrast to the reality of their own powerlessness. Various attempts have therefore been made to create models which can combine people's empowerment and effective intervention without undermining the source of NGO strength.

BINGOs versus Networks   In response to this dilemma, two main models have emerged. The first is to create big NGOs that have the potential to influence government while at the same time developing a strong institutional base. Two major criticisms are levelled at the BINGO model. First, beyond a certain size it becomes impossible to avoid setting up a bureaucratic/hierarchical structure that is less flexible, creative and participatory than smaller organisations. Second, the underlying ethos of development NGO work remains *participatory*, including the ability to decentralise decision-making to autonomous regional groups. There is a perceived tendency for BINGOs to retard the development of autonomous development NGOs because programmes are developed at the centre, and donor agencies encourage this trend because they prefer to deal with a few large NGOs only.

In response to these criticisms, most development NGOs have chosen to adopt another option – setting up networks and coalitions among networks. They feel that networks which coordinate across small- and medium-sized organisations can create the desired impact while maintaining and developing the strengths of each individual NGO. Networks encourage decentralisation, maintain the flexibility of size, maximise the development of talent all over the country and sustain a participatory approach. At the same time, because NGOs band together, impact can be achieved through common programmes and common stands on a wide range of issues.

Micro versus macro   One of the most common limitations of development NGOs is the fact that they tend to be extremely localised in scope, investing a huge amount of resources on projects which are unreplicable. But more than this, many development NGOs tend to be myopic, limiting themselves to small issues and naively refusing to acknowledge that there are structural problems that must be addressed in Philippine society. They forget that the macro-context invariably produces the problems they encounter at the community level.

Romanticist versus ideological   Traditionally, development NGOs have shunned outright political activity in an effort to respect people's right to decide on all issues affecting them. This somewhat romantic view has resulted in a failure to broaden people's horizons because NGOs fear to cross the all-important boundary between 'facilitation' and 'manipulation.' Over the past decade, development NGOs have started to clarify their own visions of a more desirable future and to share this vision with those with whom they work.

Rivalry versus unity While much has been achieved over the past few years, the painful reality is that the Development NGO community is still wracked by mutual suspicion and rivalry. This is exacerbated by a number of factors. First, government and donor agencies (primarily because of funding) wittingly or unwittingly pit one NGO against another in the battle for resources. Second, past experience and personality conflicts breed their own dynamics. Third, and perhaps most important, NGOs and networks have identified themselves with distinct political forces and formations. Because of this, they have a tendency to view each other as inheritors of the accumulated 'historical baggage' of existing political groups. Working counter to these forces have been external factors such as the emergence of GRINGOs, BONGOs, and COME 'N GOs; the need for coalitions among people's organisations that can advocate for policy changes; and threats to the autonomy of both NGOs and POs, which have greatly assisted the process of unity.

Development NGOs and the national arena

Government intervention Ironically, popular support for the ouster of the Marcos dictatorship has been transformed into a mandate for the Aquino government to define the role that development NGOs and POs should play. In a tragic repetition of recent history, the new government almost immediately turned its back on the people's movement despite its rhetoric of 'people's empowerment' and 'participation.' As development NGOs and POs started to flex their muscles in an attempt to influence events, the government tried to restrict them to being implementors of government programmes. Bills have been passed to regulate NGOs through accreditation and more stringent government monitoring of their activities. Using the insurgency as a justification, the Aquino government has labelled many development NGOs as 'communist fronts', while quietly pressuring foreign governments to extend support only to favoured NGOs. As a result, more and more GRINGOs have been created.

Autonomy versus co-optation Many development NGOs try to balance autonomy and survival by agreeing to be co-opted by government. In the past, when development NGOs were small groups hardly noticed by government and wider society, autonomy was not an issue. However, once an NGO emerges from the cocoon of purely local issues and begins to tackle problems that invariably result in face-to-face interaction with government, participates in debates on national issues, seeks to advocate for policy changes and carves out a niche for itself, the question of autonomy becomes crucial. Relations with government are always difficult. The snail's pace of bureaucracy and the interminable meetings eat up so much time, and often with little to show for it. On the other hand, every relationship is one of 'give and take', and development NGOs have found themselves in situations where they are forced into a compromise they cannot support. Despite government rhetoric about the role of NGOs, they tend to expect total support in exchange for resources and security. The process of co-optation is smooth and gradual, with many NGOs ending up as little more than extensions of government.

The military versus the insurgents   Since development NGOs are legal entities that operate within constitutional bounds, they are invariably caught in the crossfire between the military and the underground armed movement. The military is suspicious of any organisation that insists on autonomy, refuses to be a pawn in the political arena, uses participatory methods, articulates demands even when these are contrary to government policies, and engages in various forms of collective action. On the other hand, the insurgents are equally suspicious of NGOs that insist on working independently because their work is viewed as a palliative that can only delay 'the revolution.' As a result, development NGOs have been harassed, and some of their personnel threatened and killed, especially in areas where both sets of combatants are present. This is a tightrope that development NGOs have to walk.

Non-party politics versus the electoral process   Under the Marcos dictatorship, development NGOs had the luxury of disregarding rigged elections. Time and effort was spent on forming and strengthening viable POs and trying to win small victories through pressure politics and extra-legal methods. Under the present government however, the electoral arena has to be confronted. Development NGOs can no longer retreat into the obscurity of purely local issues, especially if they wish to participate actively in the national debate. And yet because the electoral arena is heavily dominated by political parties of the traditional elite, development NGOs face the reality that they do not as yet have the political clout to make much difference in the electoral arena. At the same time, the importance of safeguarding the autonomy of both development NGOs and POs poses the very real problem of how to engage directly in party-dominated electoral contests.

Empowerment versus seizure of power   Opening up the electoral arena has raised a more basic question: if development NGOs are committed to people's empowerment, why have they shied away from the issue of capturing state power? Should development NGOs content themselves forever with the role of critics, seeing what is wrong and boasting of alternatives, but refusing to take on the challenge of political power? Where do development NGOs draw the line between facilitating the empowerment of people and building a society where power does indeed rest in their hands?

NGOs and the international arena

Until recently, most donors and development NGOs viewed their relationship purely in financial terms, but now there are some signs that these links are changing in ways which reflect the aims of partnership and solidarity which CODE-NGO is trying to establish

Externally-imposed priorities versus funding needs   An analysis of NGO concerns over the past two decades will show that many shifts in emphasis have been affected by 'flavour of the month' choices or by priorities set by donor agencies. Because development NGOs are dependent on external resources, the danger of becoming driven by funding is very real. Even with the best of intentions, donor agencies can fuel this problem.

Partnership versus subservience   Especially for Development NGOs that rely heavily on foreign grants for their sustenance, a disturbing relationship tends to develop which mirrors the old colonial model, and for which both NGO and donor share the blame. The self-respect of development NGOs is undermined by agreeing to whatever the donor requires so long as the grant is secured. On the side of the donor, genuine assistance is transformed into a process of re-colonisation, whereby funds take the place of the sword, the cross, or the gun. This is apparent among Northern NGOs that insist on sending their own nationals to manage and supervise the operations of Southern NGOs as a condition for funding. In contrast, true partnership is not limited to funds but ensures a commonality of framework and vision, not only between the donor and the NGO, but also between the people's organisations that are beneficiaries of the grants and those in the donor nations who should know more about the manner in which their money is spent.

Dependence versus self-reliance   Feelings of dependence are exacerbated by the belief that development NGOs will survive because funding will always be available. There is an urgent need for development NGOs to become more self-reliant; as long as they are vulnerable financially they will find it extremely difficult to set up real partnership on the international level. Ideally, NGO services should be supported by the people who benefit from them. However, for Southern NGOs it is unthinkable to expect the poor to shoulder all the costs of their own empowerment. Perhaps, on the side of donor agencies that are equally concerned with building a relationship of solidarity, now is the time to think seriously about long-term solutions that will free development NGOs from the ritual of forever applying for funding, and donor agencies from the never-ending routine of processing proposals.

The spirit of voluntarism versus basic needs of development workers   The primary characteristic of people who enter the NGO world is commitment to service. However, no amount of selflessness can sustain development workers if they have to subsidise their own commitment. Development NGOs, by providing alternative career paths, are able to ensure at least that their personnel do not have to be destitute to be of service to the powerless. Donor agencies must therefore help to enable development workers to meet their basic needs and sustain their commitment. But because of differences in standards of living, the contraction of the employment market, and the thrust towards 'professionalising' NGO work, significant changes are occurring. As development NGOs increase in size and become more institutionalised, higher salaries, more comfortable surroundings, and a hierarchy that parallels private business, become more evident. There is a valid fear, especially among those who pioneered NGO development work a decade ago, that these trends will start to de-emphasise commitment, attract people who view the work merely as a job, and undermine the very essence of the NGO. The moment the spirit of voluntarism is eroded, development NGOs will also surrender their essential contribution to society.

CODE-NGO: Confronting the issues

The Caucus of Development NGO Networks (CODE-NGO) is a response to the specific situation confronting development NGOs in the Philippines, and is the latest stage in a series of developments aimed at maximising their impact. For many years, individual NGOs operated quietly and singly, honing their skills and building up their work. As more NGOs appeared on the scene, some reached out to each other, while others feuded bitterly. Networks emerged from this situation in order to share experience and gain greater access to funds. These networks reflect similarities in thrust, field of operation, and ideology. By 1988, there were ten major national networks with a combined membership of approximately 1,300 individual NGOs. Some of these networks already had links with each other, and six had ratified a common code of ethics for social development agencies. At the same time, coalitions of sectoral organisations (peasants, workers, urban poor, fisherfolk, and indigenous people) and issue-based coalitions (women, peace, foreign debt, US bases, environment, and children) were emerging, and development NGOs were active participants in all of these.

This experience with networking provided the base upon which wider dialogue and debate were founded. More than anything else, each individual NGO and network, after years of relative isolation, came essentially to the same conclusion: development NGOs, in partnership with people's organisations, have a great potential to be the bearers of an alternative future that places emphasis on people's empowerment – the ability of communities to define their own problems, decide on their options, and determine their own future. Development NGOs are in the best position to help create, strengthen and sustain autonomous organisations that can relate to and debate with each other, advocate and lobby for policy changes, assess the options presented by political parties and forces, experiment with alternative relations of production, concretise their vision of an alternative political order, and create participatory structures that will no longer allow the elite and self-appointed parties and personalities to speak in the name of the people.

However, this conclusion also brought with it the humbling realisation that as single NGOs, or even individual networks, there was no way in which the potential of development NGOs could be maximised; development NGOs would forever be relegated to a minor role that would fail to combat poverty and injustice in the country.

Therefore, we had to scale-up our impact. We had to confront the obstacles to development together, protect and enlarge the space within which we could operate, and consolidate our assistance to the people's organisations that were our reason for being. It was fortuitous that at about this time, the Canadian International Development Agency (CIDA), was reviewing its country programme for the Philippines. Through some of the emerging networks, a series of consultations were held, together with Canadian NGOs. Despite mutual suspicion, the development NGOs forged a consensus on mechanisms to facilitate funding as well as partnership relations with Canadian NGOs. This is what is now known as the 'Philippines–Canada Joint Committee for Human Resource Development.' This also became the major vehicle through which the networks were able to discuss other issues and agree on common stands. Realising that we all carried legacies from the past, the process was cautious and extremely slow. After two years, CODE-NGO was publicly launched at a conference on 'The Role of European Governments and NGOs in Promoting Sustainable Development in the Philippines', in May 1990. By January of 1991, a secretariat had been formed.

CODE-NGO was formed by the ten national networks in existence at the time, representing 1,300 individual development NGOs: the Association of Foundations (AF), Council for People's Development (CPD), Ecumenical Center for Development (ECD), National Confederation of Co-operatives (NATCCO),

National Council for Social Development (NCSD), National Council of Churches in the Philippines (NCCP), National Secretariat for Social Action (NASSA), Partnership of Philippine Support Service Agencies (PHILSSA), Philippine Business for Social Progress (PBSP), and the Philippine Partnership for the Development of Human Resources in Rural Areas (PhilDHRRA). The governing board consists of one representative from each network and all decisions are made strictly by consensus.

To consolidate and strengthen CODE-NGO, much emphasis was placed on consensus-building activities that tackled crucial issues affecting development NGOs, but also provided the vehicle for creating trust and mutual understanding, forging a minimum common vision based on respect for our differences as organisations.

CODE-NGO's first conference focused on peace and justice. The development NGOs' peace agenda provided an input into a national peace conference which brought together all sectors of Philippine society. The second conference focused on the role of development NGOs in the electoral process. Five major levels of participation were debated: electoral education, electoral reforms, building a people's platform, support of candidates and direct participation through fielding of candidates. CODE-NGO agreed that each NGO should get involved in the first three levels and respect those that wished to go further. The result of this conference was the recognition and strengthening of 'Project 2001', a coalition of NGOs and POs that is flexing its muscles for the elections in May 1992 and beyond.

Our third conference focused on formulating a gender-based framework for planning and evaluation, while the most recent culminated in the First National NGO Congress on December 4th, 1991. This was attended by more than a thousand delegates from all over the country, and ratified the 'Covenant on Philippine Development.' The Covenant contains our common principles, and responsibilities, goals and commitments, and an NGO Code of Ethics.

Lessons of experience

Three years on, it is easier to look back and try to systematise what was in reality an evolving rationale for CODE-NGO. The factors that led to the formation of CODE-NGO were both reactive and pro-active – reactive because CODE-NGO was a direct response to situations and problems that impinged on the development NGO community; pro-active because CODE-NGO is also the umbrella organisation that will chart the future of development NGOs in the country.

Claiming our space   CODE-NGO is a concrete response to the proliferation of organisations which devalue and debase the work of development NGOs. The creation of CODE-NGO is an attempt to define who we are, distinguish ourselves from others, and create a niche in Philippine society. This does not only mean defining who we are, but also creating a unity that is the only basis for common action. By so doing, CODE-NGO (whose membership at the moment covers about 75 per cent of all development NGOs) is able to speak out as a sector, and represent a wide range of NGOs in negotiations with government (local and foreign), international agencies, donors, and counterpart NGOs.

In addition, it is imperative that development NGOs develop their own mechanisms for self-regulation. In the case of CODE-NGO, this is the 'Code of

Ethics' which ensures that development NGOs subscribe to the same set of principles and practices even though responding differently, due to specific situations in their areas of operation.

Creating national impact CODE-NGO has been able to test practical mechanisms to balance the need to maximise impact while maintaining individual flexibility. Together with other sectoral coalitions, an alternative trading scheme has been set up that links grassroots producers directly with consumers. By eliminating middlemen, it is able to buy from peasants at higher prices and sell to low-income groups at prices below the market rate.

Another experiment run by three of the networks is the Livelihood Revolving and Capability Building Fund for Poor Women (LRFW), which provides access to resources for poor women in 40 out of 70 provinces in the country. The success of this programme is encouraging because it serves as a model for achieving national impact while maintaining the small size, flexibility and non-bureaucratic character of NGO operations.

Sharing of information and expertise CODE-NGO provides avenues through which development NGOs can learn from each other. In addition, joint training programmes, the transfer of skills from one NGO to another, and the exchange of expertise, allow NGOs to focus on specific issues and hone their skills rather than trying to develop expertise in every field. The process of learning from each other also helps to consolidate CODE-NGO still further.

Experimenting with concrete alternatives NGO work would be relegated to 'gap-filling' if NGOs did not try to link their activities to the larger issues of social structure. In addition to conceptual work on alternative visions, there is a conscious effort to weave together concrete successes and failures to flesh out a blueprint for the future. Small-scale experiments that are then tested on a national level provide people with a glimpse of an alternative but attainable future.

Increasing advocacy The successes of development NGOs are not sustainable if they do not result in policy changes through advocacy. Our experience has shown that development NGOs are taken seriously by policy makers only when they speak with one voice. CODE-NGO has provided that strength. Whether it be with our own government, with donors or with international agencies, the fact that development NGOs are organised and can take a collective position on issues, means that much more influence can be brought to bear in government bodies, negotiations with donor agencies, representation in public hearings, and lobbying for the revision and/or enactment of laws.

Assisting in the formation/strengthening of regional alliances of NGOs
Because of the archipelagic nature of the Philippines and a tradition of Manila-centered power, development NGOs outside of the capital have always been at a disadvantage. The task is to strengthen regional alliances so that they can develop more development workers, determine their own priorities and counterbalance what can easily become the domination of the centre.

Building a successor generation Because the development NGO community is relatively young, the leadership of most NGOs is still in the hands of those who pioneered the field. CODE-NGO places emphasis on developing the next generation of NGO leaders so as to transfer their vision, sustain inter-NGO unity, and check excesses that may arise because a few leaders ensconce themselves at the helm.

Standardising NGO benefits   Because development NGOs differ in size and operations, NGO personnel enjoy a wide variety of privileges and benefits. This puts smaller NGOs at a disadvantage because they cannot offer the same benefits as larger NGOs. Discussions have been underway to find some way of standardising these conditions, especially given the absence of a viable social security system in the country.

Avoiding co-optation and ensuring autonomy   Following the successes of the Philippine–Canadian NGO agreement cited above, CODE-NGO is trying to implement similar mechanisms with other donors. The Australian government has approved a similar package, USAID has approved an endowment fund for NGO activities related to the environment, and negotiations have begun with the European Community. The intention is to ensure the continued autonomy of development NGOs through funding mechanisms that are run by NGOs themselves. It is easier to approach donors by negotiating as a group. At the same time, scarce resources are more equitably distributed because the networks have a better grasp of what is happening in the NGO world. Co-optation is also reduced when NGOs relate to each other as cohesive groups. It is not as easy to use government funds as a lever for support when government has to deal with an umbrella like CODE-NGO.

Strengthening partnership   Much progress has been achieved with donors because CODE-NGO has linked up with counterpart NGOs in donor nations. There is an urgent need to relate to Northern NGOs for advocacy, joint action on global issues, sharing experience, and skills. Equally important is the building of stronger links among Southern NGOs.

Safeguarding our security   Because of the role of the military in placing development workers at risk, CODE-NGO has developed a liaison mechanism with the military that allows us to resolve conflicts at an early stage. The formal Memorandum of Agreement establishing this mechanism is due to be signed late in 1992. While this will not eliminate threats to our security, it will facilitate links so that undue harassment is minimised.

Conclusion

CODE-NGO is an experiment in scaling-up NGO impact. Development NGOs in the Philippines have organised themselves in ways which are consistent with the principles that govern grassroots organisation for the empowerment of people. In this process we have sown the seeds for strengthening and expanding individual NGOs, undertaking national programmes without centralising power, encouraging the emergence of popular and autonomous people's organisations, participating in and influencing local and national structures, and providing an alternative and grassroots-based path towards development which is not limited to small local areas.

CODE-NGO is a phase in our own development. We continue to grapple not only with national issues, but as importantly with the specific roles we have set for ourselves. Many questions continue to occupy us: the specifics of structural change in the Philippines, the pros and cons of our participation in national politics, the resolution of tensions between our own ideological commitments and the autonomy of POs, the apparent ease of the state in co-opting NGO leaders once they are placed in positions of power, and how to sustain a pluralist unity. Time will provide answers to these questions. In the meantime, we continue in our search, in the knowledge that the people's organisations we are helping to develop will, in the final analysis, determine our common future.

14

From victims to victors: NGOs and the politics of empowerment at Itaparica

Anthony Hall

Introduction

Like many other developing countries, Brazil has witnessed a substantial increase in the range and intensity of activities undertaken by non-governmental organisations. Of particular significance is the emergence of a strong advocacy role for both indigenous and foreign NGOs in support of local populations whose livelihoods are threatened by state-sponsored projects and programmes. In Brazil, the best-known of such protest movements internationally have tended to be in Amazonia, where sensitivity to environmental problems created by rainforest destruction has attracted global publicity. Notable examples include the struggles of the rubber-tappers' organisation in Acre state against encroaching cattle-ranchers, campaigns by Amerindian groups such as the Yanomami and associated NGOs for the demarcation of their reserves, and the organised opposition mounted by the Kayapó and other tribes against the Xingú river hydroelectric complex (Branford and Glock 1985; Gross 1989; Revkin 1990; Goodman and Hall 1990; Hall 1991). Yet one of the most important and potentially significant cases of NGO success in lobbying on behalf of adversely-affected low-income groups has not been in Amazonia, but in North-East Brazil.

The Itaparica hydropower scheme in the middle São Francisco valley is a pioneering example of the potentially key role of NGOs in bringing about a major reformulation of development plans in favour of a large number of people who would otherwise have suffered major losses. It is the first time that a large-scale hydroelectric project in Brazil (or Latin America, or possibly the Third World itself) has provided for the comprehensive resettlement of an entire displaced population, in this case of some 40,000 people. The relative success of Itaparica compared with similar previous experiences in the region has been due to a somewhat specific set of circumstances, centred particularly around the strength of local rural trades union organisations and their battle against the power company, together with the timely intervention of a powerful third party, the World Bank. This chapter argues that there are, none the less, important lessons to be learned from this project which have a wider relevance in terms of scaling-up the advocacy role of NGOs in support of groups threatened by similar infrastructural and related development schemes elsewhere.

Hydropower in the North-East: early experiences

Projected growth in domestic and industrial demand for electricity in North-East

Brazil led to the São Francisco valley, the region's largest, being quickly identified as a major potential hydro-energy source. The regional power authority (CHESF) was set up in 1945 and the first 120 MegaWatt scheme completed at Paulo Afonso in 1955. Generating capacity grew rapidly during the 'economic miracle' years of the 1970s, fuelled by the 'oil shocks' of that decade, increasing tenfold to 10,000 MW by 1984. Apart from earlier and smaller projects at Paulo Afonso and Moxotó, the much larger dams at Sobradinho (1979) and Itaparica (1988) have so far formed the major pillars of hydroelectricity expansion in the North-East. Brazil's military governments (1964–85) placed a heavy strategic emphasis on hydropower development, underpinned by finance from multilateral agencies such as the World Bank and the Inter-American Development Bank.

Adverse social impacts have been associated with the implementation of hydropower and irrigation projects in North-East Brazil since the early 1970s (Hall 1978). Although serious problems had been experienced at the Moxotó hydroelectric scheme, Sobradinho came to be the most disturbing example in the region during this period, if only because of its sheer size. The Sobradinho dam and reservoir project was conceived in the late 1960s and funded by multilateral and bilateral loans totalling some US$240 million. It flooded an area of over 4,000 square kilometres along the middle São Francisco valley, forming the largest inland body of water in South America after Lake Titicaca. Completed in 1979, Sobradinho displaced 70,000 people in the immediate vicinity of the reservoir. A further 50,000 farmers and dependants were affected downstream around the estuary by the permament flooding of rice-paddy due to changes in the river regime and a sharp increase in the low-flow level.

The scale and intensity of economic and social havoc wrought upon the local farming population in the São Francisco valley due to Sobradinho is worthy of more detailed comment, since it provides a telling contrast with developments at Itaparica a few years later. Provisions for compensating Sobradinho displacees were grossly inadequate, erratically planned and unequal in their impact. Some 30 per cent of the population was urban-based and was, generally speaking, successfully rehoused in new towns on the lakeside. However, the rural population fared much worse. The resettlement process was highly traumatic and, despite the rigid press censorship in force under the then military government, many reports emerged of violent clashes between farmers unwilling to leave their land and CHESF or the construction companies. Following Brazilian law, cash compensation was restricted to farmers with documentary proof of land ownership and/or for 'improvements' to properties (*benfeitorias*), effectively disqualifying *de facto* small farmer owners with no land title as well as sharecroppers, who formed the majority of the rural population. With no other means of support beyond some temporary shelter and emergency food supplies, thousands were reduced overnight to a state of penury. Many left the region altogether to try their luck in the cities of the North-East and Centre-South.

Some attempts were made to relocate the displaced population but these were poorly planned and executed. Serra do Ramalho, for example, a major resettlement scheme intended for 25,000 farmers and their families, was an unmitigated disaster. Located 1,000 kilometres upstream on infertile, dry soils, it was set up with no consultation among the intended beneficiaries. In fact, only a few hundred settlers decided to make the arduous journey overland, and were effectively left to their fate by the colonisation authority (INCRA), without agricultural support, irrigation facilities or social infrastructure. Around Lake Sobradinho itself, the remaining rural population was housed in 25 hastily constructed new villages (*agrovilas*), their numbers swollen by disillusioned returnees from the colonisation project and by small farmers who had sold or lost their properties through intense land speculation and concentration as a result of infrastructural developments associated with the new dam. The farmers' traditional irrigated farming systems were virtually wiped out by the move to unwatered, infertile plots on the lakeside, while many cultivators were simultaneously decapitalised due to the limited indemnification offered by CHESF. Subsequently, the authorities have all but abandoned these communities, whose inhabitants struggle against continuing problems of unemployment, poverty and malnutrition (IDB 1984; Hall 1989a).

In the lower São Francisco valley, an 'emergency' programme was established to offset the adverse impacts of Sobradino, based on polder-type irrigation schemes for small farmers. However, even here there was a net displacement of over 30,000 rural dwellers due to a series of factors. These included the limited labour-absorption capacity of the new irrigation projects, a delay of several years between expropriation and recruitment to the schemes which resulted in heavy out-migration, and general disenchantment with the irrigation authority (CODEVASF) following large-scale, frequently violent evictions and the limited compensation offered to the displaced population. For example, 100 larger landowners monopolised compensation payments, while 7,300 quasi-landless tenant farmers and sharecroppers received next to nothing (Barros 1985).

In summary, the Sobradinho hydropower scheme created vast social and economic problems in the São Francisco valley and beyond. About half of the 120,000 people it displaced received no compensation and were left to fend for themselves. Vociferous protests at the time from radical Catholic clergy and lay workers in the region produced no significant response 'from above', nor was there any organised grassroots opposition movement.

Itaparica: the people fight back

The experience of Itaparica stands in sharp contrast to that of Sobradinho. Situated a mere 200 kilometres downstream from Sobradinho within a broadly similar socio-economic setting, the immediate human impact of the new dam and reservoir was comparable, and involved the displacement of 40,000 people. But while at Sobradinho there was no popular response to the inadequate resettlement provisions made by CHESF for the rural populace, at Itaparica the threat to people's livelihoods posed by the scheme generated a massive social protest movement led by a new indigenous NGO, a purpose-built federation of 13 rural trades unions known as the 'Polosindical' (*Polo Sindical do Submédio São Francisco*). This social movement, spearheaded by the Polosindical, was a major factor behind the redesigning of relocation plans in favour of the rural population.

When dam construction at Itaparica began in 1978, CHESF had made resettlement plans only for the 10,000 urban population, which was to be rehoused in new towns on the lakeside, as at Sobradinho. The 30,000 rural inhabitants (or at least those eligible by law) were to be offered only cash compensation, in the expectation that people would move elsewhere peacefully. No thought had been given to providing alternative farmland or other means of support to compensate for the 60,000 hectares which would be lost underwater. By the time major negotiations over resettlement between CHESF and the Polosindical had been completed in 1987, however, comprehensive resettlement plans had been drawn up for the entire displaced rural population and World Bank funding had been secured. It is important to understand the processes which produced this positive outcome, and the possible implications of Itaparica's experience for similar NGU activities elsewhere.

Property speculation had started in the Itaparica region during the early 1970s as a direct result of the planned hydropower scheme, giving rise to land conflicts between peasant farmers and 'land-grabbers' (*grileiros*). In the absence of an effective trade union movement in the region during this period, the local Catholic Church, as the only organisation active at community level, initiated an educational campaign among villagers to warn them of the impending dangers associated with Itaparica. By 1976, a few rural unions (*Sindicatos de Trabalhadores Rurais*), with the support of the Pernambuco State Union Federation (FETAPE), had extended a National Training Programme to the Itaparica area to teach people how to organise themselves (Araújo 1990). In this task they were closely assisted by radical Catholic clergy and layworkers in the immediate vicinity practising Liberation Theology in a context of intense political repression under military rule. These, in turn, had the support of two North-Eastern regional branches of the outspoken National Conference of Brazilian Bishops and their respective Church Land Commissions. As a result of these Church and union activities, the local population started a campaign of non-co-operation with CHESF as the power authority tried to acquire land for the project, disrupting early building work at the dam site.

However, a longer-term campaign required changes in political organisation at local level. A movement to replace conservative union leaders was begun in earnest in order to transform the rural unions, most of which had been set up in 1971–72 by the Ministry of Labour, from paternalistic welfare benefit channels into organisations prepared to act decisively in support of their members' interests. Educational campaigns in rural areas by the Church, which were partly funded by OXFAM-UK, as well as by union workers, were expanded to encompass all the local municipalities affected by the dam. New and more dynamic leaders were elected and the Polosindical federation was subsequently formed in 1979 in order to lead and coordinate the Itaparica movement. As the unions grew in strength, the local Church took a conscious decision to withdraw from the struggle in order to allow the Polosindical to develop autonomously. The initial phase of isolated, fragmented local protest soon gave way to systematic and well-articulated demands by the local population.

At first, and in reaction to the power company's highly secretive attitude, these demands centred on gaining access to CHESF's plans and maps of the project area so that the full impact of the scheme could be properly gauged. The documents were finally released following an occupation by the farmers of CHESF's offices in the central town of Petrolândia. Demands soon widened, however, to include the provision of land titles for all farmers in the area, full and fair compensation, the relocation of all displacees on lands adjacent to the new lake, and post-settlement agricultural production support services and social infrastructure. Public rallies were held in Petrolândia, calling for comprehensive resettlement plans to be drawn up. Formal representations were made to CHESF, while a regular newsletter (*Boletim Terra por Terra na Margem do Lago*) was sent nationwide and even overseas. In 1982, the Centre for the Defence of Human Rights in the Lower-

Middle São Francisco (CDDSSF) was formed, funded by international NGOs, to provide agricultural, legal and other technical advice and support to the Polosindical in its dealings with CHESF.

By 1985, however, and despite a sustained protest campaign involving seven major public demonstrations by the local population with some media coverage during Brazil's incipient 'democratisation' process, CHESF had shown no desire to speak to the Polosindical. The power authority had by this stage formed a special working group to address the resettlement question, but a new management took a hard line and failed to consult the Polosindical when it finally prepared its own, somewhat incomplete and inadequate plan (CHESF 1985). In the meantime, a strong international NGO campaign led by the Washington DC-based Environmental Defence Fund (EDF) had begun, denouncing CHESF's procrastination in responding to the population's demands, which attracted a degree of worldwide media attention.

In 1985 also, a World Bank mission visited Itaparica to appraise the Environmental Sector Master Plan in connection with a US$500 million power sector loan, the first for Brazil, which concluded that there were major problems with CHESF's resettlement plan. The Bank made approval of the second and third tranches of the loan conditional upon the preparation of satisfactory resettlement provisions for Itaparica's rural population. In mid-1986, at the invitation of the Brazilian authorities, Bank staff started to prepare the 'Itaparica Resettlement and Irrigation Project'. However, further procrastination by CHESF as well as the parastatal's continued reluctance to establish a dialogue with the Polosindical, provoked an occupation of the dam site by several thousand people in December 1986, which paralysed operations and attracted widespread publicity, both at home and abroad.

Pressure both on the World Bank from international NGOs and from the Bank itself upon CHESF now reached a climax, and CHESF had little choice but to negotiate with the Polosindical. A formal agreement was signed after a few days of talks between the two, setting out the major preconditions for the resettlement process demanded by the Itaparica population. These included the fixing of firm dates for land purchase, indexation of compensation payments against rampant inflation, the provision of housing and irrigation facilities for the entire displaced rural population and the lifting of restrictions on recruitment to the new projects. Most importantly, in view of the long delay between population relocation and the coming on-stream of the irrigation projects, the Polosindical secured a commitment from CHESF to provide regular monthly maintenance support for rural displacees, pending sale of their first harvests from the new schemes.

One year later, in 1987, the World Bank approved a US$132 million-dollar loan for the comprehensive resettlement programme. CHESF formed a new department for resettlement coordination, brought in additional staff and undertook the first proper survey of the affected population. Some 5,000 rural families were transferred to 109 new *agrovilas*, where each was given a masonry house and the right to an irrigated plot once the projects became operational. Six such projects, covering a total of 18,000 hectares, are currently at various stages of implementation, although none of the major schemes were functioning by the end of 1991. A further 2,000 urban families were moved to new towns on the lakeside and given alternative housing or appropriate cash compensation. This substantial population movement took place relatively smoothly, in direct contrast to the traumatic experiences at Sobradinho and in the lower São Francisco valley a decade earlier.

Itaparica: Empowerment, politics and policy-making

There were two major, interrelated sets of factors behind the relative success of resettlement at Itaparica compared with the unsatisfactory outcome at Sobradinho. First, the educational and political roles played by the Polosindical, and second, the entry of the World Bank. The first and arguably the most fundamental factor concerns the formation of the Polosindical as a vehicle for articulating and representing popular demands. Had the Polosindical not existed, it is difficult to escape the conclusion that the rural population would have suffered a fate similar to that of their counterparts at Sobradinho. In less than a decade, from the formation of the union federation in 1979 to the closing of Itaparica's sluicegates in 1988, the Polosindical had grown substantially both in size and, particularly, in influence, enabling it to work effectively for major changes in the plans for Itaparica and winning many benefits for the displaced rural population. In effect, the inhabitants of Itaparica united to form what eventually became a powerful social movement to defend themselves against the common external threat posed to their livelihoods by CHESF.

Yet it would be a mistake to see the Polosindical as wholly a spontaneous movement which arose automatically in response to the Itaparica project. Both the Catholic Church and international NGOs were instrumental in facilitating and encouraging the formation and growth of the federation. Committed Catholic clergy, community workers and hard-core rural union officials had, since 1973, been carrying out grassroots educational campaigns in the region, focusing on the potential threat to the local population posed by the dam and the need to articulate a response. This activity was intensified in the late 1970s and given critical financial support by OXFAM-UK through small grants to the local Catholic Church. This outside support was particularly crucial during the initial stages of the movement, as the small group of activists struggled to get their message across to isolated, scattered communities which, lacking any history of political involvement and following ten years of military government in Brazil, were often suspicious of outsiders and reluctant to listen or co-operate. Without the grassroots support of the Church to help initiate and legitimise the protest in its early days it is possible, even probable, that neither the Polosindical nor the wider social movement would have existed and that subsequent developments at Itaparica might have resembled the débâcle at Sobradinho.

In terms of the categories used in this volume, the Polosindical combined 'additive' and 'multiplicative' strategies. During the early stages of the organisation, the embryonic federation concentrated on growth, on adding to its size: extending the participation of local rural trades unions in the movement, educating the public about the impending threat to their lands and livelihoods and thus mobilising popular support in the vicinity of the project. During this phase, simple confrontational tactics were adopted against CHESF, with limited success. From 1983–84, however, the Polosindical became far more sophisticated in its tactics, combining direct action at the project site with pressure further afield. Through the recently-established local Centre for the Defence of Human Rights in the Lower-Middle São Francisco valley (CDDSSF), the Polosindical took legal action and entered into direct negotiation with CHESF and other State bodies. This multiplier effect was greatly enhanced by international networking and lobbying, undertaken with the assistance of foreign organisations such as OXFAM-UK. The Polosindical's link with OXFAM, through its country representatives *in situ*, was crucial in several ways. In addition to providing early key funding to cover basic running expenses, OXFAM was able to liaise with the Environmental Defence Fund (EDF) in its lobbying of the US Congress against World Bank-financed schemes such as POLONOROESTE and Itaparica. OXFAM also lobbied the UK Executive Director of the World Bank, who raised the resettlement issue at the highest levels of the organisation, contributing significantly to internal pressure for emerging policy guidelines to be followed and for corrective action to be taken. This combination of financial aid and wider strategic support to the Polosindical and CDDSSF was a critical factor in strengthening the federation in its negotiations with CHESF and the World Bank.

In most development schemes, beneficiary involvement is limited to token consultation and cost-sharing. Yet the Polosindical and other organisations were able to extend the boundaries of participation in the planning process quite significantly. Reference to the categories of participation defined by Paul (1987) provides a useful conceptual guideline. First, 'project effectiveness' has been enhanced because the Polosindical was able to make sure that the project design was more appropriate for the needs of those affected by Itaparica. Second, 'empowerment' of the displaced population resulted from the fact the Polosindical's actions have provided them with a far greater control over resources and planning decisions affecting their lives than would otherwise have been the case. Not only did the Itaparica population win major concessions from CHESF for itself, but the Polosindical's achievements also have profound implications for hydropower development along the entire São Francisco valley. The Polosindical has made it quite clear that it will not permit the Sobradinho experience to be repeated at any of the hydroelectric projects currently planned for the valley and would, if necessary, undertake similar campaigns elsewhere to make sure that people were fully and properly compensated (Hall 1989b).

Yet in stressing the vital role of the Polosindical, it should not be forgotten than the leverage upon CHESF exerted by the World Bank was also of fundamental importance in forging a commitment by the parastatal company to the comprehensive resettlement of the displaced rural population of Itaparica. During the early 1970s, when Sobradinho was being planned and implemented, the Bank had no formal policy commitment to comprehensive resettlement of populations affected by large infrastructural projects, despite this being the decade of 'poverty-targeted' development. Partly as a direct result of Sobradinho and other similar projects in which the Bank was involved, an internal debate ensued involving, in particular, staff sociologists and anthropologists working on policy matters. Initial policy guidelines (World Bank 1980) were formulated and later substantially revised and broadened in scope to provide for a fully-comprehensive and integrated approach for dealing with involuntary resettlement in Bank-funded projects (Cernea 1988a; World Bank 1990). The existence of these policy statements on resettlement undoubtedly compelled Bank management to adopt a different approach at Itaparica (compared with Sobradinho) which included recognising the grievances and wishes of the displaced.

An additional consideration in explaining the Bank's relatively prompt intervention in the North-East of Brazil may have been the fact that the institution's sensitivity to external criticism had been heightened during the mid-1980s by the controversy surrounding the POLONOROESTE frontier development programme for north-west Amazonia. Widespread condemnation by international NGOs, and ᵃᵘᵖᵉᵈᵃˡˡʸ ᵗʰᵉ ᵖᵒʷᵉʳᶠᵘˡ US ˡᵒᵇᵇʸ ᵒⁿ Cᵒⁿᵍʳᵉˢˢ, ˡᵉᵈ ᵗᵒ ᵗʰᵉ Bᵃⁿᵏ ᵗᵉᵐᵖᵒʳᵃʳᶦˡʸ suspending loan disbursements in 1985 pending reformulation of the programme (Aufderheide and Rich 1988; Hall 1991). The decision on Itaparica was all the more significant in view of the fact that the World Bank did not directly finance the hydropower project itself and did not initially acknowledge any project-related obligations arising from the loan.

In essence, therefore, the pioneering Itaparica resettlement project can be seen as the product of two, mutually reinforcing sets of factors: political pressure from 'below' via the Polosindical, and demands from 'above' through the World Bank's policy-making machinery. The Polosindical programme for educating and mobilising the rural population, culminating in the December 1986 mass demonstration which paralysed dam-construction operations and attracted global media attention, brought matters to a head. It obliged the Brazilian State and power authorities to take the population's demands seriously and seek assistance officially from the World Bank. Without this bottom-up pressure, it is highly unlikely that Bank policy and operations staff working on their own, even with the best will in the world, would have had sufficient power to induce a course of action so beneficial to the displaced population. At the same time, however, it is also likely that the stalemate between CHESF and the Polosindical would not have been broken without the intervention of the World Bank. The Bank acted decisively both to persuade CHESF to modify its resettlement strategy, as well as by providing vital funding for the new and relatively expensive irrigation schemes during a period of economic austerity in Brazil. Neither the Polosindical nor Bank policy and operations staff, working in isolation, would at that juncture have had the strength to achieve very much. Together they formed a powerful combination of interdependent forces which has won significant gains for Itaparica's rural population and set a precedent for the future.

Despite the path-breaking achievements at Itaparica, however, all has not been plain sailing. The combined strength of the Polosindical and the World Bank has not prevented long delays in the implementation of the irrigation projects, which are designed to form the basis of people's livelihoods. By mid-1992, five years after the signing of the first Bank loan agreement, none of the major schemes were operational. The Polosindical's direct action against CHESF continues; in June 1991 some 8,000 rural workers and their families occupied the dam in protest, while in February and April 1992, groups of some 300 rural workers from the area area staged a sit-in at the regional headquarters of CHESF in Recife (*Caminhar Juntos* 1991; *Jornal do Comercio* 1992). The resettled population has suffered from social and economic problems as well as psychological stress associated with unemployment and enforced idleness. Some poorer or more impatient settlers have 'sold' their plots unofficially before irrigated production has even started, while the São Francisco valley irrigation authority (CODEVASF) is ill-prepared for the task of running the new projects when they come on stream. The Polosindical has been engaged in an on-going conflict with CHESF over adjustments to settlers' maintenance payments to compensate for Brazil's 20 per cent-plus monthly rate of inflation, while accusations against the power company over alleged mis-use of

Bank funds intended for the resettlement programme have been rife. For many months the Brazilian government refused to provide counterpart funding to facilitate a US$100 million supplemental loan from the World Bank, eventually signed in November 1991, to allow project construction to be completed.

The major initial achievements of the Polosindical, progressive World Bank policy-makers and associated forces such as the radical Church and international NGOs in bringing about the adoption of a comprehensive resettlement strategy at Itaparica must, therefore, be seen against this less encouraging and more recent background of further delays and procrastination. The precise nature and distribution of benefits which will accrue to the resettled population in the future, notwithstanding their victories so far, is still very much an open question. It also remains to be seen whether the Polosindical can maintain its resolve and unity in the face of these frustrating delays. Furthermore, the organisation will need to explore ways of adapting from the mainly combative, confrontational role adopted until now, to involvement in the management and operation of the new resettlement schemes.

Conclusion: the lessons of Itaparica

Itaparica raises a number of issues concerning the roles of NGOs in comparable situations where the livelihoods of thousands are threatened by large, infrastructural projects. This case study is especially pertinent in view of the huge expansion in hydropower development taking place not just in Brazil but elsewhere in the Third World. For example, it has been estimated that from 1979–85 alone, World Bank-funded hydropower projects involved the displacement of over 600,000 people in 27 countries (Cernea 1988b). Furthermore, development activities such as official resettlement programmes, mining and logging have spawned a rising tide of protest movements by local groups whose livelihoods are being placed at serious risk. The best known of these is probably the campaign being waged by NGOs and local groups against forced resttlement in the Narmada Valley, India, where the Sardar Sarovar Dam alone will displace 100,000 tribal people (Esteva & Prakash 1992). However, many schemes, even apparently benign projects such as social forestry, may threaten indigenous populations with summary eviction (Hallward 1992). It is therefore of the utmost importance that NGOs work as effectively as possible with community groups and progressive development policy-makers and practitioners to become a positive countervailing force.

The major lessons to be learned from Itaparica for the scaling-up of NGO activities may be summed up as follows:

NGOs as new social movements

Hybrid organisations such as the Polosindical can play a pivotal role in building up grassroots movements around specific, livelihood-threatening issues by making populations aware of impending dangers, and acting as a channel for people's demands where other forms of locally-based political organisation may be weak or non-existent. New social movements (Scott 1990) may thus be generated by uniting previously fragmented and disorganised groups around external threats posed by large-scale development schemes, empowering disaffected groups from 'below'. Following successful resolution of the conflict, such movements may develop alternative or additional functions based on the need for organisational efficiency in areas such as management of new communities or production-related activities.

International NGO support

The financial and logistical support of international NGOs is often critical in enabling such local movements to be established and to prosper. Two major stages in such assistance may be distinguished: in the earlier or embryonic phase, when other domestic sources of assistance are frequently few and far between, it can mean the difference between the movement being stillborn or being allowed to grow. NGOs therefore need to identify such needs very quickly and act decisively to provide financial and other support so that such movements can develop. Once they are established, international NGOs can perform a valuable role by networking and lobbying internationally in favour of people's interests. In the light of growing adverse social and environmental consequences arising from large-scale development programmes, foreign NGOs will have an increasingly crucial lobbying role to play. It is also, therefore, essential that they become more efficient and effective in refining their strategies to achieve greater influence.

External policy leverage

At the same time, such local movements are unlikely to win significant concessions unless they can count on support from 'above'. Since it is improbable in most countries that these groups will enjoy strong, institutionalised political links at national level, top-down pressure probably has to come from outside institutions. Based on reformulated policy directives which lay greater emphasis on social and environmental concerns, bilateral and multilateral institutions have a duty to exert leverage and impose conditionalities in order that satisfactory provision be made for people affected by schemes like Itaparica. In this connection, the emerging links currently being forged by official multilateral and bilateral aid bodies with NGOs will become increasingly significant and will need to be enhanced. The expertise and specialised knowledge of NGOs of grassroots situations will have to inform the official processes of policy-making and -implementation in a more systematic and serious way than has hitherto been the case.

Legitimising NGO-backed social protest

Growing evidence of mass protests against projects involving large-scale population displacement, such as India's Sardar Sarovar dam (Rich 1989), suggests that official aid agencies will in future have to come to terms with social protest movements and recognise the legitimacy of local demands for the provision of adequate compensatory measures. Consequently, appropriate channels for negotiation and consultation between NGOs, bilaterals and multilaterals will be necessary if aid donors are to maintain their credibility as development institutions concerned for people's welfare. Official development bodies, whether bilateral or multilateral, must take due note and harness the power of new social movements as constructive forces for the design and implementation of economically, socially and environmentally sustainable projects.

Complementarity from 'below' and from 'above'

The relative success of resettlement at Itaparica was determined by the interdependent action of both the Polosindical and the World Bank. In the final analysis, the empowerment of disaffected local populations such as at Itaparica depends upon a strategic combination of mutually-reinforcing factors operating both from 'below' and from 'above'. Indigenous and foreign NGOs will need to bear this in mind when devising their operational strategies. The capacity of unaided social movements working on their own to induce positive change will surely be limited in most cases. Conversely, progressive policy-makers within official development organisations must recognise the contribution of beneficiaries and grassroots organisations. The whole is clearly greater than the sum of its parts.

The overriding message from Itaparica is one of cautious optimism and hope for the future. If the joint efforts of indigenous and international NGOs can be combined with those of forward-looking, influential planners and policy-makers in key official funding and executive agencies, we have the recipe for a powerful formula which could improve the design and implementation of development strategies in which the livelihoods of thousands are at stake. Itaparica is a path-breaking example of how the predetermined shape of official development can be successfully contested, turning once passive victims into victors. As far as Itaparica is concerned, the challenge now is to ensure that these initial gains are not lost with the passage of time. More generally, however, ways need to be explored of how this model of complementarity for achieving greater impact can be replicated or adapted to further the interests of populations at risk from similar schemes in other parts of the developing world.

Mobilisation and advocacy in the health sector in Peru

Elsa Dawson

Introduction

The Villa El Salvador Health project illustrates two main areas in which Peruvian NGOs can be seen to have a potential comparative advantage in relation to government as a channel for development assistance:

- the capacity to develop innovative and more appropriate policy proposals from field experience, for eventual use by the public sector, by other NGOs and by community organisations. Peru is an extremely heterogeneous country, and government officials in Lima often have little information and understanding of the reality experienced by the population of the rest of the country, even in Lima's shanty towns.
- the development of a much closer relationship with the population of a given area, which enables NGOs to strengthen popular organisations, respond to people's needs, facilitate meaningful participation by 'beneficiaries', and target their assistance at the poorest sections of the population (Tendler 1982).

The health project in Villa El Salvador provides an example of scaling-up impact via the exploitation of these comparative advantages, and also by uniting the efforts of different NGOs around a similar objective – health improvement in the district of Villa El Salvador. The project is based on two concepts: first, *primary health care* – the installation of a basic range of health services, with voluntary health workers from the community viewed as the lowest rung in the health system hierarchy; preventive health and health education; and democratic control of health systems by beneficiaries, in order to ensure that they are appropriate to real needs. The Villa El Salvador Health Project represents an attempt to make a reality of this approach by working for effective community participation in decision-making related to health.

The second guiding concept is *popular education*, a strategy for strengthening people's involvement in their own development by raising understanding and awareness of the causes of their problems, and by increasing their self-confidence, ability to assert their own point of view, and pride in their cultural identity. Participatory surveys feed local ideas into action plans, which are then evaluated collectively in order to improve future activities. Findings and viewpoints are communicated to the general population via street theatre, neighbourhood newspapers, posters and other techniques.

The project and its context

The health project is supported by INCIDES, a local NGO funded and partly launched by Save the Children Fund-UK. It aims to develop an appropriate primary health care system for the district of Villa El Salvador, located in the desert sand-hills to the south of Lima, and a typical example of the low-income, peri-urban areas which have multiplied in recent years throughout Latin America.

Emphasis was placed on beneficiary participation in the planning and execution of health activities, as part of a general effort to achieve the democratisation of decision-making in health in Peru. The project's centrepiece was the development of a 'Unified Health Plan' (UHP) for the district. Through its representative organis-ation CUAVES, the population of Villa El Salvador were to direct and manage their own district health system, in coordination with the municipality and local state health centres and hospitals, while drawing on technical assistance from all the NGOs working in the area. The idea of the project was also to avoid duplication by involving in a single system NGOs who had previously worked independently.

The UHP provided a framework within which all the actors involved in health in the district could coordinate, under the direction of the CUAVES Health Council – the body elected by the community to take charge of its affairs related to health. Programme-planning commissions were set up, each consisting of NGO representatives, Ministry of Health staff, municipal officers and community health promoters, so that appropriate and coordinated programmes with uniform criteria could be agreed and implemented. Commissions were formed for each of the following: Child Health, Women's Health, Immunisation, Environmental Health, Tuberculosis, and Human Resource Development. The resulting programmes were coordinated with the health plans at block level.

The residential area of Villa El Salvador was divided into four sectors. Each was made up of 15 or 16 residential units, but each of these units was too small to warrant one NGO team (a doctor, a nurse, and a social worker/health educator). It was therefore decided to group four or five together into 'operational units', each of which encompassed approximately 15,000 people. INCIDES covered four of these operational units and assigned a health team to each.

Weekly meetings were held in each operational unit, attended by Health Secretaries, voluntary health workers and other CUAVES officials, during which the specific health problems of the locality would be discussed, and relevant activities planned – for example, the distribution of food hand-outs to families which needed them most, the organisation of rubbish-clearing campaigns, and the establishment of a community medicine store based on a rotating fund.

The team also provided curative services four times a week in each operational unit; trained voluntary health workers from the community (one for each block of 24 homes); undertook health education for mothers' clubs, soup kitchen groups and 'glass of milk committees'; and provided technical support for the weekly meetings of community leaders and voluntary health workers.

Under the guidance of INCIDES, a survey was carried out by voluntary health workers to identify 'high-risk family units' for targeting in all the programmes that were established. The inhabitants of Villa El Salvador were divided into three socio-economic strata according to criteria related to housing, occupation, number of children and level of education. The lowest stratum contained the high-risk family units, while the highest were judged able to purchase private medical assistance.

Achievements

Despite many hindrances (frequent desertions by voluntary health workers, changes in community leadership and Ministry of Health staff, and increasing economic difficulties among beneficiaries) INCIDES consider that good progress has been achieved overall. Gradually, responsibility for management of the health system is being assumed by members of the community. In terms of beneficiary participation, many voluntary health workers are actively involved in health education using participatory methods, to encourage the growth of self-confidence and creativity amongst the community in their search for solutions to health problems. There have been some examples of groups of beneficiaries developing activities on their own initiative. For example, one group of health workers decided sex education was a priority in its area, and organised a series of workshops on this subject. Another group conducted a campaign on violence against women, and another on children's rights.

Health-planning and evaluation meetings are now held regularly at both the operational unit level and by the CUAVES Health Council, and many district health planning conventions have been organised. Ministry of Health staff accept decisions made by these meetings to a growing extent.

In terms of service-provision, INCIDES reports show a consistently higher rate of immunisation coverage (around 85 per cent of the target population) than areas of Villa El Salvador which are not directly covered by their teams (60–70 per cent), and very few cases of children suffering from diseases against which immunisation has been given. In terms of replicating the model that has been developed, many aspects of the Unified Health Plan have been adopted by the Ministry of Health. These range from details such as the forms produced for registering children for immunisation and child growth monitoring, to the way in which officials now talk explicitly of working towards the UHP, and adhering to the mandate of CUAVES.

Motivated by the example of Villa El Salvador, others have pursued the concept of participatory planning as an important goal in order to improve the health of the populations of Lima's shanty towns since 1985, when under the leadership of the then Mayor (Alfonso Barrantes), the Lima Municipality began to think in terms of district health plans. This project represented the first time that the idea of district health plans had been put forward in Peru, and INCIDES were the first group to attempt to put this idea into practice. Two other districts of Lima (Ate-Vitarte and El Augustino) also began to develop district health plans (Mendoza 1991). In 1985, a district health convention was held in Ate-Vitarte with support from INSAP (the Institute of Popular Health) and the idea of a district health plan was launched.

This was the first time that attempts had been made to plan participatory health systems at a district level in Lima, bringing together previously-isolated efforts in the areas where each NGO was operating. INCIDES played an important role in showing that these efforts were feasible, at least in one district, and in trying to establish mechanisms for coordination at the district level. In the district of Chorrillos, a multi-sectoral committee has been set up by members of the local education and health authorities in order to coordinate work in health and in aid of children.

President Fujimori's first Minister of Health, Dr Carlos Vidal, was a member of the Cayetano Herredia University, where the Director of INCIDES studied. Under Dr Vidal's leadership, the Health Ministry began to coordinate closely with

INCIDES in the development of the Unified Health Plan in Villa El Salvador. Both the Director and the Programme Director of INCIDES have been invited to join local health authorities in Lima as advisers.

The project's success in coordinating all Villa El Salvador's health resources became apparent during the campaign to control the cholera epidemic which hit Lima in the first half of 1991. The Director of the South Lima Health Authority has given credit to the high level of coordination, community awareness and organisational capacity in Villa El Salvador which lay behind the rapid decrease in mortality rates during the cholera epidemic after the first preventive measures were taken (Arca 1991).

However, there have been problems as well as successes. Drop-out rates among voluntary health workers are high. For example, in 1985 64 per cent abandoned the project. Many were selected or had volunteered for the wrong reasons – for example, young, single and more highly-educated women who did not have direct experience of the health problems of young children. Others volunteered in the hope of acquiring saleable skills (such as giving injections) and then left to set up their own practices. Attempts were made to overcome this problem by concentrating more on existing community organisations such as mothers' clubs, glass of milk committees and soup kitchen groups.

In addition, strikes among Ministry of Health staff were frequent, and there were constant shortages of vaccines and essential drugs. There were also frequent changes of leadership among CUAVES, especially in the membership of the Health Council, so that new members had to be remotivated in support of the Unified Health Plan. Conflicts and rivalries existed between CUAVES and the municipal council. Because INCIDES worked closely with the former, the municipal health officer was automatically opposed to their work. Finally, some of the INCIDES team members lacked proficiency in the methodology of popular education.

Lessons learned

INCIDES and 'comparative advantage'

Has INCIDES exploited the two areas of comparative advantage identified at the beginning of this chapter – innovation in policy reform, and closeness to people and their organisations? Certainly, INCIDES has explicitly focused its work on the development of innovative policy proposals and their replication by state and other organisations. The model has had widespread influence, as will be examined in detail below. Not only is the project itself aimed at developing models in order to influence government policy, but members of INCIDES have also accepted roles as part-time advisers to the local health authority.

In addition, INCIDES has strengthened the capacity of CUAVES leaders to manage health activities at district level in Villa El Salvador. The organisation now produces its own health plans, and launches initiatives such as campaigns (against the cholera epidemic, for example), and district conventions (on TB, for example). However, a recent evaluation of INCIDES' work shows that they have not managed to make CUAVES much more than an organisation of community leaders. It still lacks real participation from the majority of beneficiaries. As noted above, INCIDES carried out an extensive survey to identify high-risk families in the project area, in order to improve the targeting of their work. However, a review of the average level of education of those attending INCIDES clinics showed that this was equivalent to the average level of the population of Villa El Salvador. If educational levels are taken as a major indicator of levels of poverty, INCIDES are not managing to target their work at the poorest families.

The ultimate proof that INCIDES has fully exploited its comparative advantage would be evidence of significant change in public-sector policy that favoured the project's beneficiaries. Progress in this area is described below.

Scaling-up impact

In their efforts to exploit their comparative advantage, INCIDES has been involved in a number of strategies to scale-up the impact of their work. The first of these is 'micro-policy reform' – influencing health policy among the Peruvian Ministry of Health, other NGOs and grassroots organisations, on the basis of their experience in Villa El Salvador. The project is concerned primarily with the development of a model primary health care system for Villa El Salvador, which might also be replicated elsewhere. To promote the model, INCIDES participate in inter-NGO networks in Lima aimed at the exchange of ideas and experiences, such as Intercentros de Salud ('Health NGO Interchange'), in which 30 NGOs participate. They have also published articles in Peruvian journals such as *Salud Popular* ('Peoples' Health'), produced by INSAP, the Institute of Popular Health.

The Villa El Salvador project has just been evaluated by a consultant, Ivan Mendoza, who has specialised in a new concept being promoted by the Pan-American Health Organisation – 'Local Health Systems.' The Unified Health Plan developed by INCIDES for Villa El Salvador is the most advanced operational example of a Local Health System in Peru. The evaluation found the Plan to represent a valuable attempt at the construction of a Local Health System, and it is hoped that PAHO will help to promote the replication of the model elsewhere.

Whether the model has made a significant impact on health status in Villa El Salvador is difficult to judge. Even if accurate information on children's health in Villa El Salvador were available, it would be impossible to attribute any improvement solely to the project's activities, owing to the number of other sources of assistance in the district. Moreover, the project's main efforts have been directed at improving coordination between these different sources of assistance.

Nevertheless, as noted above, credit for the rapid descent in mortality rates in Villa El Salvador during the recent cholera epidemic has been attributed to the generally high level of coordination, community awareness and organisational capacity in the district. Another indication of success is the high rate of immunisation coverage that has been achieved. As described above, the local Health Authority has already incorporated many aspects of the systems designed by INCIDES. Whether the model in the precise form in which it has been developed in Villa El Salvador could be replicated in other areas seems doubtful, mainly because the strength and degree of centralisation of community organisation there is not found in other districts of Lima. Nevertheless, the advantage of setting up the model in Villa El Salvador was that it would have a greater chance of functioning well precisely *because* of the level of awareness and commitment to collective, voluntary activity which existed among the population.

Another serious drawback of the project in terms of sustainability and replicability is its cost. Currently, INCIDES provides a doctor, nurse and social worker/educator for every 15,000 people, each of whom receives a higher salary than public-sector health staff. It is doubtful whether this level of service can be sustained in Villa El Salvador, let alone be repeated in other districts. INCIDES find that this level of staffing is required in order to maintain community interest in the project.

Hence, although the concept of district health planning based on community decision-making has been taken on by many other bodies in Lima (including the Ministry of Health), it is too early to say for sure whether the project has been successful in reforming policy at the micro level. This depends on the progress of community capacity-building, and the commitment of the Ministry of Health, other NGOs, and the Municipality, in promoting the model in Villa El Salvador and elsewhere.

The second strategy employed by INCIDES to increase the impact of its work is the strengthening of people's capacity to pursue their own development strategies independently of outside assistance. INCIDES consider that they have used the strategy and methodology of popular education to improve the capacity of the population of Villa El Salvador, and in particular that of CUAVES, to design and conduct their own development activities in the field of health, and to develop autonomous initiatives. But have their efforts really stimulated independent thought and action on the part of the population?

Tendler (1982, p 74) exposes what she sees as the myth of the 'participatory' project in which 'outsiders [are] making decisions for subsequent local acquiescence'. How does the Unified Health Plan stand in relation to this criticism? In defence of the project's work, one should note the following:

- Weekly meetings of voluntary health workers and community leaders in each of the operational units certainly do decide the detailed arrangements for carrying out health activities. They also work out local health plans, which feed into the District Plan.
- Local planning conventions, well-attended by community leaders, have now become an integral part of the South Lima Health Authority administrative structure (Arca, 1991) and INCIDES has contributed towards the development of this important stage in the decentralisation of decision-making in health in the capital.
- Although meetings do tend to be taken up with administrative detail and inter-party and institutional rivalries, PAHO consider this appropriate, seeing it as precisely what a Local Health System should do – resolve conflicts between different actors concerned with the health of a district[1].
- INCIDES report that many women leaders of mothers' clubs, 'glass of milk' and soup kitchen committees have gone on to become leaders in health, which would indicate that increasing numbers of ordinary community members are progressing up the ladder to higher leadership positions.
- INCIDES has done much to contribute to the ability of CUAVES to plan health activities. The structure it built up under the aegis of the Unified Health Plan has permitted extensive involvement on the part of community leaders in health planning, if not of the poorest members of the population.

However, the following shortcomings should also be noted:

- Despite the population's involvement in planning, evaluation and campaigns,

---

[1] Dr Patricio Hevia, PAHO Lima: personal conversation, 1991.

meetings have tended to concentrate on the details of programmes which have already been established by professionals from government or the private sector, and not in the main of activities originating from the community.

■ Many inhabitants of Villa El Salvador are recent immigrants from the Peruvian Highlands where indigenous concepts of ill health and appropriate cures are quite different from those of modern western medicinal practice. Because people have few resources for the purchase of drugs and the improvement of sanitation, and because the climatic and geographic environment of Lima differs from that of Europe, traditional practices and concepts may be more appropriate than those proposed by modern medicine, especially given the cost of the latter in relation to average income. One would expect therefore to see such practices and concepts appearing in the health plans. In practice this has not happened, perhaps because the population now considers itself urban and 'modern' and therefore rejects the traditional beliefs of the Andean Highlands.

■ community members (other than active community health workers) seem unaware of the Unified Health Plan and often do not identify with its proposals.

■ INCIDES has tended to concentrate on coordination with community leaders. 'High-risk' families (mainly single mothers and their children) do not take part in the project. This is because they are too occupied with the immediate problems of everyday survival to be able to take on extra tasks.

■ the recent evaluation by Alfaro (1991) points to a tendency to lend greater importance to the development of *organisation around health*, rather than the resolution of *concrete health problems* as perceived by voluntary health workers themselves. It may be that INCIDES has tended to idealise community leaders and to defer overmuch to their ideas and wishes.

Contextual factors in the success and failure of strategies to increase impact

In general, the strategies outlined above are directed at long-term processes, and it is not therefore possible to make a final assessment of their success at this stage. However, certain factors can already be detected which are facilitating or hindering the degree to which they have been successful.

Factors contributing to success

In as far as real community participation has been achieved in the management of the Unified Health Plan, this has been due to:

■ the long history of social and political organisation and general commitment to the collective good of the population of Villa El Salvador;

■ the commitment of the staff of INCIDES, who have been prepared to work inordinate hours of the week.

The success of the coordination achieved in Villa El Salvador with regard to the control of the cholera outbreak can be attributed to the decision of the directorate of the Lima South Health Authority under President Fujimori's Minister of Health to co-operate with NGOs in the area, and their efforts to involve the population in active, participatory decision-making.

The dissemination of the concept of a District Health Plan was due to:

- the political will of the Mayor of Lima (Alfonso Barrantes) between 1983 and 1986, and of President Fujimori's health ministry under Dr Carlos Vidal;
- the interest of PAHO in developing similar models.

In general, a climate of relative political continuity, and gradual opening-up on the part of the national government to the policy proposals emanating from NGOs, have favoured the level to which the project's policy-reform objectives have been successful. This has been accompanied by relative continuity of policy-making in the health sector, which has broadly followed the lines set by the Alma Ata Conference on Primary Health Care in 1978.

Factors hindering progress

The principal obstacles have been:

- the previous (APRA) government's Social Assistance Programme of temporary employment on public works, which, by offering immediate material benefits, tended to take community health workers away from participating in the UHP;
- the increasingly difficult economic situation in Lima which has forced many voluntary health workers to abandon their work in order to concentrate on day-to-day survival. The increasing cost of food and medicines has also been important;
- constant changes in the leadership of the community organisation, the Municipality, and the Ministry of Health, and inter-party rivalries and differences affecting these bodies and co-operation between them;
- the lack of centralised and established community organisations in other districts of Lima, similar to CUAVES.

Conclusion

It is not possible to say at this stage whether the Villa El Salvador Health Project has been successful in achieving policy reforms in favour of the poorest people in Lima. However, it has already served to encourage greater coordination of health resources at the district level in Lima by demonstrating the feasibility of alternative structures for this purpose. It has also demonstrated workable mechanisms for the decentralisation of decision-making in health down to the level of community leaders.

INCIDES has made significant progress in exploiting its comparative advantage as an NGO. Its members have been willing to risk experimenting with innovations in an area urgently requiring policy reform – urban health in developing countries – which have had widespread influence in Lima. The task INCIDES took on – to develop effective mechanisms for community participation and the coordination of a unified district plan involving many different actors – was formidable, and their courage and idealism in taking on this important challenge deserves recognition in itself.

Thanks to adequate remuneration and a commitment to social change, INCIDES staff have been able to work closely with the leaders of the community in the development of local health plans, and to set up structures for feeding into the district-level plan, thereby adding much to the skills of these leaders.

Table 15.1:

SUCCESS FAVOURED BY:	SUCCESS HINDERED BY:
1. Community level:	**1. Community level:**
■ History of community organisation and commitment to the collective good.	■ Little history of community organisation or commitment to the collective good.
■ Centralised community organisation.	■ Atomised, localised community organisation, divided politically.
■ Members enjoying relative economic stability.	■ Suffering severe economic difficulties.
2. Government level:	**2. Government level:**
■ Stable with political continuity.	■ Unstable, frequent changes in leadership.
■ Continuity in policy-making related to sector concerned.	■ Changing policies in the relevant sector.
■ Open to co-operation with NGOs in their efforts to gain community involvement in decision-making.	■ Social assistance programmes providing immediate benefits without a long-term perspective.
3. Implementing agency:	**3. Implementing agency:**
■ Commitment of members to social change.	■ Lack of genuine commitment to social change.
■ Capacity to conduct real education processes.	■ Isolated from beneficiary community, no studies undertaken.
■ Understanding of and close relationship to beneficiaries.	■ Ideological rigidity.

The evidence indicates that the degree to which scaling-up has been successful in the case of this project has been due largely to the nature of government and society in Peru, which has favoured the adoption of innovations from the NGO sector and allowed new models to develop relatively unhampered by state control. Villa El Salvador has, at least until recently, been relatively free of the political violence and natural disasters which have hindered similar efforts in other parts of the country. It is also clear that increased economic hardship on the part of the population limits the degree to which effective beneficiary participation can be developed. Strategies to increase impact must therefore consider macro-level constraints such as 'structural adjustment' and their effects on poverty and government services.

Overall, micro-level and macro-level action by NGOs can be seen to be complementary and mutually-reinforcing strategies aimed at redirecting government policy and redistributing national resources in favour of the poor. These links are shown diagrammatically in Figure 15.1.

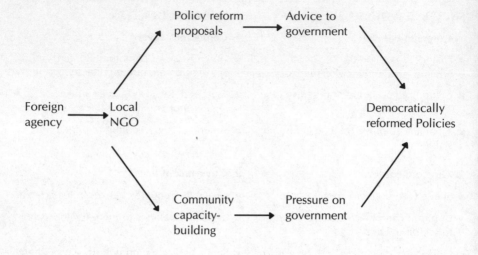

Figure 15.1:   *Micro- and macro-level action in Peru.*

Scaling-up in urban areas[1]

Diana Mitlin and David Satterthwaite

Introduction

In most urban areas in the Third World, a substantial proportion of the population lives in poor housing with inadequate or no basic services and infrastructure. This is a major factor in the high levels of ill-health, disablement and premature death of these populations. In most instances, local governments lack the power and resources to address these deficiencies. Neither national governments nor aid agencies appear to be able (or willing) to respond. However, low-income groups have demonstrated remarkable ingenuity in developing their own shelters and they are responsible for most new housing in Third World urban centres. There are an increasing number of intermediary institutions (most of them Third World NGOs) which provide technical, legal and financial services to low-income households for shelter construction or improvement or which work with community organisations in basic service and infrastructure provision. This chapter offers an analysis of the mechanisms and processes through which Third World NGOs have undertaken such tasks. It also considers the ways in which such NGOs effectively multiply the impact of community initiatives: how they stimulate the formation of community organisations; how they support their work, and the role of credit in such initiatives.

The scale of need

By 1990, an estimated 1.5 billion people lived in urban centres in the Third World[2]; of these, at least 600 million are estimated to live in 'life and health threatening' homes and neighbourhoods because of the inadequacies in the quality of the housing and in the provision of infrastructure and services.[3] The conventional

---

[1] Drawn from a report prepared for UNDP/UNCHS, 'Funding community level initiatives' by Silvina Arrossi, Felix Bombarolo, Jorge Hardoy, Diana Mitlin and David Satterthwaite (IIED and IIED-AL). The information in the boxes is extracted from IIED and IIED-AL reports.

[2] See for instance Cochrane (1983), Stren (1989), and the special issue of *Environment and Urbanisation* on 'Rethinking local government: views from the Third World' (Vol. 3, No. 1, April 1991).

[3] In order to further this discussion, IIED-America Latina and IIED's Human Settlements Programme has been considering the possible role of intermediary institutions (including NGOs) in working with small-scale community organisations in order to initiate, fund and support housing and neighbourhood improvements. The work has included the analysis of 17 case studies of (mainly) NGOs with a strong emphasis on support for the development of community organisations and an interest in new strategies for addressing urban poverty. The case studies cover a wide range of different experiences including: organisational type; their focus for tackling poverty; the services provided such as technical support, funding, community development and training; and the exact client group of the organisation. This chapter is taken from this longer report, 'Funding community-level initiatives', and the case studies contained within the boxes are drawn from longer profiles.

model for the development of urban residential areas within market or mixed economies assumes that most housing will be designed by architects and constructed by building enterprises on sites with basic infrastructure. It also assumes that a range of public authorities and agencies will ensure the provision of infrastructure and services to all developments and lay down a planning and regulatory framework to ensure that buildings are healthy and structurally safe. This model of urban development does not work in the vast majority of urban centres in the Third World.

Most investments in the built environment in all but the central districts and rich neighbourhoods in urban centres in the Third World come from a large and varied multiplicity of individual and household investments. Most of these are unrecorded and are made outside any legal building or planning regulations. Only rarely does public policy support this investment and it may constrain or hinder it. The gap between reality and 'the conventional model' is such that, in most Third World nations, the number of conventional dwellings constructed annually is between two and four per 1,000 inhabitants, while the actual increment in the housing stock (including all illegal and informal housing) is likely to be between 15 and 30 units per 1,000 inhabitants.

Government agencies in the South often have similar roles and responsibilities to those in the North. But the authorities who in theory are responsible for investments in infrastructure and services lack the power and resources to do so[4]. Public investments in infrastructure and services are at best inadequate and at worst non-existent. Private companies are unable to respond to the need for infrastructure and services which is constrained by low levels of demand (reflecting a lack of income) but also by the difficulties of funding and organising investments which can only feasibly be made on a neighbourhood or district basis. The result is large areas within each urban centre, city or metropolitan area with no paved roads or pavements, no piped water systems and no electricity supplies, no sewers or drains; and serious deficiencies in services such as garbage collection, health centres, schools and day-care centres.

The cost of ensuring adequate provision for all of those in need is large, even if it is restricted to water and sanitation. Estimates suggest that providing 100 million urban households with new or improved sanitation and water supply systems would result in a total cost of US$62 billion simply for the initial capital investment: no additional maintenance or operating costs are included. In order to place these figures in perspective, total official development assistance from OECD members states was just under US$50 billion in 1988. But even if major additions could be made to capital investment in water and sanitation, the weakness and inefficiency of existing public-sector institutions with responsibilities for water and sanitation would severely constrain their efficient use.

Although these costs are so large that it is unlikely that many Third World governments will be able to meet them, the scale of investments being made by low-income households and communities is often substantial. It is therefore essential to change the traditional model of financing urban growth to one which supports and works with the most dynamic force currently operating in this area: low-income households and their community organisations. This implies new models for public intervention which recognise the right of residents to participate in the planning, execution, maintenance and control of projects. Traditionally, plans to deal with poverty revolved around the planning and action of central or state governments (in some cases acting together with multilateral agencies), or private institutions. These were generally expensive and only reached a small number of people, often of middle or even upper income. There is an urgent need to consider how the great majority of the poor can be supported to develop their own strategies, making best use of their scarce resources to obtain housing, basic services and infrastructure.

The nature of housing, basic services and infrastructure investment

In considering the capacity and actions of individuals and community organisations working for the improvement of local neighbourhoods, it is important to differentiate between investments such as housing construction or improvement which can be made on a individual basis, and most kinds of infrastructure and services which can only be supplied cost-effectively on a settlement wide basis.

Most urban housing in Third World cities is built and financed by individuals, with little use of formal banks or housing finance institutions. The total cost of any housing unit is likely to be large relative to the income and assets available and capital for such investment is generally needed over several years. In some cases, an incremental approach to housing development may be appropriate.

Most basic services and most forms of infrastructure can only be supplied at a community or neighbourhood level. Individual households can make limited improvements to some forms of infrastructure and services – for instance pit latrines dug to improve sanitation. However, problems such as poor site drainage and unpaved roads cannot be solved by individual households. Individual household solutions for water supply and sanitation are often inappropriate for urban areas, especially in high-density settlements, and unit costs per household served are usually far cheaper for community-wide solutions.

Basic service and infrastructure investment generally involves significant capital investments and long depreciation periods. Cost recovery for such investments should be spread over the life of these assets. However, this may be difficult; for instance, if the future of the settlement is uncertain because of its illegal status or if a high proportion of the inhabitants are tenants and neither they nor their landlords (who may live elsewhere) want a long-term commitment or an increased cost.

It may be possible to fund improvements in roads and drains, piped water systems and improved provision for sanitation with costs being fully recovered from users. The unit costs of many forms of infrastructure and services are much lower if provided to all those within a particular area – for instance paved roads and paths, street lighting, electricity, piped water and drainage systems.

However, the costs per household of what might be defined as a minimum package of infrastructure and services (eg water piped to the house yard, the cheapest appropriate sanitation system, drains, paved roads, garbage collection and primary schools and health centres) are still relatively high in comparison with the incomes and assets available to poorer groups. For instance, supplying a household with water piped to its yard and the cheapest adequate sanitation system may be between US$500 and US$800 assuming comprehensive coverage in the neigh-bourhood. This is more than most poor households can afford. Costs are particularly high for established low-income settlements because it is much cheaper to invest in piped water, sanitation, drains and roads during the preparation of the site.

While investment in housing, basic services and infrastructure does not often add directly to household income, it can be an important contributor in several respects. Improvements in water systems can often provide better quality and greater quantities of water at costs well below what residents previously paid to water vendors, and paving roads often brings significant improvements in bus services. Many small informal enterprises operate from the home and better facilities may increase earnings. Improvements in housing conditions reduce the incidence of illness and injury which can in turn ensure that income is not lost through illness. The increase in the house's value may provide an asset to secure a loan for a business investment when borrowing from conventional sources.

Working with community organisations

Establishing community organisations

Many case studies of community-based programmes to improve housing and living conditions are drawn from settlements where the community organisation was already established prior to the programme being initiated. However, in many low-income urban settlements no community organisation exists. NGOs and external agencies working in such areas have to get involved in establishing community organisations. Three possible routes into working with such communities are described in this subsection: a long-term programme of integrated support for a single community, the establishment of potentially independent housing co-operatives, and the formation of small groups from individual households for a programme of activity with the NGO.

Establishing community organisations takes considerable amounts of time and requires much sensitivity. Box 1 describes this process in a low-income illegal settlement to the north of Buenos Aires, Argentina. The NGO found that it was important to maintain a momentum of activities and a continuity of advice and support in a community which had grown disenchanted with offers of support from ineffectual external sources.

Box 1: Barrio San Jorge – the process of initiating a community organization

Barrio San Jorge is located in San Fernando, a municipality on the periphery of Buenos Aires. The barrio contains 630 households and 2,926 inhabitants within a site of just under 10 hectares. A high proportion of the inhabitants are infants, children and adolescents.

When the International Institute for the Environment and Development – Latin America (IIED-AL) became involved with the construction of the mother and child centre in September 1987, only 16 people in San Jorge (mostly women) were interested in community activities. The great majority of the population looked upon the construction of the centre with scepticism. Some of the members of the original group joined forces with IIED-AL from the outset and became the main support in the construction and management of the mother and child centre. In late 1989, residents became more interested in the activities being introduced in the barrio. Attendance at meetings increased as did participation in decisions about work priorities. But few people were prepared to contribute to building tasks unless they received payment.

During early 1990, the consolidation of a community organisation continued. In August 1990, elections were held in the barrio to choose representatives to join a commission which was to develop a long-term programme for the improvement of the barrio. This commission included representatives from the government of the province of Buenos Aires, the local municipality and IIED-AL. Subsequently the newly-formed community organisation of San Jorge has requested the transfer of the public land they occupy to the settlers and has pressed the municipality of San Fernando to organise the rollrrtirn and disposal of garbage.

The most important lesson learnt in the process was the need for the external agency to have a permanent and continuous presence in the community.

A different kind of process is described in Box 2. Concentrating on less well-established communities and focusing on the provision of credit for housing construction, the work of Catholic Social Services in Pakistan has resulted in the establishment of potentially independent housing co-operatives.

Box 2: Catholic Social Services – establishing autonomous housing co-operatives

Catholic Social Services provides credit in squatter settlements in Karachi through a revolving fund to residents. The organisation has experimented with several different mechanisms and has developed a system which offers loans to groups of borrowers who collectively guarantee the repayment of individual loans. When people approach the society for a loan, they are organised into a co-operative. Each member is asked to contribute Rs 50 (US$2.40) a month into a common fund, and for at least a year this amount cannot be touched. Thereafter, the funds are available for members of the group requiring small loans with the consent of other members. Members of the co-operative who require a housing loan are asked to increase their contribution to the common fund to Rs 300 (US$14) a month for a six month period. In addition, every prospective borrower is required to attend a basic loan and co-operative education course. Loans of up to Rs 10,000 (US$475) are granted. Recently Catholic Social Services have been encouraging several of the original co-operatives to become autonomous organisations. This will enable them to raise their own funds from new sources, and allow the revolving fund and Catholic Social Services to concentrate on newly-formed or potential co-operatives.

Korangi Christian Co-operative Society was the first group with which the Society started work. The area is a resettlement site for those evicted from other parts of the city. The co-operative began with just 12 members in 1984. By June 1989, 45 members had purchased plots and most had completed the construction of houses with permanent roofs. The group has also purchased land and built a community centre using the resources of their common fund. The Korangi Christian Co-operative Society was formally registered in 1989, and since then has begun to work autonomously.

Offering opportunities for credit may be a key mechanism to attract community support and involvement. Several credit initiatives have experimented with group-development techniques in order to establish a mechanism for securing repayment. There are two additional advantages in using this mechanism for supporting programmes in housing, basic services and infrastructure. First, it establishes a group which can work together on the more difficult parts of construction work, and second, it begins a process of collective decision-making which can be essential for implementing some basic service and infrastructure programmes. Box 3 illustrates this process in one Chilean case study. However, one disadvantage is that it is not quick – the Bangladesh Rural Advancement Committee estimate that, in a new area, it takes about four years before its credit programme can operate without subsidies.

Box 3: The Housing and Local Management Unit – small group development in housing

The Housing and Local Management Unit is a non-profit-making organisation in Santiago, Chile. Since becoming independent in 1987, the Unit has worked with low-income groups. One of its current programmes is a package offering credit and technical assistance for housing improvement. Groups are formed of between five to eight people (heads of the family) with some previous knowledge of and trust in each other. For three months, each participant deposits a monthly sum in a bank which is equivalent to the instalment that they will pay once the loan has been authorised. The members of the group each have to apply for the same amount of credit and repay it over the same period. A technical team gives assistance to enable each participant to draw up their project and offers socio-organisational support aimed at consolidating the group. Once a loan has been approved, each member places the initial amount saved in a long-term deposit account (the term being the duration of the loan), endorsing it in the bank's name as a group guarantee. This guarantee represents 25 per cent of the loan.

   The group members receive the money in the form of a promissory note which they make out to the team, which buys and distributes the materials for each family. Once they have the materials, the participants begin the construction (sometimes individually, sometimes collectively) with the support of the team. The loans are repaid over a period of between 12 to 18 months. Once the repayment is complete, the participants can automatically take out a new loan, or withdraw their contribution from the security fund, which is returned to them with interest.

Supporting community organizations

NGO support for community initiatives might include any one of a number of possible measures. Some of these are undertaken in conjunction with credit (the focus of the following sub-section) and continuing support for community development. Most NGO programmes for community initiatives involve a package of measures considered appropriate to the specific context in which the NGO is working. Such packages include technical training, bulk purchase of materials and legal assistance to acquire tenure over land. For example, FUPROVI, a Costa Rican NGO assists families and communities to carry out improvement programmes and community development. FUPROVI works through participating communities which provide organisation and labour. In return, FUPROVI supplies credit for construction materials, housing extension and improvements; assistance, training and practical support; a fund for basic services and common activities; equipment and tools to facilitate community work; and support for institutional development.

The use of credit

The large amount of capital required for many housing, basic services and infrastructure programmes mean that there is a potential role for credit and this has been used successfully by a number of NGOs. A number of aspects of the successful operation of credit schemes in relation to housing, basic services and infrastructure investment are discussed below.

Relationship to the formal sector   The relationship of innovative funding programmes to the formal sector differs greatly. In some cases, institutions have been set up to facilitate the integration of low-income groups within the formal sector. In other cases, the credit scheme involves the establishment of an alternative institution, resulting in the withdrawal of the poor from the formal sector. Box 4 illustrates three different strategies which have been used. There are no obvious lessons emerging in respect of whether one strategy is more successful than another – the necessary conditions for success appear to be dependent on the context within which the programme operates.

Box 4: Housing loans and NGOs

Loans provided by an NGO, transferred on legalisation of land

FUPROVI (Costa Rica) is a private non-profit-making institution which offers loans to low-income households and assists them to achieve the legalisation of their land. Once legalisation has been secured, participants join the national housing financing scheme. This scheme then takes over the loan and FUPROVI recovers its investment, returning it to a rotating fund.

Loans guaranteed by NGO provided by commercial bank

The Chilean Housing and Local Management Unit is a non-profit-making organisation which offers loans through a commercial bank to groups of families. The initial loans were backed by a security fund provided by the Unit which equalled 100 per cent of the loan value and the bank was only a formal intermediary for credit. Later the security fund was dispensed with and the bank now risks its own funds.

Loans given by an 'alternative' bank

Members of the Grameen Bank who borrow money for income-generating activities are also eligible for housing loans. Borrowers receive a package of materials including concrete pillars, galvanised iron sheets, a sanitary latrine and material for the walls and roof. Some of these supplies are produced in manufacturing units supported by the Bank. This programme is integrated into the Bank's other credit programmes and prospective loanees have to secure the approval of their group and regional centre.

Subsidies and grants A number of credit programmes involve an element of subsidy in the loan. Programmes normally differentiate between reductions in the cost of individual credit and the financing of an additional programme to facilitate and support the operation of the credit programme. There is a general, although not universal, consensus in income-generation schemes that subsidised credit should be avoided. However, the same degree of agreement does not exist in respect of housing, basic services and infrastructure investment. Many organisations offering credit for housing, basic service and infrastructure construction do not charge a commercial rate of interest. A difficult question is whether or not the resources spent on subsidising the loans might better be spent on alternative programme support; for example, directly meeting part of the programme costs such as in the provision of support services, or paying part of the capital investment required.

Savings Many programmes involve the generation and use of recipients' savings as an integral component of a credit programme. Savings may be particularly important in the case of loans for housing, basic services and infrastructure investment because no direct increase in income results from the loan. A programme of saving before the commencement of the loan will ensure that the household can make the required repayments. In some cases, savings can be invested in the same programme as the loan; in others, savings must be retained in order to provide a minimal form of collateral.

Risk and repayment   Overcoming and reducing the risk of loan default is a critical element of NGOs' work in the area of credit. In some cases, through the use of guarantee funds, NGOs' intervention in this area is simply to take on some of the risk and thereby open up access to formal credit institutions. However, NGOs usually become involved in managing the credit and thus in designing cost effective systems. Several mechanisms used to ensure high rates of repayment are described below.

The group guarantee scheme made famous by the Grameen Bank has been used (albeit with slight alterations) in many different programmes throughout the world. Such programmes organise borrowers into groups of about five people. Each individual is eligible for loans but the granting of each loan is staggered over some specific period of time. Repayments by all members must be up to date in order for the next person to receive a loan. The group is collectively responsible for ensuring that each individual member continues to make repayments.

An alternative is to offer only small loans and make further loans conditional on successful repayment. The effectiveness of this procedure relies on the scarcity of the available credit to provide an incentive for borrowers to maintain repayments. The small amounts (and market interest rates) generally ensure that only those on low incomes are interested; richer individuals borrow elsewhere.

Some NGOs have kept losses to a minimum by only lending to a small group of people which they know very well, or who have received a reference from someone well known to the organisation. While this method has been successful, it obviously greatly reduces the potential growth of the credit scheme. The challenge to those operating credit schemes for individuals or households on low incomes is to reduce the costs associated with each individual loan, such as the costs of chasing up those who default. Generally those on low incomes only want to borrow small amounts and so individual transactions costs are high relative to aggregate lending. This is one of the reasons why such lending is unattractive to the formal sector. If market interest rates are to be maintained, the NGOs have to ensure high repayment rates with only little additional expenditure on overheads. The evidence from many different programmes is that, if the programmes are carefully designed, high repayment rates can be secured in different situations and cultures.

In housing, basic services and infrastructure programmes, there are a number of special characteristics relevant to repayment considerations. The cost and slow depreciation of the capital asset mean that repayments may need to be made over an extended period. In some cases, this is not possible, and this obviously constrains the scale of the investment that can be made. Such programmes do not often add directly to household income. The requirement for savings at a rate equivalent to future repayments for a period before obtaining a loan may be particularly important in ensuring that households who cannot afford the repayments do not join. Residents may wish to invest in a property for which they lack legal tenure. For this reason, programmes need to assist participants to gain this status or find ways round this problem.

Conclusions – going to scale

Devoting more external and/or government resources to investments in shelter, infrastructure and services is one of the most frequently cited 'solutions'. Yet even if the scale of such resources was multiplied several fold, without changes in the approach, there would only have limited impact. It is critical that official policies and programmes respond to the needs and priorities of the individuals and community organisations who are currently responsible for most investments in shelter and infrastructure in urban areas and who generate the demand for most services – virtually all of which is outside official policy and receives little official support.

Scaling-up to improve housing and urban services is not simply the replication or expansion of a successful project. Rather it entails providing support for a large range of community initiatives, each rooted in the specific needs and priorities of that community. Intermediary institutions, including NGOs, have an important role to play – not so much by implementing large programmes but by acting as multipliers, providing support and guidance to hundreds of community-level initiatives. Through a successful programme of support, NGOs can begin to increase the effectiveness of community organisations in house and site improvements, service provision and support for income generation.

In supporting the work of community organizations, three areas are of particular importance:

- better use of existing, under-utilised resources
- increasing representation and accountability
- new partnerships in the development of low-income settlements.

The use of resources

In working with community-level organisations at every level, successful NGOs have focused on identifying and developing potential resources. In general, such resources are un-utilised and under-utilised. Through drawing out such resources with small, well-chosen, investments, significant achievements can be made. In general, the resources fall into one of three categories.

Technical and organisational skills. For the individual household building or improving their home, technical advice can help improve health and safety standards and reduce costs. Legal advice can also help those living in illegal settlements negotiate more secure tenure or even transfer of ownership or tenure rights. Technical advice can ensure the best possible use of local resources – for instance the harvesting of rainwater for household use, or the best use of local – springs and the means to improve the environment generally – for instance by improving drainage.

Financial resources. Successful credit schemes can permit relatively modest sums of money to mobilise people's own financial resources to more effectively secure their livelihood. Guarantee schemes can permit both individuals and groups to obtain loans from the formal financial sector which previously denied them credit. The use of material banks and bulk purchasing of construction materials, fixtures and fittings can help optimise the use of scarce income.

Productive capacities. In many low-income settlements, there is an important synergy between improving services and job creation – as in nurseries and daycare centres which employ some local staff and which also permit the mothers to spend more time on income-earning activities. Support for local workshops producing building materials and fixtures can create local employment and also lower the cost of improving housing.

Increasing representation and accountability

The poor are not only poor in a financial sense. The continuing struggle for resources and the stress associated with providing for themselves and their dependents has its own costs. A strong local community organisation can be a route through which many forms of deprivation can be addressed.

Many local communities have little control over the provision and operation of basic services and infrastructure. The role of local government in regulating and monitoring housing, basic services and infrastructure is essential and needs to remain and be developed. But it can be enhanced through the active involvement of community organisations. Such community organisations have a threefold role. First, they can realise tangible programmes, raising money and other resources to undertake works prioritised by the community. Second, they act as pressure groups on local government, securing infrastructure and services for their members and ensuring that their interests are not forgotten. In such a role they can support the democratisation process which is critical to ensuring that government at all levels is more responsive to the needs of the poor. Third, community organisations are also important in developing the fabric of the community so that it can be an effective support for its members, many of whom suffer the extreme stresses which result from poverty.

New partnerships

New partnerships are required to develop the work of community organisations. The list of potential external partners is large: national or state governments, local governments, NGOs (international, national and local), religious groups, private business organisations, commercial financial institutions, official multilateral and bilateral development assistance agencies, international private voluntary organisations. In many projects, more than one partner is involved in joint collaboration.

Such new partnerships are likely to be critical in ensuring the more effective use of resources. Support for individual and community level initiatives within low-income settlements will need the support of a wider network of NGOs who can provide training, advice, representation and a host of other services. It will also require a new role for many local governments who will have to start working effectively with such community organisations, many of whom will be autonomous, decentralised bodies. Private-sector financiers and existing and potential suppliers of services will be needed to support such new initiatives.

Successful partnerships need their pace and coordination determined by the community organisations. This implies changes to the way that many potential partners operate since there is often a mismatch between outside agencies' modes of working and dispersing funds and the needs and priorities of low-income households and community organisations. In particular, such partners will have to recognise the need to take new risks and delegate responsibilities both to NGOs and community organisations. Donors must accept that NGOs cannot be effective implementors without having access to adequate funds committed over several years, thereby reducing the resources presently allocated to fund-raising activities. All partners must recognise that the community organisations have an essential role to play and must be able to control resources and take decisions in respect of their own future. The consequences of a lack of community involvement are best illustrated by a quote from a paper about one such community 'Failures are almost inevitable when outsiders try to impose their points of view' (Hardoy, Hardoy and Shusterman 1991).

It's not size that matters: ACORD's experience in Africa

Chris Roche

Introduction

In 1972, a group of European NGOs established a consortium to respond to the difficulties faced by the people of Southern Sudan after so many years of civil war. Two years later, another NGO grouping came together in the wake of devastating famine in the West African Sahel. The two structures amalgamated in 1976 to form the consortium known today as ACORD[1] through which 20 NGO member agencies from Europe and Canada pool their experience, resources and expertise.

ACORD was created in order to work in those parts of Africa where local structures were weak or non-existent, to benefit from the collective experience and fund-raising potential of its membership and to establish an international platform to discuss development issues. The creation and reinforcement of local institutions has therefore always been at the heart of ACORD's programmes in Africa. Implicit in this approach was the wish to see if by providing more resources than is usual for an NGO programme, a greater impact could be achieved while at the same time respecting an NGO philosophy based on participation and contact with the grassroots. ACORD therefore started as an initiative to scale-up the impact of a group of NGOs and to do this worked closely with government. Around 1980 the strategy shifted to what one might term 'operational expansion' as the relationship with the state became more problematic. Since 1986 the emphasis has switched to what has been termed 'scaling up through supporting community initiative' (Edwards and Hulme 1992).

Learning: 1972–85

The development of ACORD between 1972-85 can be divided into two main phases. The first lasted for most of the 1970s and was characterised by institution-building at the regional or district level and involved close links with government. The second started in about 1980 and involved operational scaling-up, with ACORD 'doing it itself', and an increased accent on production as opposed to institution-building.

The early years

The Kiu centre in the Ngara District of Tanzania, the AMADI institute in Southern

---

[1] The Agency for Co-operation and Research in Development (ACORD) is a broad-based international consortium of European and Canadian NGOs working together for long-term development in Africa.

Sudan, and the rejuvenation of the Co-operative Movement in Mali typified the organisation's work in the 1970s. All depended on close collaboration with local government and all assumed that these centres or organisations were either providing services required by the rural poor or, in the case of Mali, were representative of the rural poor. All were assumed to be capable of having an impact at a regional or district level which surpassed a typical NGO micro-project approach. The state was perceived as being more than a monolithic block with individuals and departments which were committed and capable of complementing ACORD's work and above all were seen to be the logical partners to which much of the programme activities would eventually be 'handed over'.

In the early 1980s it became increasingly clear that due to external pressures (from the IMF and World Bank in particular) the capacity of local government structures to play the role originally envisaged by ACORD was progressively compromised. In addition it also became clear that the accountability of these intermediary local structures (such as the co-operatives in Mali) as well as that of local government, towards the rural poor, was deficient. In effect the way the 'scaled-up' approach had been executed was flawed, starting as it did from an intermediary perspective rather than from the bottom up.

The middle years

Between about 1980 and 1986 therefore, ACORD began to 'do it itself'. A rapid increase in expatriate staff was paralleled by an increased emphasis on productive activities (irrigation, market gardening, agricultural and livestock projects) and a diminishing level of support to institution-building. ACORD in essence swung away from collaboration with state technical services, because of the problems it had faced, and replaced this input with its own (usually expatriate) staff. As such its lack of confidence in the state was mirrored by its lack of confidence and awareness of the skills, resources and knowledge of the people it aimed to support.

The results of this approach were that programmes became much more expensive, tensions with government departments increased (particularly among those who had previously been supported by ACORD) and management became more complicated. The concomitant bureaucratisation that this expansion involved tended to increase overhead costs as well as stifle initiative and flexibility. In addition the need to cover relatively large budgets pushed ACORD into more fund-raising from bilateral and multilateral donors, and to the verge of becoming sub-contractors for them in certain cases. The threat to the organisation's independence and to its mandate, in terms of supporting the emergence of local structures in areas where they were weak, became evident as the pendulum swung away from institution building to economic production-oriented development initiatives.

The example of Mali

The ACORD programme in Mali exemplifies these two phases. The programme was established in the Gao Region of northern Mali following the 1973/4 drought. The idea was to tackle the 'organisational' aspects of development, with a view to long-term structural change through a programme of relaunching of the state-inspired co-operative movement. The co-operatives were considered, at the time, to be the only existing structures capable of absorbing rehabilitation and development activities in the region. The programme at this stage essentially worked through regional government services as it was felt that the strengthening of marginalised regional government structures was important in addressing the imbalance between the north of the country and southern dominated central power.

As frustrations with the capacity of local government emerged and as it was thought that the co-operative structures needed a better economic base on which to build, ACORD began to hire expatriate technical staff to run technical components of the programme (irrigated rice cultivation, livestock, market gardening, well construction etc). Budgets increased dramatically as did the management problems relating to the supervision and monitoring of a large and geographically dispersed team.

Evaluations in 1983 and 1987 considered that the programme had made impressive quantitative and technical achievements. However in terms of local institutional development the results were very much less impressive. Since 1987 ACORD has therefore shifted its support to more informal groups (producer/marketing/women's groups), encouraged an on-going process of decentralisation of what were very large and in many cases inappropriate co-operative structures, reduced drastically the number of expatriate staff and revised completely its methodology so as to incorporate more fully the groups with whom it works at each stage.

1986 – a change of emphasis

The mid and late 1980s saw, therefore, ACORD's emphasis switching to the support of informal, grassroots organisations (eg village groups and pastoral associations in northern Mali, village groups and women's groups in Burkina Faso, mutual savings groups in Uganda, micro-businesses in Port Sudan). However it was realised that, in order to avoid a simple juxtaposition of micro-projects, encouragement should be given to the establishment of alliances, federations and unions of these informal groups. The important thing being that these be based on activities and mutual support as determined by the individual groups rather than by ACORD. ACORD sees its current role, therefore, as one of facilitating the emergence of such structures but not speeding-up or directing the process. The two case studies presented below exemplify this approach.

The Burkina Faso programme

ACORD's programme of support to socio-economic village organisations in the Sahel region began in 1983. Its main aim has been to strengthen men's and women's village groups and encourage links between them, while at the same time facilitating their access to financial and other support from other agencies. ACORD, through a process of 'animation' using the locally developed GRAAP methodology[2], and an important training component, managed to build up village

---

[2] This methodology has been developed by the Groupe de Recherche et d'Appui pour l'Autopromotion Paysanne (GRAAP) in Burkina Faso. It aims to assist groups to recognise change as one way to improve their situation. This is achieved through a continuing cycle of analysis, reflection and action. A trained animator encourages this process through posing questions on different themes: the different types of people living in the village; constraints to production; and areas of conflict between groups. These discussion sessions are held in sub-groups and use clear simple pictures to aid visualisation of the issues discussed and the

continued on p.183

portfolios, that corresponded to the individual needs of the groups, into a coherent regional planning document that allowed funders to subsequently invest in the diverse areas of support that were required.

An initial survey by ACORD of the 330 village groups existing in 1983, showed that many of these groups failed because; villages did not consider many of the projects funded at the time as their own, but as externally imposed; limited management capacity hindered implementation; and some village groups had internal problems which were further aggravated during project implementation. At the regional level there was no overall policy to tackle the particular needs of the area and few criteria for the establishment of projects. ACORD believed that state structures were sincerely trying to help rural communities, and that instead of by-passing or emphasising the negative aspects of local government, ACORD's strategy should be to support those structures to become more effective, eg through assistance with planning rather than material resources. Thus the programme in its first phase aimed to support training for animation and project development with village-level workers and state extension workers.

In the period 1983–90 the number of groups supported by the programme rose from 330 to 540 (of which 23 per cent were female and 8 per cent mixed, as opposed to 16 per cent and 1 per cent respectively in 1983), the number of members increased from 13,860 to approximately 45,600, and the proportion of groups with funds greater than 80,000 FCFA (£160) grew from 13 to 37 per cent.

More interestingly, the development of alliances and federations of such groups has occurred, with 25 unions of village groups who have in turn created three provincial union committees and one regional union committee[3]. This structuring of the groups has not been completely spontaneous. However, in recent years the majority of departmental unions were created by the village groups themselves, and the Sahel Regional Union Committee came about as a result of many of the groups and unions deciding to undertake themselves in 1990 a large-scale cereal and livestock marketing exercise owing to the very poor rains of the previous year.

This operation, which was designed and executed by the unions with modest support from ACORD, combined the purchase and distribution (at cost) of cereals from outside the area with the purchase of livestock from within the zone in order to inject capital into the economy and thus facilitate cereal purchases. Despite the limited impact in terms of the estimated regional cereal deficit in 1990 (about 35,000 tonnes) the unions showed their capacity to determine, execute and manage an appropriate intervention as well as the potential to undertake similar operations

---

continued from p. 182
relations between different people or groups of people. An important element of the GRAAP method is the iteration between sub-group sessions and plenaries when the groups come together. This is particularly important to ensure the participation of women and youth. The spokesperson for a group is much more likely to speak up on behalf of a group than on behalf of him/herself. Proverbs, stories and songs are also used. The training helps animators to provide a discussion framework for the role of religion, modern science and indigenous knowledge, inter-generation conflict, dependency relationships, and the role of an outside catalyst or animator.

[3] The programme covers the three Sahelian provinces of Oudalan, Seno and Soum, which each have their own provincial union committee. The Regional Union Committee covers all three provinces and represents the old Region of the Sahel.

at a larger scale. The degree of political empowerment of the unions was also evidenced recently by their negotiating successfully, at presidential level, for a reduction in the price of cereals sold by the state marketing board in the region.

The final stages of ACORD's support to the unions and village groups in the Sahel are now beginning. By 1995/6 it is hoped that these groups and their representatives will be capable of negotiating from a position of strength with government and development agencies. In order for this to be achieved ACORD will be concentrating in the next few years on management training and institutional support at all levels. This will include developing the network of partners with whom unions can liaise.

There are, of course, outstanding problems that need to be addressed in the next few years.

Gender issues   Despite an increase in the number of women's groups in the area, these remain weak and women's representation at the higher levels of the unions is very low. Support to women's practical and strategic needs will need to be increased and the question of their representation at departmental, provincial and regional union committees will have to be discussed with these groups. A continuation of ACORD's support to literacy training for women as well as their economic activities is crucial for them to gain the skills and resources necessary to challenge existing gender relations.

Livestock   Despite the importance of herding in the area ACORD has not to date adequately supported herders' initiatives. The reinforcement of village groups, many of whom are made up of pastoralists, has led to demands for increased support in areas of animal health, water supply and marketing.

Self-financing and access to formal credit   Increased self-financing and access to other sources of credit are key to the unions becoming a truly independent local organisation. Training in financial management, accounting and report writing, exchange visits, workshops and the introduction of the unions to other partners will be essential.

The Uganda programme

ACORD has been working in Gulu District since 1979, in the Nebbi District since 1983 (both in the north of the country), and the Oruchinga Valley in the south-west of the country since 1987. The early years of ACORD's work in the north were characterised by efforts to rehabilitate productive activities (fishing, agriculture) and social services (mainly health). Both the northern programmes were disrupted by insecurity on several occasions. In 1987 all programmes, including the initiative in Oruchinga valley, adopted new three-year programmes initialling a change in methodology. These three-year programmes were understood to be the first phase of a nine-year time-frame divided into the *establishment phase*, characterised by the recruitment, training and consolidation of three teams of change agents; the *development phase*, characterised by the increasing consolidation of emerging groups and *member-controlled* associations and federation of groups; and the *localisation phase*, where the associations of groups will be strengthened and ACORD withdraws. The encouragement and strengthening of member-controlled associations of interest-groups capable of promoting and protecting the interests of their members and of the association as a whole was to be a key element of the programme.

Group development   In quantitative terms the development of groups in the Uganda programmes has been impressive, rising from 194 in 1988 to 388 in 1990. Membership has increased from 2637 to 6533 and women's participation has risen from 35 per cent to 44 per cent. Funds under group control have rapidly grown.

There is great variation between groups. In Pakwach there are at least ten groups undertaking collective commercial investments through owning shops. Another 20 or so are directly involved in productive activities such as fishing, boat-building, tools production, group farming, beekeeping and textile dyeing. In Oruchinga groups of potters, brick-makers and beekeepers exist. Most of ACORD's partners, therefore are organised in small groups but many have begun to ask for assistance in association-building. Others have expressed an interest in assistance with creating bigger interest groups for social purposes, for example to cope with the problem of orphans, digging a well, and lobbying the district authorities.

Associations   In Pakwach six group associations have emerged which are investing up to one million Ugandan shillings or more (approximately £1000). This will enable the associations to take on more demanding activities and will increase their economic power considerably. The oldest is the Paroketo Fishermen's Association which emerged as an association of smaller groups in 1987. There is another similar association emerging called the Boro Fishermen and Farmer's Association. There are also groupings like the Pakwach Fishing Group, the Alwi Women's Association and the Janam Small-Scale Industries Association which have already been established.

In Oruchinga three associations have been formed in the programme area, for the marketing of bananas and also among beekeepers. Associations of traders are beginning to form and these purchase commodities in Mbarara for sale in the Valley. Associations of tree planters have emerged and the founding of BIEPO (the Bukanga and Isingiro Environmental Protection Organisation), has resulted in the creation of a central nursery and four branch nurseries expected to produce 130,000 seedlings in 1991.

In Gulu some groups are planning to form producer associations to purchase rice hullers and to form producer associations to deal with problems of transporting agricultural produce. In addition the Community-Based Health Care Association has been created. Some of these associations have plans to operate at the County level, so as to pool together the resources of groups facing similar problems.

Credit Associations   In all the programmes the rationale of pursuing development through promoting cash savings and credit groups has been questioned. However, the assumption that external credit and extension services will be available to groups has proved to be untenable. Thus, ACORD has established its own credit scheme in each of the programmes managed by elected representatives of the groups. The scheme has so far operated efficiently, with more than 85 per cent loan recovery in Pakwach. By the end of 1990 a total of 7,519,600 Uganda shillings had been lent out to 30 groups (32 per cent for agricultural production, 17 per cent for boat-building and fishing and 51 per cent for commercial purposes). In Oruchinga about 7 million shillings have been lent out since the end of 1990 to 30 groups. Currently 101 groups are working with ACORD to organise a credit association which will eventually take over the ACORD credit scheme. In December 1990 the individual groups had a total of 13 million shillings (approximately £10,000) out in loans to members. They shared profits of 1.4 million shillings (£1,080) and invested 8.2 million shillings (£5,500) in group assets.

In Gulu the ACORD Rural Development Credit Association was established in 1991, with 132 groups joining as founding members. Links have been established with local banks in order to encourage them to consider providing credit to groups in future. A special effort has been made to ensure the participation of women in the committee structures by providing for the election of at least one woman group-representative to each of the three county loan committees and four women out of the nine members of the district executive committee.

In addition a variety of advisory, producer-association and planning committees and councils have been established at sub-county, parish and district levels, elected from group members. These are all efforts to create a sustainable process that is controlled by the partners. The objectives of these committees will be reflected in ACORD's planning framework for the remainder of the programme period. These structures are an important step towards establishing a resilient self-evaluation mechanism by which the community and ACORD can evaluate their common contract.

Lessons learnt

There is now a healthy network of economic and social development activities operating with various degrees of success, run and controlled by individuals and groups. As a result, many more groups are forming daily and old ones are consolidating. However several significant problems still confront the programme.

Gender issues   Despite the fact that those women the programme reaches have grown in confidence and are taking some joint decisions, the majority of women still live under oppressive patriarchal relations, whereby they are not able to participate equally with men in terms of major decision making. This was initially compounded by the reluctance of ACORD to work with individuals. This alienated ACORD from a large body of potential beneficiaries, including the poorer sections of the population, especially women.

The external environment   The Structural Adjustment Programme continues to squeeze commercial and government expenditure. Banks are starved of liquidity; crop financing and purchase is poor and unreliable; government's capability to rehabilitate infrastructure and motivate its staff is low; the country's dependency on aid for development is growing rather than reducing and the control of inflation seems to be eluding the government.

The problem of AIDS   Although the programme has been educating the change agents about AIDS, has trained some as counsellors with TASO (The AIDS Support Organisation), and tested the TALC flannel graphs for AIDS in some parishes, the degree to which the programmes feel that ACORD can do anything faced with this pandemic is very low. There is a general sentiment from the local staff that they are powerless in the face of such a dramatic process.

Problems with the initial methodology   In terms of the relationship between the change agents and the community there is a clear question-mark over the likelihood of the change agents being supported by the community in the long term. The fact that the change agents were not identified and employed by the community means that they are not answerable or accountable to the community. The problems revealed in relation to the conceptualisation of the change-agent element in the methodology are carried over into the conceptualisation of the participation element. The notion of the community being provided with opportunities, as far as possible, to participate in planning and implementing its own development is symptomatic of top-down thinking and assumed that the people in the community were not already engaged actively as subjects of their own development. The community was assigned a role which had been defined for them by someone else. As such the community was not allowed to participate in deciding upon its own participation!

Problems, conclusions and prospects

Scaling-up

ACORD has moved from scaling-up through working with government, through operational expansion, to support to grassroots mobilisation. This experience suggests that scaling-up is possible if it builds upon interest groups and their needs, to create alliances and federations. Where perhaps we have the most positive developments in terms of scaling-up impact (the Burkina Faso experience with Unions of Village Groups); this has been in large part possible because of the conducive political climate.

The experience has been much slower and more difficult in countries where the political climate was inimical and a positive relationship with the state has proved difficult to construct. There is a need to work with the state in order to create the space necessary for the emergence of autonomous local structures. Although the state is not monolithic, and there are parts of the structure and individuals within it committed to the development of the zones in which they work, it is structured to become monolithic in times of crisis. NGOs need to identify how best they might support but not substitute themselves for what exists. They need to exploit their comparative advantage over the state in terms of the different relationship they can have with intended beneficiaries and their capacity to organise themselves in an appropriate manner, rather than compete (Fowler 1987). Ignoring the role that the state plays and will continue to play, like it or not, in promoting or suppressing the strengthening of the civil society, is short-sighted and possibly dangerous for those who actually take the risks.

Accountability and decentralisation[4]

It is difficult to achieve the right balance between support to different levels (grassroots organisations, federations and intermediate structures) as well as between institutional support and support to 'activities'. It is also difficult to ensure that the least powerful or unheard voices (women and minority groups) are listened to and represented within such structures without interference. In the same way that Africa is looking for partners that will allow it to recapture the development process, micro-organisations are looking for support that will help them become self-reliant, not more dependent on donor support. Apart from technical, organisational and financial support this means political backing and protection where necessary. One of the main lessons that ACORD has learnt is that its institutional set-up was inappropriate to continue promoting the interests of the

---

[4] See ACORD (1990).

poor. Its accountability remains, almost exclusively, to its funders and members who in turn are accountable to their own boards and public. Despite some work on mutual evaluation processes there is no real mechanism whereby the consortium is also accountable to those with whom we work. In addition its decision-making, management, support and platform for debate on development issues are too distant and too alienated from its work in Africa and the short-term nature of its funding is contradictory to the long-term objectives that have been set.

In recent years various international organisations have attempted to overcome some of the problems associated with the lack of involvement of those that they wish to support in decision-making by decentralising functions and a limited amount of power to local offices or local NGOs. However one of the major difficulties of this has been the problem of developing local accountability. Nobody has the answers. However, there is a danger that the difficulties that have been encountered up to now will be used as an excuse not to proceed further. It is crucial that bolder, more experimental steps are taken to permit a real devolution of power to the groups and individuals that are confronted by the problems outlined above and that such a process is carefully evaluated and the lessons and mistakes made widely available. Experience suggests that a decentralised structure with semi-autonomous, self-managed, federated units coupled with information and co-operative learning is perhaps the most appropriate organisational design for supporting micro-development (Fowler 1987).

Educating donors

The kind of work described above is necessarily of a long-term nature (10–15 years) and guaranteed funding for such a period is difficult if not impossible to come by. The lack of rapidly visible results, a flexible approach and such a long time-frame tend to turn donors off. In addition, such processes require sensitive support of a varied nature depending on the ecological zone, the socio-political environment and the stage of development of the informal groups. This means that support must be location- and organisation-specific and therefore, although certain principles are the same in each programme, no blueprint or simplistic replication plans can be drawn up. The donor clamour for replicability and quick results goes against such an approach.

Much remains to be done by NGOs themselves as well as those academics interested in influencing official donors, to persuade policy-makers to adopt more flexible and long-term approaches for funding support.

Monitoring and evaluation

NGOs have often been reticent about setting clear objectives and evaluation criteria for grassroots mobilisation activities. Some have argued that the outcome of such projects is not quantifiable, others that they do not want to fall into the trap of executing sophisticated cost-benefit analyses and some that the results are less important than the processes involved in achieving them. This has three main dangers: first it leaves NGOs open to the subjectivity of external evaluators, who will, in the absence of any clear programme objectives, determine the criteria for evaluating the success of a project. Secondly, if NGOs do not develop more appropriate and innovative evaluation and monitoring systems they may be forced into adopting procedures alien to their very philosophies. Thirdly it means that little is being learnt about successes and failures to the benefit of future action.

Several ACORD programmes, and many by other agencies, have been experimenting with innovative forms of participatory self-evaluation which have provided interesting insights into potential methods of analysing processes hitherto thought to be difficult or impossible to evaluate due to their non-quantifiable nature. There is a need to develop more systematic, practical and accessible appraisal, monitoring and evaluation processes which look at how best to integrate internal participatory processes and external evaluation procedures as well as clarifying feedback and learning mechanisms. This process should lead to the development of clearer indicators of the degree of NGO achievement in facilitating the development of local structures, as well as increasing the capacity of local structures to monitor and evaluate their own work and organisational development.

Coping with change and the image of Africa[5]

The importance of external factors in affecting the development of local structures needs to be more carefully analysed. Although there are examples from our work in Burkina Faso and Uganda where such events have in fact produced positive and lasting developments as local groups coalesce to counter or mitigate the effects of drought and civil war, it is necessary to help local groups cope with such rapid change. A first step in this is understanding how they already cope while at the same time helping them to understand and analyse those factors that are hindering or enhancing their development.

Just as at micro level we have to take into account existing survival strategies and strengthen these, so too at the macro level Northern NGOs have to pay more attention to positive developments emerging from Africa itself. The way that NGOs raise money, and therefore the way that they portray Africa, gives the impression that if the public respond adequately then famine will become a thing of the past and 'development' will occur. This is a gross distortion of reality. First, the vast majority of people who survive droughts, famines and wars and undertake 'development' do so on their own. Secondly, the work that NGOs do is infinitesimal in terms of need and goes only a small way to changing the underlying structural causes of poverty, vulnerability and injustice. If NGOs carry on pretending that they can 'feed the world' or continue to undertake 'long-term development' while ignoring the factors that make this so difficult, then they will become part of the problem rather than part of the solution.

This is not to argue that a 'miserabilist' image of Africa should be portrayed but rather to argue for a depiction of Africa that makes more of what people do so brilliantly already; survive and organise their lives under the most adverse circumstances that are not of their making. A corollary of this must be a portrayal by NGOs of their work that is more modest, more honest and more explicit when it comes to explaining why those adverse circumstances come about. The strength of NGOs lies in their ability to form opinion based on their experience on the ground. If our own financial survival strategies become more important than those of the people we claim to help, there is a danger that the image of Africa portrayed will continue to ignore the fact that most Africans survive successfully without us or, as some argue, despite us.

The current pluralistic developments in much of Africa suggest that a more

---

[5] See ACORD (1991c).

favourable political environment could come about. However the dangers associated with the establishment of cosmetic multi-party democracies, which will be deemed sufficiently oriented to 'good governance' in the eyes of western donors, are real for the kinds of processes that NGOs aim to support. Unless democratic grassroots structures are part and parcel of civil society and have the capacity to influence state action, then democratic process at a national level will be built on weak foundations.

18
Policy influence, lobbying and advocacy
John Clark

Introduction

If maximising profit is the paramount objective of the private sector, maximising impact is the paramount objective of NGOs. Conventionally this is achieved, as in the private sector, through growth – the 'additive' approach. However many strategically-minded NGOs find expanding and replicating projects too slow. They seek to move into the fast stream of social change by 'influencing' attitudes, policy and practice, and have been inspired by the success of the women's movement, the environment movement and other prominent campaigns which have succeeded in doing this.

Development NGOs can seek to influence change amongst the poor (for example raising awareness of their exploitation or increasing confidence), among other aid agencies (for example encouraging diffusion of techniques to the larger agencies), in the actions of local governments (for example seeking to reform state services on the basis of NGO experience), or in the policies of Northern governments (for example reforming practices which contribute to the root causes of poverty). Such influence can be achieved organically as the message of the NGO spreads by word of mouth – the 'diffusive' strategy – but it will be more powerful if it is planned, and this requires a 'multiplicative' approach to scaling-up (Edwards and Hulme, this volume).

For most NGOs, maximising influence requires new skills and new ways of working. They must overcome their tendency to insularity, become more confident with analysis and research, and learn to locate their grassroots programmes in a macro context. They must learn the skills of dialogue, communications and strategic planning.

All of this requires a different relationship between Northern and Southern NGOs. In particular Northern NGOs are increasingly expected to help Southern NGOs in their advocacy, and to lobby directly for the policy changes NGOs of both

---

[1] The opinions expressed in this paper represent those of the author alone and do not necessarily reflect the views of OXFAM or of the World Bank.

North and South agree are necessary. Particularly for Northern NGOs, effective lobbying requires a two-pronged strategy, combining careful analysis and reasoned professional advocacy with mobilisation of public opinion and use of the popular media.

This chapter looks at the experience of development campaigning over the past 20 years, and how the influence of Southern NGOs has become increasingly prominent. This has caused a shift in the focus of campaigning to more grassroots concerns and has changed the cast of actors engaged in campaigns. Some conclusions are also drawn about how to maximise effectiveness in lobbying and campaigning.

Achieving influence

To evolve to a more strategic 'influencing' role, NGOs must seek to broaden their skills, activities, and partnerships. The traditional NGO approach is to concentrate on service delivery and local-level interventions, often disconnected from a broader, national context. The language of 'participation' and 'empowerment' conventionally refers to the poor's relationship with the project itself and to decisions and practices at the local level. As ANGOC (the Asian NGO Coalition) says, 'questions of development theory and official policy were left largely to the experts' (Lok Niti 1988).

Increasingly, however, NGO leaders are recognising that they and the poor themselves have an equal right to be regarded as 'experts'. As the condition of the poor continues to decline it is evident that we need to reshape our ideas of development. NGOs could play a critical role in this revision. To quote ANGOC again:

> [NGOs] are now questioning official policy processes, existing development theories, and their own inclination to wholly accept government leadership in setting the directions of national development policy ... Broader effective participation in the decision-making process by which both local and national development decisions are shaped is increasingly seen by NGOs as the key to future development progress in South and South East Asia (Lok Niti 1988).

The challenge for NGOs therefore is to learn how to influence key aspects of a wider development process rather than seeking to control micro-development projects from beginning to end. They must learn how to *facilitate* as well as *deliver*.

New styles and skills

There is a tendency towards insularity within the NGO sector, to talk only with those who 'speak the same language', but influencing policies and practices clearly necessitates forging new working relationships – for example with government and other officials at both national and local levels. This may require changes in the NGO's own staffing. For example, staff involved in advocacy should not be closely identified with any anti-government factions and should appear politically mature. Those who are well connected to senior decision makers or who command broad public respect are important allies. The NGO, if it has an open mind, may also find that the issues are not quite as clear-cut as they seem on the surface, and that it has a lot to learn from others who know the issue or the country well. These factors indicate the need for NGOs to build much broader coalitions than they are accustomed to, working closely, for example, with the academic community, with the business sector, with politicians, trade unionists, religious leaders and others who have access to the ears that need bending or to the knowledge that the 'bending process' requires.

Avoiding dialogue because this risks compromising one's position is unrealistic and immature. Social change is about compromise because it is about balancing opposing forces – typically the tension pulling towards reform versus the resistance of the status quo. A pressure group which achieves a significant reform may be well satisfied with the progress – and say so publicly – even if only 20 per cent of its demands have been met. This does not imply that the group has dropped or lost faith in the remaining 80 per cent, rather that it considers it politic to consolidate the initial gains.

Strategic NGOs need to convince others on the development stage of the validity of their new influencing role. They must seek to be consulted on policy issues and be prepared, for example, to serve on government commissions. This process can have major ramifications for NGO leaders. In some countries they have been persuaded to leave the NGO sector and to move into government. This should not be seen as a 'selling-out' but as building a more effective platform on which to make the NGO case. As Eduardo Garilao says (1987), 'Third World NGO leaders will begin to enter into public service and politics because, in addressing the structural problems of poverty, it is the logical next step'. Likewise with official aid agencies NGOs must manoeuvre into a closer relationship so that they can help formulate policies and project design.

Some within the official agencies are advocating this new relationship. Cernea (1988) points out that a World Bank impact study of 25 projects concluded that the principal reason some Bank projects failed to be sustainable was non-involvement of grassroots organisations. When local organisations were involved the projects endured. Evidence such as this is leading many aid officials to recognise that allowing NGOs negotiating space, in particular to introduce ideas of popular participation, will strengthen their own projects.

NGOs of the 'Information Age'

NGOs, like businesses, are moving into the information age. The 'software' of their trade – ideas, research, empowerment, and networking – are rapidly becoming more important than their 'hardware' – the time-bound, geographically fixed projects, such as wells and clinics. In this new age, information and influence are the dominant currencies rather than dollars and pounds. A failure to recognise this is likely to lead Southern and Northern NGOs into an anachronistic relationship.

Just as they must take on new responsibilities in order to preserve their relationships, Northern NGOs must also relinquish others. The 'crucial issue is the transfer of power' to Southern NGOs (ICVA 1989). In particular decisions over project-funding should increasingly be transferred to Southern specialists. It is lamentable that, as the century draws to a close, there is a colonial residue which still believes that decisions concerning poverty alleviation in India can be better made in London or New York than on the spot, where the real expertise lies.

The North–South NGO partnership must not be a jealous one. It must allow room for others. It is important to build new alliances with environment, human rights and women's groups, with consumers' associations, trade unions, professional bodies, academic institutions and others, all of whom have an important contribution to make towards influencing. Northern NGOs must be prepared to move to a more secondary place. If the influencing role is to become significant then the closest partners of the Southern NGO must be indigenous institutions and the government itself, rather than Northern NGOs as is usually the case at present. The latter, as Garilao says (1987), must help Southern NGOs to define what they want to do, rather than define the agenda for them. They must look beyond their traditional resource-transfer role to invest in the capacity-building of their Third World partners.

This relegates Northern NGOs to a lesser role in devising grassroots development strategies. However in other areas a much higher profile is called for, particularly in the field of international lobbying. The reluctance of many funding NGOs to adopt this enhanced advocacy profile is leading to a shifting of allegiance within the NGO community. Many Third World NGOs are moving away from their traditional partners who fund them and striking up closer bonds with Northern advocacy organisations such as the environmental pressure groups. For example, grassroots NGOs working with indigenous tribal people in India and Brazil are coming to identify more closely with human rights organisations such as Survival International and with lobbying organisations such as the Washington-based Environment Defense Fund than with their longer-standing Northern funders. They are one step ahead of their funders in recognising that well placed pressure for international policy change is a more precious development resource than money.

International lobbying

Most Northern NGOs spend a small portion of their budgets on 'development education' – to influence their own societies about Third World issues. They seek to give a more accurate impression of the Third World. Though with schools NGOs avoid overt bias, NGOs are adopting a more propagandist, action-oriented approach with the general public, calling on their supporters to join in campaigns. They deliberately seek to influence decision-makers into changing some aspects of policy or practice.

For this a two-prong approach is needed. No matter how well-researched their case and articulate their presenters, significant political change is unlikely unless there is a groundswell of public opinion demanding those changes. The converse is also the case. If a campaign skilfully mobilises public opinion but does not have a water-tight argument, the decision-makers will find it easy to dismiss it as little more than hot air. Hence an NGO needs skills of both lobbying and public campaigning. Their supporters must be informed about the issue in question, invited to join the lobbying (for example by raising the issue with their local Member of Parliament or by writing letters to decision-makers), and asked to help mobilise public opinion (for example through publicity stunts or writing letters to newspapers).

Effective lobbying affords a powerful and increasingly important means for NGOs to multiply their impact on significant development questions, ranging from the design of specific World Bank projects to the debt crisis. Until recently, such international lobbying has been largely dominated by Northern NGOs, with Southern NGOs concentrating their efforts on influencing decision-makers within their own countries. This is, however, beginning to change.

Northern NGOs are increasingly being challenged by their Southern partners to put more resources into education, campaigning and advocacy. The 'Manila Declaration' issued by Southern NGO leaders in June 1989, for example, called on their Northern counterparts to monitor and campaign on issues such as official aid and multinational corporations. African NGOs meeting at the UN Special Session on Africa in 1986 drafted a declaration which, inter alia, called on Northern NGOs to 're-orientate their activities' towards development education, advocacy and information flows, and in particular to attack 'policies of their governments, corporations and multilateral institutions ... which adversely affect the quality of life and political and economic independence of African countries' ('Declaration of NGOs on the African Economic and Social Crisis'). In 1989 a larger gathering of African NGOs and others meeting in Arusha made similar points (the 'Arusha Declaration'). And many Latin American NGO leaders have called for a new relationship with Northern NGOs in which influencing is the shared goal. For instance Mario Padron (1987) criticises the majority of Northern NGOs for their reluctance to spend money on development education, saying that they 'accept too easily the idea that funds are only for the poor'. A new, genuinely two-way relationship between Northern and Southern NGOs, in which development education in the North is a shared responsibility, is essential, he argues, for moving 'from development aid to development co-operation'.

Southern NGOs are saying that it is not enough to give money, what is needed is political action to help them in the struggle to get the rich North off the backs of the South's poor. In effect they are saying, to quote Larry Minear (1987), 'Don't just do something. Stand there!' Many Northern NGOs have assumed the role of ambassadors for the world's poor. With this goes a responsibility to represent the political concerns of the poor. This entails helping to make the political and economic institutions of the world more broadly accountable, injecting the voice of • the traditionally voiceless into international decision-making, and facilitating the two-way flow of information that might both improve decision-making and improve the capacity of the poor to influence those decisions. Progressive NGOs may agree with this in theory, but in practice neglect to act. Advocacy may be seen as *important* but it is not *urgent*. Consequently it is easily squeezed out by the day-to-day dilemmas and crises arising from the project activities, from donor pressures and from media enquiries.

International factors are not necessarily the most important root causes of poverty but they are ones which Northern NGOs should not ignore. If they do so they must expect to be viewed with increasing suspicion by their Southern partners. The latter are increasingly making it clear that they want a more equal partnership. As donors expect regular financial and progress reports from the projects they fund, so Southern NGOs are starting to ask their donors to report to them on the action they are taking to educate Northern publics and to tackle the international causes of global poverty.

'Street-view' credibility

Sometimes Northern NGOs are reluctant to take on this new responsibility because they have a sneaking disrespect for their own evidence. When pitted against great volumes of statistical data, their own evidence can seem flimsy and anecdotal. This lack of confidence is unwarranted. To obtain a portrait of a city there are two approaches. The first is to charter a plane and take photographs of the city from the air. This shows the main housing areas, industrial complexes, buildings, communication routes and physical terrain. It is a complete view but it only allows guesses to be made about the condition of life in the different quarters. The alternative approach is to visit particular communities or work-places, talk to the community workers or residents and stay with them long enough to appreciate their concerns and aspirations. This gives a more accurate portrait of the human condition, but a patchy view – a snapshot of a few streets, districts or ethnic groups.

Since development is essentially about the human condition, the 'street view' is at least as valid as the 'aerial view' and one in which the NGO has unchallenged advantage. The street view is perhaps less scientific but it may reveal serious problems and important issues which are not picked up by the aerial view. Whether or not these issues are general or unique to the community studied is important, but the uncertainty should not prevent the NGO from making its experience known. NGOs should make little apology for the somewhat anecdotal nature of their evidence, infuriating as development economists often find it.

For example in 1987 through its work in two poor districts of Malawi (Phalombe and Mulanje), OXFAM became concerned about the costs to the poor of closing down the marketing depots run by ADMARC, the agricultural parastatals. As part of the World Bank-funded structural adjustment programme, the Government of Malawi had agreed to start dismantling a number of parastatals, including ADMARC. There is no doubt that some changes in ADMARC were required, since it was losing money heavily. However, most of the losses were on its estate-management and food-processing operations. The 'bread-and-butter' task of basic agricultural marketing was widely regarded as one of the more efficient examples of state marketing operations in Africa. Traditionally ADMARC bought cereals after harvest, sold some to the cities and stored the remainder in its rural depots. Some months later the rural poor would have run out of food they kept back after harvest for their own use and they would engage in wage labour activities. They would then purchase food back from ADMARC depots. When the World Bank-backed programme of market liberalisation was introduced, licences were given to private merchants to buy and sell cereals and other crops. In the regions where it was felt that there were sufficient private traders to fill the gap, the ADMARC depots were closed down. ADMARC was to be reduced to a 'trader of last resort'.

From its contact with poor farmers in these areas, particularly with female-headed households, OXFAM became concerned that the valuable 'food security' role played by ADMARC would be lost. OXFAM relayed these concerns to the World Bank, but the closure of depots continued. Come the harvest, most of the sales in Phalombe and Mulanje were to private merchants. As the NGO had predicted, when farmers came to buy back food they found they simply could not afford the prices. Whereas traditionally the buying price would be about 20 per cent higher than the sale price at harvest time, the merchants were charging up to seven times the sale price. It was proving more profitable to sell the food in the nearby city of Blantyre. This resulted in immense difficulties for the poor in that region (Trivedy 1990).

When this fresh evidence was presented, the Bank investigated the claims and found them to be accurate in certain districts of the country. Generally, the Bank maintained, the new system was working well but recognised that mistakes had been made which should be corrected by strengthening the 'food-security' role played by ADMARC in vulnerable regions. This is an illustration of how NGO evidence, based on day-to-day contact with poor people in a dozen villages in one region, revealed a problem which had been overlooked by the 'aerial view' and led to the authorities pledging to take corrective action.

Examples of NGO advocacy

The combined influence of NGOs and public opinion has initiated major policy changes by Northern governments on a number of issues including:

- a code of conduct for the marketing of baby milks
- the drafting of an international essential drugs list
- removing restrictions on the importation of certain clothing manufactured in the Third World (such as shirts from Bangladesh)
- establishing an emergency reserve so that EEC food surpluses become more readily available for famine relief
- concerted action on international environmental issues such as global warming and rainforest destruction
- affording special debt relief to the poorest countries
- the imposition of sanctions to combat apartheid.

If it were possible to assess the value to the poor of all such reforms they might be worth more than the financial contribution made by NGOs. Yet only a tiny fraction of NGO resources are directed to such work. The range of issues has developed over time as the profile of lobbying NGOs has evolved and the increasing contribution of Southern NGOs to international lobbying endeavours has shifted the focus of this activity from the macro concerns of Southern governments to issues which are of more direct relevance to Southern people.

Campaigning in the 1970s

In the early 1970s the major campaigning activities of Northern NGOs followed an agenda which was largely determined by the UN system, and in particular by the objectives declared for the Second Development Decade and by the FAO's Freedom From Hunger Campaign. This trend continued throughout the decade with attention generated by the World Food Conference in 1974 and UNCTAD IV in 1976 (Lemarasquier 1987). Much NGO campaigning was rather untargeted in nature. It sought to bring about more caring attitudes amongst Northern publics and decision-makers, and to describe the immoral contrast between Western opulence and Third World misery, rather than to lever for specific changes or new policies. Where specific targets were set they again reflected the UN offered agenda. Examples were campaigns to reach the 0.7 per cent of GNP target for official aid, to increase the multilateral (as opposed to bilateral) component of official aid, to set up specific commodity agreements and to support proposals for the New International Economic Order.

Running in parallel to these campaigning activities was a more politically-charged strand, which attacked multinational corporations for exploiting the Third World. These campaigns were poorly financed and run by highly committed but inexperienced volunteers, but were highly effective at capturing the public imagination. One of the earliest examples of this was a British campaign in which the World Development Movement and War on Want joined forces to challenge the below-starvation wages paid by UK food giants to tea pickers in Sri Lanka and elsewhere. This achieved massive media coverage and forced some of the major tea companies to revise their employment practices. Another British campaign, which subsequently spread to other countries, was the attack on coffee multinationals by the specially formed Campaign Co-operative. This group financed their venture by selling instant coffee they imported directly from a government-owned factory in Tanzania. The coffee also formed the vehicle for their message – 'political packaging' – and for action. Their supporters set up stalls to sell the 'Campaign Coffee', persuaded their student unions to switch to it, got local shops to stock it, and organised coffee mornings to use it.

This was an early example of an NGO importing a basic commodity. Similar ventures during the 1970s, particularly in Holland, have influenced an important category of NGOs which are today known as the Alternative Marketing Organisations. For example the 'Max Havelaar' campaign in Holland has now captured some 2.4 per cent of the country's coffee market for its own brand name. In this case the consortium of NGOs license the name, they do not import the coffee themselves. Instead they persuade major Dutch coffee roasters to import from suppliers on a list they provide, and offer some collateral to safeguard imports and arrange the advertising and promotion.

In the late 1970s, lobbying became considerably more sophisticated, a landmark being the international baby milk campaign which culminated in an International Code of Conduct governing the marketing activities of baby milk companies, adopted by the World Health Assembly in 1981. There has been no evaluation of this campaign, but were one able to calculate the global results – in terms of infant lives saved, reduction in infant diarrhoea and marasmus, the return to breast feeding and the wasted foreign exchange saved – it would almost certainly be shown that the combined effort of NGOs, WHO, Unicef and others has been one of the most cost effective ventures in infant health care ever.

Campaigning in the 1980s

Lobbying and campaigning continued to become more sophisticated and targeted throughout the 1980s. The campaigns tended to focus on aid, trade, international finance and foreign policy in the governmental domain; and buying, selling, investing and employment practices in the corporate sphere. The major trends have been an *increasing strength* of the 'NGO lobby', a more *strategic approach* to advocacy, closer *integration* of lobbying and public campaigning/education, and more attention to the use of the *media*. The increasing strength of the NGO lobby comes in part from the substantial resources some of the larger Northern NGOs with overseas operations have begun to put into advocacy activities and from the growing credibility of the NGO sector as a whole.

Learning how best to use democratic channels has led to more strategic lobbying. For example many US groups and coalitions regularly present evidence to congressional committees and draft bills for individual congressmen and senators (the structure of the US political system gives greater opportunities for this than in most other countries). In the UK NGOs frequently submit evidence to Select Committees or to other parliamentary bodies and distribute briefings to MPs prior to debates on international issues. Furthermore, events on the mainstream political calendar are used more systematically as fora to present NGO concerns (for example the World Health Assembly on the marketing of pharmaceuticals, the

World Bank Annual Meeting on 'problem projects', the 'Group of Seven' summit on debt).

NGOs have become more forthright in inviting their supporters and the public at large to join in the lobbying. Their publicity materials regularly suggest action in addition to making donations. This, together with public concern generated by the African famine and mounting environmental crises, has sharply increased public support for NGO campaigns. For example the 'Fight World Poverty' lobby of UK parliament in 1985 set an all-time record for the number of people who met their MPs in a single day. Westminster was besieged for the whole day, every meeting room in the Commons was booked for the occasion, some 16,000 people managed to meet their MP and several thousand more took part in other meetings.

NGOs have also formed closer links with journalists and the broadcast media. Their causes are, as a result, more likely to be the subject of documentaries and feature articles. And their events are more likely to be planned with a view to being 'media-worthy'.

Key actors in advocacy

Operational NGOs have been slow to move into lobbying. Until the early 1980s their educational activity (house newspapers, leaflets, slide sets and so on) tended to emphasise the NGO's own project experience rather than the political issues of development. And their development education work in schools avoided an action agenda (though it frequently dealt with controversial issues such as the actions of multinational corporations). NGOs did little public campaigning. This is unfortunate because they are well-placed to influence Northern governments. The public at large knows them, trusts them, and has faith in their motives. Politicians and 'experts' respect the field-level evidence they bring. The media like the first-hand nature of their experience. Official aid agencies want to build closer connections and so are disposed to listen carefully to what they have to say. And celebrities stand ready to be identified with their causes. Experience of numerous campaigns shows that a modest input of time and resources can lead to quite significant policy shifts. In spite of this, the largest NGOs, especially in USA, have put very few resources into such activities.

Throughout the 1980s, however, this began to change and operational NGOs started taking more courageous steps towards lobbying. Their principal umbrella organisation, the International Council of Voluntary Agencies, has drafted a policy briefing, 'Making Common Cause Internationally', to help and encourage member agencies to formulate their individual policies on campaigning and advocacy. Operational NGOs are having to change. They are under increasing pressure from their Southern partners to become more active in both educational and campaigning activities in their home countries. The famine in Africa of 1984–85 demonstrated more clearly than ever the need for closer interaction between NGOs and official aid agencies, and the futility of NGO efforts if not combined with much bolder efforts to change development priorities. And they have seen that the pioneers of NGO lobbying have not found the consequences of their lobbying too threatening; neither their charitable status nor their donor base has been eroded – and in fact they appear to enjoy increased media coverage and public support as a result of these new activities.

What is more, the increasing environmental consciousness of politicians and the general public has heralded a new sense of realism. Conventional NGO project activities are manifestly 'finger-in-the-dyke' responses to problems that require nothing short of worldwide and whole-hearted governmental commitment to combat. This commitment is only likely to arise from concerted public pressure and hence NGOs have a special responsibility to do what they can to galvanise public opinion.

There are other trends which allow for optimism for the future of NGO lobbying: the growth of campaigning activities among Southern NGOs, new alliances with campaigning groups outside the development sphere and the emergence of highly specialised campaign groups and networks. Some Southern NGOs have prioritised lobbying in recent years (particularly in Latin America and Asia). Most of their attention has focused on domestic rather than international issues, but this is changing, especially as many of the problems they address have clear Northern connections. These NGOs may, like their Northern counterparts, comprise highly educated, politicised staff and have a Western outlook and communications style. Or they may be grassroots organisations which have direct experience of the problems. For example, the rubber tappers' union and a number of tribal indian groups in Brazil have led worldwide action for international responsibility for the protection of the Amazon rainforests. Village-level health workers have provided much of the evidence on which campaigns against the marketing malpractices of baby milk and pharmaceutical manufacturers have been based.

Many of these grassroots organisations have long had connections with Northern NGOs, but the funding relationship has been the basis for them. They now seek a different form of partnership in which Northern NGOs lend their name, media skills and contact with people of influence to help champion the cause they are fighting. The increased prominence of Southern NGOs has both strengthened international lobbying and changed its focus. Campaigns for the New International Economic Order, for official aid targets and for commodity agreements have given way to campaigns against environmentally-damaging logging operations, against marketing malpractices by Western companies and against adjustment programmes which hurt the poor. The former dwell on the unjust treatment of poor nations by rich ones, and the latter on the injustices done to poor *people*. The former demand Northern institutions 'to *do* something', implying that their sin has been past *failure to act*, rather than the active causing of damage. The latter call for harmful practices to be stopped.

These trends have not only fostered new allegiances between Northern and Southern NGOs but have also opened doors to movements outside the development sphere. At the same time as development NGOs have become more concerned with other social issues, so too various social movements have become more concerned with development and international issues.

International action on hazardous practices in the marketing of pesticides first brought a group of development and environmental NGOs together from the North and South. This was followed by concerted action against careless planning of large dams, and later by the launch of international campaigning on the rainforest issue. Similarly the analysis by NGOs of gender relationships in development has engaged the interest of the women's movement. They have helped campaign against male bias in development planning.

Campaigns to reform or scrap projects which involve the displacement of large numbers of people have been greatly strengthened by the support of Northern human rights groups. For example Survival International and other Northern NGOs have joined forces with Indonesian NGOs to press for changes in the World Bank-funded Transmigration Programme. In this scheme tens of thousands of people have been moved from the densely-populated islands – especially Java – to the sparsely-populated territory of Irian Java where the culture and environment of the indigenous tribes has become severely threatened. Other campaign issues have brought developmental NGOs together with labour unions (for example regarding the conditions of Bolivian tin miners), and with consumers organisations (for example regarding the dumping of hazardous products in the Third World).

Conclusions

The experience of the last 20 years allows us to conclude that there are five important areas to be attended to in the planning of effective lobbying and campaigning activities.

Balance macro-analysis with the use of first-hand experience   A solid understanding of the views of academics and official agencies is essential if the received wisdom is being challenged, but the NGO must also become confident in the use of its own direct experience, however anecdotal this may seem. If observation does not fit with the theory then it is the theory that is wrong, not the reality. The street view is every bit as important as the aerial view.

Choose the issue carefully   The campaign focus must genuinely be relevant to the poor, it must be supported by Southern partners, it must arise from the direct experience of the NGO, and it must be a subject on which the NGO is generally viewed as an authority. There must be clear policy objectives, which are conceivably winnable, and this may mean, pragmatically, the setting of intermediate goals. For Northern NGOs there should be some evident connection between their own countries and the issue.

Construct the expert case   Use extensively the analysis of known authorities on the subject, recruit convincing allies to the cause (for example involve respected academics in meetings with officials), ensure that all analysis and statements are scrupulously accurate, ensure that prescriptions proffered are realistic and workable. Often, NGO authors will spend months researching and writing a report, but will throw together some recommendations with relatively little thought; most readers will give much more attention to the recommendations than to the analysis.

Generate public support   No matter how well-argued the case, decision-makers may not be persuaded to change the policy in question because they are preoccupied with matters they perceive as higher up the political agenda. Hence the second prong of an effective advocacy strategy is often essential: mobilisation of public support. For this a 'human-interest' angle is necessary for attracting media attention, support from TV celebrities and other communications specialists should be sought, and a comprehensive communications strategy should be carefully planned. Sometimes it will be considered desirable to urge the NGO's supporters to undertake campaigning action. For this the degree of commitment must be carefully gauged. Strategies billed as mass campaigns should be resisted unless widespread support can be confidently anticipated; otherwise an unfortunate impression of public indifference will be conveyed. Conversely the judicious use of a small band of well motivated and carefully guided public campaigners can make a powerful difference. For public campaigning it is important to decide carefully the tone to be adopted, appropriate 'pegs' must be selected (such as demonstrations alongside official meetings, or specially planned events). Actions that supporters are asked to take must be carefully selected, realistic, and adequately resourced, including systems of 'rewards' so that the supporters feel valued and valuable.

Strive for bargaining power   Identify who are the key decision-makers or people of influence, and work strategically to achieve meetings with those people. Invite respected academics and other figures of authority who are known to support the case to join those meetings. It is equally important to listen carefully as to preach persuasively. Take careful notes, particularly of decisions reached or areas of agreement, and write afterwards to thank those met and to remind them of the decisions and agreements. After an appropriate time, follow up on those points, for example by requesting progress reports or a return meeting. The objective is to achieve official recognition that the NGO has become a party in the negotiations over the issue in question. This may be a difficult status for an isolated NGO to achieve, which is why national or international networks of NGOs are increasingly important.

By applying these formulae, it is possible for NGOs to achieve vastly greater impact in improving the situation for poor people than they can through conventional project work alone. Projects will continue to have an important place. They are innovative models from which others may draw lessons, but they are also vantage points from which the experience needed for influencing work can be derived. This experience can be vital ammunition in campaigns against the root causes of world poverty and injustice which lie in the orbit of Northern governments and institutions.

British development NGOs and advocacy in the 1990s

Chris Dolan

Introduction

During the 1980s and early 1990s donor governments and official institutions have increasingly channelled development aid through NGOs. Various reasons have been suggested for this, including a general shift in development thinking about the importance of human capital formation (World Bank 1990), and a shift from a materialist to a more humanist conception of development[1]. However, the most significant factors are the general ascendance of free market economics (Toye 1987) and its corollary, a belief that government agencies are ineffective[2]. Whatever the reason, NGOs find their credibility enhanced and their responsibilities increased; this includes a responsibility to themselves to decide where their own priorities lie.

This chapter discusses the likelihood and feasibility of British development NGOs scaling-up their impact through lobbying for and advocating systematic change rather than piecemeal reform. This would involve intensified and sustained lobbying on macro-issues such as aid, trade, debt and the environment, rather than lobbying about very specific policy issues (eg the response of the Overseas Development Administration (ODA) to an emergency in a particular country). Such an approach can be advanced for practical and theoretical reasons. At a practical level, and despite the recent increases in their funding, NGO resources remain far too small to achieve more than relatively small cases of success in operational work. At a theoretical level, if the problems of the developing world are seen as rooted in the practices, attitudes and ideology of the developed world, then operational work is no better than 'Band Aids', treating the symptoms of poverty rather than attacking the root causes: what Clark (1991:147) calls a 'curative' rather

---

[1] 'Countless projects have failed because the people whose labour was needed were unwilling participants. The technocentric as opposed to ethnocentric approach to development is doomed to failure; it ignores tastes, habits, customs, knowledge and experience. What is required is nothing less than a complete re-evaluation of the human element in development, shifting from a materialistic to a humanistic approach'.

('Giving Development a human face' – Idriss Jazairy, President of the International Fund for Agricultural Development, in *International Herald Tribune*, 23 May 1989).

[2] 'Successful programmes have not relied exclusively on government agencies, which can provide effective central support but often lack both the field staff and the flexibility to work at the local level. Instead, they have employed a mixture of institutions – NGOs, private operators, and local groups' (World Bank 1990:71).

than a 'preventive' approach to development problems.

A key proponent of such lobbying and advocacy is David Korten (1987). He argues that historically most NGOs pass through three generations of programme strategy. They start by doing relief and welfare work, move on to small-scale self-reliant development programmes, and finally involve themselves in sustainable systems development. For Korten the role of Northern NGOs (NNGOs) in sustainable systems development is to support Southern NGOs (SNGOs) technically and financially, and to engage in advocacy and lobbying of their own countries' governments and of international institutions. NNGOs should have little or no direct involvement in operations overseas.

The reasons for adopting this strategy are presented in his 'Global Realities' paper (Korten 1989), where he argues that there is among NNGOs an 'emerging new vision' based on attacking the '... underlying causes of underdevelopment rather than the symptoms': with this new vision[3] he argues that it is possible to draw a distinction between *humanitarian* assistance to the victims of global systems failures and *development* assistance that attacks the causes of those failures. Korten is critical of NNGOs which allow humanitarian concerns to dominate their agenda, and suggests that advocacy and lobbying are the most meaningful form of development assistance NNGOs can provide.

Korten's model is initially attractive for several reasons. By identifying a regular dynamic of change in NGOs it appears to have some predictive power. It also appears to have normative or prescriptive power; later generations of NGOs are better than earlier ones, as development assistance is better than humanitarian assistance. Thirdly, it stresses the distinction between governmental and non-governmental organisations, making governments clear targets for blame, and NGOs advocates for necessary changes.

This chapter assumes that for British NGOs to lobby effectively for systematic change they would need to reach a high degree of consensus. This is because any agency advocating radical changes in isolation would be vulnerable to the withdrawal of support from funders, and the impact of an individual agency is likely to be marginal, in any case.

Given this assumption Korten's model raises the question of whether or not British NGOs actually have the 'shared vision' of global systems failure which would be needed to mount a concerted and effective critique of Western governments on matters such as aid, trade, debt and the environment? If they do not currently have such a vision, what is the likelihood of it emerging?

A second question is whether the socio-political environment in which British NGOs operate allows such a critique to be raised or take root? Even if within NGOs there are those who subscribe to the view that what is needed is an attack on the root causes rather than symptoms, what is the economic and political feasibility of a strategy which focuses on advocacy and lobbying at the expense of more direct involvement in the field?

The internal dynamics of NGOs

To answer the first question, the internal dynamics of NGOs, and of the NGO sector (defined by its legal status) were examined. Fourteen in-depth interviews were

---

[3] How 'new' is open to question, resembling as it does the dependency theories of the 1960s.

conducted with individual senior staff of British NGOs. The focus was mainly on operational agencies, because a change in their approach would be indicative of an emerging new vision in which British NGOs move to a support role.

One potential indicator of a shared vision of development would be a common response to the recent rapid increase in official funding. For example, the ODA's Joint Funding Scheme for NGOs has risen from £2.25 million in 1983/84 to £22.8 million in 1991/92 and is planned to reach £28 million in 1992/93. This is the fastest-growing part of the aid programme, but it only represents a part of ODA's support for NGOs. Some agencies choose to restrict income from official sources to a set proportion of total income. However, although the dangers of co-optation by government were mentioned by interviewees several times, NGOs generally seem to have taken money when it is available, as a glance at many annual reports shows. ACORD saw its income leap from £3,600,803 in 1984 to £6,243,673 in 1985. SOS Sahel reports a 78 per cent increase in annual income in its 1990 Annual Report, while Water Aid's 1990 Annual Review states that 'in 1981/82 Water Aid's income was £25,000. Eight years later that figure has grown more than one hundredfold to £2.7 million'. SCF's income has grown from about £6 million ten years ago, to £60 million in 1991.

Such funding opportunities may force agencies into thinking more strategically and identifying high performing activities to expand. Not necessarily a bad thing. On the other hand, such increases may stretch an agency's absorbtive capacity to the point where it threatens to become funding rather than programme led. In particular, funding application procedures often involve thinking through the planning and reporting process in a specific way[4]. This is a bureaucratic inevitability, but ensuring that satisfactory fundraising systems and systems of accountability to donors are in place may become a higher priority than, say, the evaluation of a project's contribution to a broader poverty-reduction strategy. Indicators of agencies being funding-led include their failure to increase funding of research at the same rate as the funding of operations overseas, and a tendency to focus on particular areas of competence. Both tendencies may make it more difficult for agencies to obtain the sort of macro-perspective which lobbying for systematic change would demand.

A second indicator of a shared vision of development would be a shared (and relatively politicised) language. With this in mind, interviewees were asked to explain how they understood a number of terms which frequently appear in NGO reports and describe activities or processes that NGOs are believed to be better at than governments: *scaling-up, participation, empowerment, sustainability, linkage* and *co-optation.*

The responses suggest that these words have almost as many different interpretations as users. Although the *scaling-up debate* is an attempt to consciously and positively address the fear that NGOs create little islands of success but have no major impact, relatively few people interviewed had come across the term before, let alone formed strong views about what it might entail. *Participation* was interpreted more as a homespun psychology of motivation to enhance operational effectiveness than a development goal in its own right. *Empowerment* was a term avoided by some interviewees as being dangerously

---

[4] See for example the ODA's recommended 'Project Framework', Appendix E of *The Joint Funding Scheme Guidelines on Project Proposals.*

political, but embraced by others as the key to meaningful development. The case of *sustainability* was an interesting one as, given that environmental destruction is a powerful motivation for an 'emerging new vision', one might expect environmental sustainability to be a high priority. In fact sustainability was generally explained by interviewees in terms of *institutional* rather than *ecological* survival.

Asked directly whether they saw lobbying and advocacy as a key concern, respondents expressed differing opinions. Some thought that being non-governmental should be taken to mean *no* input into 'governmental' issues. For some types of relief and development work an apolitical image is a pre-requisite, the most obvious example being the International Red Cross. Those who felt that lobbying and advocacy was important diverged on whom to lobby (governments and institutions, key individuals), what to lobby on (sanctions, debt, structural problems, geo-political issues, ODA's emergency response) and how to lobby (on the basis of a macro-perspective or on the basis of evidence collected at the micro-level).

These differences are expressed in the internal structures of individual NGOs, in particular the degree to which information systems are prioritised. Christian Aid, for example, restructured several years ago into a matrix system whereby each region has its own aid specialists, educationalists, journalists, fund-raisers, etc., rather than the organisation having discrete functional divisions. This is still relatively unusual for NGOs, however.

Such divergences in approach and prioritisation are large enough to throw into question the notion of a shared vision, or of a strong sectoral identity which it was suggested earlier would be necessary to achieve significant lobby impacts. On the contrary, it seems to be a case of survival of the fittest in which the promotion of individual agencies' distinctive images rather than the image of the sector as a whole is of prime importance. This contributes to the professionalisation of the aid business, and, by default, to the closer integration of NGOs into officially approved activities.

This situation is illustrated by a reluctance to exploit complementarities to any degree. Consortia, which in theory would exemplify a shared vision, are shied away from as soon as there is an open development agenda (such as trade or aid policy) rather than a specific humanitarian emergency to respond to. Few people are willing to work alongside those from other NGOs, because both individual careers and agency profile are at stake. Ironically, even the ICRC finds situations where individual Red Cross societies will go it alone rather than co-operate with sister societies.

Overall then, the internal dynamics of NGOs and the NGO sector do not appear conducive to a scaling-up of impact by lobbying and advocacy work. One common and very important point which does emerge however, is a belief that advocacy and lobbying must be anchored in an agency's work in the field if it is to have any weight with the official institutions. In other words it should take place alongside and 'as a natural extension of its project work' (Clark 1991:147), rather than in isolation from project experience. Such an approach makes critiques of specific policies more likely than radical systematic critiques, and also suggests that Korten's support role is not likely to be realised in the current climate.

The external context

The argument now turns to the second question raised by Korten's model: does the socio-political environment in which British NGOs operate allow a fundamental critique of official policies and strategies to be raised or to take root? Supposing British NGOs wanted to, could they shift from the current emphasis on overseas programmes and projects to a more explicitly educative and political role at home?

Of the several constraints on British NGOs, charitable status and the public perception of charitable giving are the two which most obviously deter them from such a shift. Both can be seen to have more leverage in a climate of competition for funds. Charitable status brings with it tax concessions worth up to 30 per cent of an agency's income, and also allows them to tap into a rich vein of charitable giving by the British public.

Charitable status

A letter sent by the Executive Director (UK) of the International Freedom Foundation (IFF) to its supporters exemplifies the sort of problem that UK development NGOs presently face:

> ... the report details the systematic transformation which has taken place within many British-based 'development charities' in the 1980s. It traces the emergence, under the cloak of famine relief and development aid, of highly politicised 'charitable' organisations whose traditional functions have been relegated to a secondary role, behind a narrow political agenda. Organisations such as Christian Aid and Oxfam seem to have been 'captured' at their centres by small cliques of ideologically motivated individuals who see such organisations, with existing positive reputations, as ideal vehicles for their new agendas.
>
> Radical socialist and Marxist campaigns are now a daily occurrence from some of Britain's largest charities and all of this benefiting from the taxpayer's subsidy. This situation is not only morally distasteful, but breaches the very (charitable) laws which allow these organisations to prosper financially.

> (IFF 1989)

The difficulty is that British charity law has evolved over the centuries on a case-law approach, on the grounds that it allows flexibility as new needs arise or old ones become obsolete or are satisfied. The effect is that charitable NGOs are at the mercy of the Charity Commissioners' interpretation of what constitutes appropriate political activity. The National Council of Voluntary Organisations (NCVO 1989:para 9) states that, 'charities have both the right and the duty to undertake responsible political activity on issues relating to their particular charitable objects'. However the distinction between objects and means of achieving them is not clear and is open to interpretation on a case-by-case basis by the Charity Commission. Although the Commission is not over-eager to remove charitable status, the financial implications of such a move are well understood by NGOs and the possibility of deregistration serves as a considerable implicit discouragement to testing the boundaries of 'responsibility'.

The paradoxical outcome of this is that while the British government begins to make noises about tying aid to good governance, and welcomes indigenous NGOs as a source of pluralism[5], British NGOs are not allowed to campaign on issues such as apartheid and sanctions[6]. It also means that they must refer all advocacy to humanitarian motivations[7], the very opposite of Korten's recommendation that the humanitarian motivations should be dropped in favour of developmental ones.

Clearly, charity law is something which could be lobbied about, though as Gladstone (1982:7) suggests, '... little is likely to change [in the charity laws] without at least a degree of consensus and solidarity about what changes are needed'.

Public perceptions

Public perceptions of the purpose of charitable giving are also a constraint on British NGOs. In a report on development education in Britain, Arnold wrote that

> ... any realistic assessment suggests that development education is still a very marginal activity in Britain, and has not succeeded in getting development issues anywhere near the mainstream of government policy concerns or public consciousness.

(Arnold 1988:187)

This is partly due to what Arnold describes as

> ... a lack of clarity of purpose, leading to a variety of sometimes conflicting messages about what the Third World is like and what should be done about it ... Development educators are quick to point out, of course, that development issues are highly complex ... But the wide variety of messages does lead to confusion, and probably reinforces the marginal status of development education by enabling critics to dismiss it as soft or unprofessional.

(Arnold 1988:184)

Arguably, the immediate effect of a lack of shared understanding of development issues between agencies, and between agencies and their constituents, is that their room for manoeuvre (both in their overseas work and their advocacy at home) is

---

[5] 'In a comment that appeared to signal Britain's willingness to take a more active part in encouraging individuals and parties who sought to reform corrupt governments, Mr Hurd said "we should also look out for countervailing sources of power where it makes sense to do so along with NGOs"' (Michael Holman, 'UK strengthens linking of human rights to aid', *Financial Times*, 1 October 1990).

[6] 'It cannot be acceptable for any charity to run public campaigns against the policy of any government (whether at home or abroad) nor can a resulting increase of support and donations ever be a justification or an amelioration of the offence' (Charity Commission 1991:15).

'The charity should not be lending its name to securing the abolition or otherwise of apartheid in general or the continuance or otherwise of sanctions in particular. These are political questions which are not within the remit of charity' (ibid:16).

[7] See, for example, a recent letter to *The Guardian* from CIIR, CAFOD, Christian Aid and OXFAM in response to criticism of their work on the GATT agricultural trade talks:

'As you acknowledge, the issues involved are complex. They are also of profound humanitarian significance. Increased food self-reliance is vital if the spectre of hunger and famine is to be banished from sub-Saharan Africa and other developing regions ...' (*The Guardian*, Monday 26 August 1991).

restricted. Private donors wish to feel that their money is producing immediate tangible benefits rather than being spent on lobbying and advocacy, the ultimate outcome of which is unpredictable. Faced with the evidence that their generosity is only having a tiny impact, private donors may well succumb to compassion fatigue rather than trying to find out why their compassion is not working

Given their charitable history, British NGOs are unlikely to abandon, or even seek to modify their status while the British public continues to hold the view that the problems of the Third World can be solved by donations to charity. The pressure to raise funds for operational activities means that NGOs are more likely to want to be seen as charities and to seek to ensure that they capture as large a share as possible of public donations, than to try and change public perceptions by prioritising development education.

However, as a long-term strategy for enhancing their capacity to engage in more politicised debates the British NGOs do need to look very seriously at the level of development education they offer both to supporters and the wider public. The relatively low level of development education today will ensure that it is difficult to increase it in the future, even though scaling-up development education is a necessary concomitant for scaled-up lobbying and advocacy work. For such work to be successful requires a wider spread of popular support if politicians are not to dismiss NGOs as fringe political activists of little consequence to their own careers. NGOs have increased the scale of their funding and overall activities in recent years but their lobbying power will not increase until they have more informed constituents.

Further issues

In the course of this research two further themes were identified which challenge Korten's 'emerging new vision' and suggest that British NGO activity is more appropriately understood within an alternative interpretive framework. First, individual British NGOs do not operate in a standard fashion throughout the globe. They are far more likely to fund indigenous agencies in Asia than in Africa because it is easier to find SNGOs adapted to Northern donor requirements in terms of management and administrative capacity in Asia.

Second, the major British NGOs are finding themselves under increasing pressure either to augment their emergency and relief work, or to become involved in it for the first time. While it is possible to explain what seem to be increasing numbers of disasters as the product of unforeseeable 'acts of God', an alternative explanation, certainly in Africa, is that many of the problems are associated with long-term processes of integration into the global economy and the political influences of the world's most powerful states. The current situation in the Horn of Africa is an obvious example of this.

In operational terms, the result is that the development/relief dichotomy becomes increasingly blurred, further undermining Korten's proposition that NGOs move away from a humanitarian ethos towards a development one. If, as some predict, the rate of man-made and natural disasters increases in the 1990s, there will be increasing calls for large NGOs to prioritise rather than abandon their original humanitarian ethos.

Conclusions

Four particular points must be noted in conclusion.

- The internal dynamics of British NGOs are characterised by a wide variety of underlying philosophies expressed in divergent approaches, different internal structures, and a tendency to enter into competition rather than collaboration.
- This is compounded by a tight financial situation following a period of rapid growth in funding. NGOs with charitable status are wary of engaging in political activities because loss of charitable status would entail both loss of substantial tax concessions and, perhaps, the loss of public support. Even where they do not engage in activities which could be labelled political, agencies' freedom of manoeuvre is restricted by the general public's understanding of the function of charitable development organisations.
- The fact that individual British NGOs do not work in a standard manner throughout the globe suggests that instead of their being seen as advocates for significant change they are better understood as 'midwives' in the processes of cultural transition which occur as regions are integrated into the capitalist economic and political system.
- The above conclusions suggest that the distinctions between governmental and non-governmental agencies that many assume are too sharply drawn. British NGOs will tend to seek constructive collaboration with governmental organisations rather than analyse and criticise their policies and operations. To the extent that they professionalise their working practices and image, they will become closer to rather than more distanced from official agencies.

The factors outlined above suggest that in the 1990s British NGOs will not shift towards advocacy and lobbying as the principal way to scale-up their impact. This does not, however, mean that British NGOs will become quiescent public-service contractors. As competition forces organisations to more clearly identify and specify their strengths a trend is likely to emerge towards enjoying distinct areas of competence. This is already occurring to an extent in disaster relief work – OXFAM are the water specialists and SCF the health specialists. This will contribute to greater operational impact. International aid institutions will seek to replicate successful NGO initiatives, and NGOs' credibility with official institutions as advocates of reform for specific official policies, especially in social development, will be enhanced. Thus NGOs will survive institutionally and can expect to have some success in achieving piecemeal rather than systemic reform. Perhaps, they can then be a little 'unreasonable', but from within the mainstream rather than from outside it.

Part VI
Conclusion

20
Making a difference? Concluding comments
Michael Edwards and David Hulme

Introduction

What, then, are we to conclude from the rich diversity of experiences presented in this book? The most obvious point to note is that there are no straightforward answers to the question of how to enhance the developmental impact of NGOs. There are strong arguments for adopting all, or any, of the strategies represented. But each strategy faces significant obstacles that must be overcome if it is to be effective, and the efficacy of each can be challenged by critical counter-arguments. There is, therefore, no such thing as an 'optimal' strategy for all NGOs, even given similarity in context and background. This does not imply that all choices are equally valid, for NGOs have considerable 'room for manoevure' in their decisions and there will be more and less effective approaches for achieving impact in particular situations.

A summary of the lessons which we feel can be drawn from experience thus far, and a listing of the key issues that must be considered when a choice is being made, is presented in Table 20.1. This list is not comprehensive, and it only partly illuminates the costs and benefits of the three approaches identified in our Introduction: additive, multiplicative, and diffusive. It is not yet possible to produce definitive judgements about these approaches, but the following conclusions can be inferred from the evidence currently available.

First, whatever strategy is chosen to increase impact must be subjected to rigorous analysis before and during implementation, to ensure that decisions are based on the strongest possible foundation and that effectiveness is measured over time. NGOs will have to be much more systematic about appraisal, monitoring and evaluation. More emphasis will need to be placed on research and the documentation and dissemination of experience. The need for these changes will increase as agencies move towards multiplicative and diffusive strategies in their work. As Chambers (this volume) stresses in relation to 'self-spreading and self-improving', NGOs who are successful in this respect will have to develop the openness, self-criticism and co-operative spirit characteristic of a learning organisation. Developing these attitudes and approaches will help NGOs to build

Table 20.1:   *Scaling up NGO impact: some lessons of experience and key issues*

1. Scaling-up via working with government

Lessons

■ NGOs must work within the constraints of government systems – poorly-resourced, poorly-motivated usually bureaucratic agencies that are resistant to change;
■ Personal relationships with key staff are crucial;
■ The problems of employing expatriate staff – unsustainability, problems of handover – must be thought through in advance;
■ High mobility of government staff reduces impact of advice and training – tackle this issue directly if feasible;
■ Allow government to take the credit for success;
■ Plan for very long time-horizons;
■ Concentrate on policy reform at central government level;
■ Recognise that larger donor influence on policy reform outweighs that of NGOs and select a complementary strategy to lobby donors.

Key issues

■ Can governments be reformed? If so, which types should one focus on?
■ How should Northern NGOs relate to Southern governments?
■ How should NGOs cope with the practical difficulties of working within government systems?

2. Scaling-up via operational expansion

Lessons

■ NGOs adopting this approach must anticipate dramatic strains as organisational culture is changed and they restructure;
■ Sustainability should be planned from the start in financial, manpower and legal terms;
■ Extensively pursuing donor preferences for service delivery is likely to convert NGOs from agencies with a 'mission' into public-service contractors;
■ This strategy may require trade-offs from other strategies – the tone of advocacy work and the nature of support for local initiatives may be compromised.

Key issues

■ Does operational expansion automatically reinforce existing power structures?
■ Does the 'donor view' of NGOs define a narrow role for them in terms of strategies and activities? Does it reduce accountability to intended beneficiaries and supporters?
■ Can NGOs expand operations without becoming bureaucracies?
■ Does operational expansion by NGOs displace the state and strengthen policies of liberalisation and unfettered markets?
■ Are there some services that *only* NGOs can provide, so that operational expansion is the only option?

3. Scaling-up via lobbying and advocacy

Lessons

■ To date NGO influence has been confined to projects rather than fundamental attitudes and ideology;
■ Donors are keen to see NGOs as project implementers, not actors in a policy dialogue;
■ NGO knowledge of donors is partial and this limits their impact;
■ A practice base is important for UK NGOs to legitimise their lobbying work with charitable status;
■ UK charity law will significantly determine the future influencing work of UK NGOs with charitable status.

Key issues

- How to carry out successful influencing while remaining within charity law?
- How to balance programme work with influencing, and link the two more closely together?
- Which issues and targets are most important for influencing?
- Should NGOs seek to influence symptoms or causes, programme design or underlying ideology?
- How can Northern and Southern NGOs combine to influence donors more effectively?

4. Scaling-up via supporting local level initiative

Lessons

- The opportunity for effective involvement in such work is very dependent on state sanctioning. Where such approval is denied NGOs must carefully analyse their options for becoming 'apolitical' or partisan;
- Official aid agencies are unwilling to support serious initiatives to mobilise and empower disadvantaged groups;
- Many NGOs are happy to obfuscate the extents to which their social mobilisation programmes are intended to empower or deliver services. At times this may be a tactical device (to hide intentions from the state) but commonly it is based upon an unwillingness to make this key decision.

Key issues

- Should strategies of social mobilisation be the major role for Southern and Northern NGOs in the future?
- What steps can be taken to ensure that grassroots organisations are member-controlled and do not merely follow the dictats of their 'parent' NGO?
- Are the regional patterns of social mobilisation very different? If so, what might Africa or Asia learn from Latin America?
- Should networks of local organisations remain politically unaffiliated or should they openly ally with political parties?
- What are the trade-offs between empowerment and welfare, when 'parent' NGOs become heavily involved in mounting donor-financed service-delivery activites?
- How can cadres of professional social mobilisers be developed without a reduction in the quality of relationships with intended beneficiaries?

---

credible alternatives at micro- and macro-levels to conventional economic thinking, surely one of the major tasks of the next ten years. Claims to NGO 'success', 'comparative advantage' and 'impact' must be demonstrated in a systematic way to those outside the NGO community.

Second, all strategies for scaling-up have implications for the linkages (to 'the poor', 'partners', supporters or volunteers) through which NGOs base their claim to legitimacy ie their right to intervene in the development process. Indeed, NGOs should not attempt to scale-up anything before identifying what role or roles are legitimate for them as international NGOs, national NGOs or grassroots movements, in different contexts. The degree to which a strategy or mix of strategies compromises the logic by which legitimacy is claimed needs to be considered carefully, and can provide a useful means of testing whether organisational self-interest is subordinating mission when a choice is being made. International NGOs need to be particularly careful here, given the increasing scale of resources available to them and the opportunities they have for influencing Northern donors and governments. The choice to work directly (ie operationally) at grassroots level in other peoples's countries, or to work within or alongside their governments, needs to be based on a clear analysis of the strength and role of local institutions and the comparative advantages of local and international agencies in promoting positive change. Similarly, NGOs who claim to represent the 'voice of the poor' in Washington or Brussels must specify how this authority is derived and ensure that grassroots experience is not misrepresented or distorted by intermediaries. In this respect, multiplicative and diffusive strategies for scaling-up may be easier for international NGOs to justify than the additive approach (this theme is taken up below). One clear conclusion which emerges from all the case studies represented in this book is that *institution-building* is the critical task facing all NGOs in their search for sustainable development. This applies as much to the institutions of government and civil society as it does to themselves. Building effective, representative and sustainable institutions at different levels implies a much longer time-horizon in funding and other support than many NGOs are used to.

Third, the roles of different types of NGO are changing rapidly in response to forces and trends within and outside the voluntary sector. As grassroots movements and national NGOs become stronger and more confident in their work, international NGOs can concentrate more and more on supportive advocacy at the level of their own governments, public opinion in the North and global institutions, a development articulated very clearly in many of the chapters in this book. But such a move poses considerable challenges for NGOs, particularly those based in the North. They will have to develop new skills (in information and communication), and new partnerships – both with each other (to forge more powerful alliances on common themes) and with their 'partners' in the South (on whom they will rely for information, experience and their claim to legitimacy). This will be a particular challenge to international NGOs who see a 'practice base' (ie concrete initiatives controlled by them in the South) as a pre-requisite for institutional learning, legitimacy (in the eyes of their donors and supporters) and credibility in lobbying. Clearly, no strategy for scaling-up can be effective without concrete improvements in people's lives at grassroots level. The question NGOs must ask themselves is who carries responsibility for direct support of such initiatives, and for those organisations that do not or cannot be directly involved, how to link grassroots experience more powerfully with their own activities on the national and international stage? However, it is not just the NGOs themselves who will need to be convinced of the need for such changes, but also, and perhaps more importantly, the individual and institutional donors on whom they depend for financial support. At present it is difficult to see mass public or government support for a move away from concrete intervention 'overseas' to advocacy and education in the countries of the North. This transition, if transition it is, will need to be very carefully managed, and will require considerable work by international NGOs to legitimise their changing roles in the eyes of their own supporters and governments. Few NGOs (at least in the UK) are prepared for this challenge.

In addition, increasing interest and support for NGOs among official donor agencies may foster a predisposition towards operational and organisational expansion. While NGOs themselves may see a logical progression from additive to multiplicative and diffusive strategies, pressures from the donor community may force them in the opposite direction. A fundamental choice all NGOs will face is whether to scale-up along the lines that aid donors and host governments prefer, or whether to keep some distance, and accept the reduced access to official funding that this will entail. Donor incentives need to be treated cautiously because the decision to expand with official finance may foreclose potential courses of future action, orient accountability upwards (redefining the relationship between an NGO and its intended beneficiaries) and support policies for wholesale economic liberalisation, which may not be in the longer term interests of the poor. The increasing dependence of many development NGOs in the USA on US government funding is not unrelated to the decline of the voluntary sector there as an independent and critical influence on official policy.

Fourth, the interactions of different strategy mixes need to be considered carefully. Combinations of strategy offer the possibility of mutual re-inforcement, as Hall, Dawson, Mitlin and Satterthwaite, and other authors in this volume show in relation to policy lobbying and the strengthening of local initiative. This mutual reinforcement of strategies seems to be especially significant where NGOs have a particular sectoral specialisation (eg health, housing, forestry). NGOs need to investigate more systematically ways in which such 'complementarities' can be strengthened and exploited. Equally, certain combinations of strategy within the same NGO can generate internal conflict and reduce effectiveness significantly – as when advocacy annoys the state or donors so much that permission to mount field operations, or future access to funds, are denied. Experience shows that it is difficult (though not impossible) to combine additive, multiplicative and diffusive strategies in the same organisation, because of the very different implications of each of these approaches for internal systems, structure, management, attitudes and priorities.

Finally, the biggest challenge facing all NGOs is how to achieve greater impact (with all that this implies in the way of evaluation, strategic thinking, and improved systems) while maintaining their traditional strengths such as flexibility, innovation and attachment to values and principles. The processes described by Karina Constantino-David (this volume) in relation to NGOs in the Philippines are mirrored very closely on the international NGO scene: with greater access to resources comes a preoccupation with growth, a tendency towards bureau-cratisation, and an increasing danger of becoming 'contractors for the international system and its agenda.' These pressures are well-known to NGOs in the UK, who have seen their income grow dramatically over the last ten years. The recruitment of professional accountants, computer experts, fund-raisers and other 'managers' to support organisational growth comes as something of a shock to NGO staff who are used to working on a smaller and more informal basis, and this induces tensions explored by Billis and MacKeith, Hodson and other contributors to this volume. Sooner or later, calls for 'performance-related pay' and other attributes of the commercial sector rear their head and internal organisational issues, rather than mission, may begin to determine decisions. Of course, such trends are not inevitable, but they do need much more careful planning and consideration than most NGOs have thus far been able or willing to give them. There is a particular danger that multiplicative and diffusive approaches to scaling-up will be frustrated by organisational growth because they depend so much on openness, innovation, flexibility and learning. Yet it is clear from the experiences related in this book that no approach will be successful in organisations which cannot be self-critical, creative and open to change. The NGO of the future may look very different from the NGO of the present, but in all cases a fundamental requirement will be how to retain a sense of humility while celebrating and building on what is successful. NGOs need to be careful that the increasing resources and attention they are receiving from the international community do not lure them into a sense of complacency or self-delusion, when their real impact on world poverty still remains very limited.

Clearly, scaling-up NGO impact is not synonymous with expanding the staff and budgets of NGOs. The choices facing NGOs are complex, since all options seem certain to generate internal difficulties and all require careful analysis to gain an insight into 'who gains and who loses' when a particular option is selected. Either by design or default all NGOs will have to make these strategic choices in the coming years. Whether or not they 'make a difference' will be determined by the quality of the choices they make.

References

Chapter 1

Bratton, M (1990) 'Non-governmental organisations in Africa: can they influence public policy?,' *Development and Change* 21, pp. 87–118.

Brown, D and Korten, D (1989) 'Understanding voluntary organisations: guidelines for donors', *Policy, Planning and Research Working Papers*, no. WPS 258, World Bank, Washington DC.

Clark, J (1991) *Democratising Development: The Role of Voluntary Organisations*, Earthscan, London.

Copestake, J (1990) 'The scope for collaboration between government and PVOs over agricultural technology development: the case of Zambia', mimeo, Overseas Development Institute, London.

Dichter, T W (1989) 'NGOs and the replication trap', *Findings '89*, Technoserve.

Edwards, M (1991) 'Strengthening government capacity for national development and international negotiation: the work of Save the Children Fund in Mozambique', paper presented to the Annual Conference of the Development Studies Association, Swansea.

Edwards, M (1989) *Learning from Experience in Africa*, OXFAM, Oxford.

Esman, M and Uphoff, N (1984) *Local Organisations: Intermediaries in Rural Development*, Cornell University Press, Ithaca.

Fowler, A (1991) 'The role of NGOs in changing state–society relations: perspectives from East and Southern Africa', *Development Policy Review* 9(1), pp. 53–84.

Fowler, A (1990) 'Doing it better? Where and how NGOs have a comparative advantage in facilitating development', *AERDD Bulletin* 28.

Fowler, A (1988) 'NGOS in Africa: achieving comparative advantage in relief and microdevelopment', *IDS Discussion Paper* no. 249, Institute for Development Studies, University of Sussex.

Goldman, I, Mellors, R and Pudsey, D (1989) 'Facilitating sustainable rural development – an experience from Zambia', *Journal of International Development*, 1(2), pp. 217–230.

Hashemi, S (forthcoming) 'NGOs in Bangladesh', *Journal of International Development*.

Hirschmann, A O (1984) *Getting Ahead Collectively: Grassroot Experiences in Latin America*, Pergamon Press, Oxford.

Jha, S (1989) 'Internationalising national decisions', *Mainstream*, 8 July 1989, Delhi.

Korten, D (1990) *Getting to the 21st Century: Voluntary Action and the Global Agenda*, Kumarian Press, West Hartford.

Korten, D (1980) 'Community organisations and rural development: a learning process approach', *Public Administration Review* 40, pp. 480–511.

Leonard, D (1982) 'Choosing among forms of decentralization and linkage' in D Leonard and D Marshall (eds), *Institutions of Rural Development for the Poor*, University of California, Berkley.

Morley, D, Rhode, J and Williams, G (1983) *Practising Health for All*, Oxford University Press, Oxford.

Myers, R (1992) *The Twelve Who Survive*, Routledge, London.

Nagle, W and Ghose, S (1990) 'Community participation in World Bank-supported projects', *SPRIE Discussion Paper no. 8*, World Bank, Washington DC.

Palmer, R and Rossiter, J (1990) 'Northern NGOs in Southern Africa: some heretical thoughts', paper presented to the Conference on Critical Choices for the NGO Community: African Development in the 1990s, University of Edinburgh.

Sa'di, A H (1992) 'The role of research in NGOs', paper presented at the workshop on 'Scaling-up NGO Impact', at the University of Manchester.

Salmen, L and Eaves, A (1989) 'World Bank work with non-governmental organisations', *Policy, Planning and Research Working Paper*, no. WPS 305, World Bank, Washington DC.

Tendler, J (1987) *Livelihood, Employment and Income Generating Activities*, Ford Foundation, New York.

Thomas, S (1992) 'Sustainability in relief and development work: further thoughts from Mozambique', *Development in Practice* 2(1), OXFAM, Oxford.

Toye, J (1987) *Dilemmas of Development*, Blackwell, Oxford.

Uphoff, N (1986) *Local Institutional Development*, Kumarian Press, West Hartford.

Wood, D and Palmer-Jones, J (1991) *The Watersellers*, ITDG, London.

World Bank (1991) *Co-operation between the Bank and NGOs: 1990 Progress Report*, International Economic Relations Division, World Bank, Washington DC.

Chapter 2

Clark, J (1992) 'Policy influence, lobbying and advocacy: lessons of experience from global advocacy work', in this volume.

De Coninck, J (1992) 'Evaluating the impact of NGOs in rural poverty alleviation: Uganda country study', *ODI Working Paper no. 51*, Overseas Development Institute, London.

Edwards, M and Hulme, D (1992) 'Scaling-up the developmental impact of NGOs', in this volume.

Muir, A (1992) 'Evaluating the impact of NGOs in rural poverty alleviation: Zimbabwe country study', *ODI Working Paper no. 52*, Overseas Development Institute, London.

Randal, J (1992) 'Scaling-up and community capacity: some experiences of ActionAid Uganda', paper presented at the workshop on 'Scaling-Up NGO Impact' at the University of Manchester.

Riddell, R (1990) 'Judging success: evaluating the impact of NGO poverty-alleviation projects', *ODI Working Paper no. 37*, Overseas Development Institute, London.

Riddell, R C and Robinson, MA (forthcoming 1993) *Working with the Poor: NGOs and Rural Poverty Alleviation*, James Currey, London.

Robinson, M A (1991a) 'Evaluating the impact of NGOs in rural poverty alleviation: India country study', *ODI Working Paper no. 49*, Overseas Development Institute, London.

Robinson, M A (1991b) 'Participatory impact evaluation: reflections from the field', paper presented at the annual conference of the Development Studies Association, University College of Wales, Swansea.

Roche, C (1992) 'It's not size that matters· ACORD's experience in Africa', in this volume.

White, S (1991) 'Evaluating the impact of NGOs in rural poverty alleviation: Bangladesh country study', *ODI Working Paper No 50*, Overseas Development Institute, London.

Chapter 3

Bunch, R (1985) *Two Ears of Corn: a guide to people-centered agricultural improvement*, World Neighbors, Oklahoma City.

Campbell, J, Shrestha, R, and Stone, L (1979) *Uses and Abuses of Social Science Research in Nepal*, Research Centre for Nepal and Asian Studies, Tribhuvan University, Kirtipur, Kathmandu.

Carruthers, I, and Chambers, R (1981) 'Rapid appraisal for rural development', *Agricultural Administration*, vol. 8 (6) pp. 407–422.

Conway, G (1985) 'Agro-ecosystem analysis', *Agricultural Administration*, vol. 20, pp. 31–55.

Forsyth, R (1991) 'Towards a Grounded Morality', *Changes*, vol. 9 (4) Morality and Method: II, pp. 264–278.

Gill, G (forthcoming) 'Participatory methods in policy analysis for natural resource management' in *Natural Resource Economics for India*, New Delhi, Oxford and IBH.

Grandstaff, S, Grandstaff, T, Limpinuntana, V, Simaraks, S, Smutkupt, S, and Subhadira, S (1990) *Report of an International Training Workshop* held in Northeast Thailand April–May 1990, Southeast Asian Universities Agro-ecosystem Network, Khon Kaen University.

Gypmantasiri, P et al., and Conway, G (1980) *An Interdisciplinary Perspective of Cropping Systems in the Chiang Mai Valley: Key Questions for Research*, Faculty of Agriculture, University of Chiang Mai, Thailand.

Khon Kaen University (1987) *Proceedings of the International Conference on Rapid Rural Appraisal*, Farming Systems Research and Rural Systems Research Programs, University of Khon Kaen, Khon Kaen, Thailand.

Kumar, S (1991) 'Anantapur experiment in "PRA" training', RRA Notes 13, pp. 112–117.

Mascarenhas, J et al., eds. (1991) 'Proceedings of the February 1991 Bangalore PRA trainers workshop', *RRA Notes*, 13. Mascarenhas, J, and Kumar, P (1991) 'Participatory mapping and modelling: a user's note', *RRA Notes* 12, pp. 9–20.

McCracken, J (1988) *Participatory Rapid Rural Appraisal in Gujaret: a trial model for the Aga Khan Rural Support Programme (India)*, International Institute for Environment and Development, London.

McCracken, J, Pretty, J, and Conway, G (1988) *An Introduction to Rapid Rural Appraisal for Agricultural Development*, International Institute for Environment and Development, London.

Meals for Millions (1988) *Rapid Rural Appraisal for Project Analysis planning*, Meals for Millions, Kenya.

Mettrick, H (1988) 'Uses and abuses of rapid rural appraisal', mimeo, Wageningen.

Moris, J (1970) 'Multi-subject farm surveys reconsidered: some methodological issues', paper presented for the East African Agricultural Economics Society Conference, 31 March to 4 April 1970, Dar es Salaam.

NES et al. (no date) *Participatory Rural Appraisal Handbook*, National Environment Secretariat, Government of Kenya, Clark University, Egerton University and the Center for International Development and Environment of the World Resources Institute.

Peters, T (1987) *Thriving on Chaos: handbook for a management revolution*, Pan Books in association with Macmillan, London.

PID and NES (1989) *An Introduction to Participatory Rural Appraisal for Rural Resources Management*, Program for International Development, Clark University, Worcester, Mass and National Environment Secretariat, Ministry of Environment and Natural Resources, Nairobi.

Porter, D, Allen, B, and Thompson, G (1991) *Development in Practice: paved with good intentions*, Routledge, London.

Pottier, J (1991) 'Representation and accountability: understanding social change through rapid appraisal with reference to Northern Zambia', mimeo, Department of Social Anthropology, SOAS, University of London.

Pretty, J (1990) *Rapid Catchment Analysis for Extension Agents: notes on the 1990 Kericho training workshop for the Ministry of Agriculture, Kenya*, International Institute for Environment and Development, London.

RRA Notes, Numbers 1–14 continuing, International Institute for Environment and Development, London.

Shah, A (1991) 'Shoulder tapping' *Forests, Trees and People Newsletter*, no. 14, pp. 14–15.

Theis, J and Grady, H (1991) *Participatory Rapid Appraisal for Community Development: a training manual based on experiences in the Middle East and North Africa*, IIED and Save the Children Federation, London.

Van Steijn, T (1991) 'Rapid Rural Appraisal in the Philippines: report of a study on the application of RRA by Philippines NGOs, GOs and University Institutes', draft version for comment, Council for People's Development, Manila.

Chapter 4

Aguirre, F and Namdar-Irani, M (1992) 'Complementaries and tensions in AGRARIA-state relations in agricultural development: a trajectory', *Agricultural Research and Extension Network Paper no. 32*, Overseas Development Institute, London.

Bebbington, A J, Prager, M, Riveros, H and Thiele, G (eds) (1993) *Reluctant partners? NGOs, the State and the rural poor in Latin American agricultural change*, Routledge, London.

Bebbington, A J (1991a) 'Planning rural development in local organisations in the Andes. What role for regional and national scaling-up?', RRA Notes, no. 111 (May 1991): 71–74, IIED, London.

Bebbington, A J, Carrasco, H, Peralbo, L, Ramon, G, Torres, V H and Trujillo, J (1991). *Evaluacion del impacto generado por los proyectos de desarrollo de base auspiciados por la Funcaion Inter-americano en el Ecuador*. Report to Inter-American Foundation, Rosslyn, USA.

Berdegue, J (1990) 'NGOs and farmers' organisations in research and extension in

Chile', *Agricultural Administration (Research and Extension) Network Paper 19*, Overseas Development Institute, London.

Biggs, S (1989), 'Resource-poor farmer participation in research; a synthesis of experiences from nine national and agricultural research systems', *OFCOR Comparative Study Paper No. 3*, International Service for National Agricultural Research, The Hague.

Buck, L *NGOs, Government and Agroforestry Research Methodology in Kenya*, (In preparation), Overseas Development Institute, London.

Buckland, J and Graham, P (1990) 'The Mennonite Central Committee's experience in agricultural research and extension in Bangladesh', *Agricultural Administration (Research and Extension) Network Paper 17*, Overseas Development Institute, London.

Cardoso, V H, Caso, C and Vivar, M (1991) 'A public sector on-farm research programme's informal relationships with NGOs: the PIP's growing interest in collaboration', paper presented at Taller Regional para America del Sur: Generacion y Transferencia de Tecnologia Agropecuaria; el Papel de las ONGs y el sector Publico, 2–7 December 1991, Santa Cruz, Bolivia.

Carroll, T (1992) *Intermediate NGOs: Characteristics of Strong Performers*, West Hartford, Kumarian Press.

CESA, (1991) 'La relacion de CESA con el estado en la generacion y transferencia de la tecnologia agropecuaria', paper presented at Taller Regional para America del Sur: Generacion y Transferencia de Tecnologia Agropecuaria; el Papel de las ONGs y el sector Publico, 2–7 December 1991, Santa Cruz, Bolivia.

Chambers, R, Pacey, A and Thrupp, L A (eds) (1989) *Farmer First: Farmer Innovation and Agricultural Research*, IT Publications, London.

Chakraborty, S, Mandal, B, Das, C and Satish, S (1991) 'NGOs, on-farm research and external linkages: A case of Ramakrishna Mission, Lokasiksha Parishad, Narendrapur, West Bengal', paper presented at the Asia Regional Workshop 'NGOs, Natural Resources Management and Linkages with the Public Sector', 16–20 September 1991, Hyderabad, India.

Clark, J (1991) *Democratising Development. The Role of Voluntary Organisations*, Earthscan, London.

Copestake, J G (1990) 'The scope for collaboration between government and private voluntary organisations in agricultural technology development: the case of Zambia', *Agricultural Administration (Research and Extension) Network Paper 20*, Overseas Development Institute, London.

De Janvry, A, Marsh, R, Runsten, D, Sadoulet, E, and Zabin, C (1989) 'Impacto de la crisis en la economia campesina de America Latina y el Caribe', pp. 91–205 in F Jordan (ed) (1989) *La Economia Campesina: Crisis, Reactivation, Politicas*, Instituto Interamericano de Cooperacion para la Agricultura, San Jose.

Farnworth, E G (1991) 'The Inter-American Development Bank's interactions with non-governmental environmental organisations', paper presented at the Third Consultative Meeting on the Environment, Caracas, 17–19 June 1991.

Farrington, J, Bebbington, A J and Wellard, K (1993) *Between the state and the rural poor: NGOs and agricultural development*, Routledge, London.

Farrington, J and Lewis, D (eds) (1993) *Reluctant partners? NGOs, the State and the rural poor in Asian agricultural change*, Routledge, London.

Farrington, J and Bebbington, A (1991) 'Institutionalisation of farming systems development – are there lessons from NGO-government links?', paper presented at FAO Expert Consultation on the Institutionalisation of Farming Systems Development, Rome, 15–17 October 1991.

Farrington, J and Biggs, S (1990) 'NGOs, agricultural technology and the rural poor', *Food Policy*, December 1990, pp. 479–492.

Fernandez, A (1991) 'NGOs and government: a love–hate relationship', paper presented at the Asia Regional Workshop 'NGOs, Natural Resources Management and Linkages with the Public Sector', 16–20 September 1991, Hyderabad, India.

Fowler, A (1991) 'The role of NGOs in changing state–society relations', *Development Policy Review* 9 (1), pp. 53–84.

Fox, J (ed) (1990) *The Challenge of Rural Democratisation: Perspectives from Latin America and the Philippines*, Frank Cass, London. This is also published as a special issue of *Journal of Development Studies*, Volume 26 (4).

Gilbert, E (1990) 'Non-governmental organisations and agricultural research: the experience of The Gambia', *Agricultural Administration (Research and Extension) Network Paper 12*, Overseas Development Institute, London.

Gonsalves, J and Miclat-Teves, A (1991) 'Collaboration between the International Institute for Rural Reconstruction and public sector agencies in the development of natural resources technology and training materials in the Philippines', paper presented at the Asia Regional Workshop 'NGOs, Natural Resources Management and Linkages with the Public Sector', 16–20 September 1991, Hyderabad, India.

Henderson, P and Singh, R (1990) 'NGO–government collaboration in seed supply: case studies from The Gambia and from Ethiopia', *Agricultural Administration (Research and Extension) Network Paper 14*, Overseas Development Institute, London.

Jordan, F (ed) (1989) *La Economia Campesina: Crisis, Reactivacion y Desarrollo*, Instituto Interamericano de Cooperacion para la Agricultura, San Jose.

Khan, M, Lewis, D J, Sabri, Asgar, Alia and Shahabuddin, Mohammed (1991) 'NGO work in livestock and social forestry technologies in Bangladesh – the case of Proshika', paper presented at the Asia Regional Workshop 'NGOs, Natural Resources Management and Linkages with the Public Sector', 16–20 September 1991, Hyderabad, India.

Kohl, B (1991) 'Protected horticultural systems in the Bolivian Andes: a case study of NGOs and inappropriate technology', *Agricultural Research and Extension Network Paper No. 29*, Overseas Development Institute, London.

Korten, D (1987) 'Third generation NGO strategies: a key to people-centred development', *World Development*, 15, (Supplement), pp. 145–159.

Mung'ala, P and Arum, G (1991) 'Institutional aspects of environmental research and extension in Kenya: the Department of Forestry and Kenyan energy and environment organisations', *Agricultural Research and Extension Network Paper no. 22*, Overseas Development Institute, London.

Mustafa, S, Rahman, S, Sattar, G, and Abbasi, A (1991) 'Technology development and diffusion: a case study of collaboration between BRAC and the Government of Bangladesh', paper presented at the Asian Regional Workshop 'NGOs, Natural Resources Management and Linkages with the Public Sector', 16–20 September 1991, Hyderabad, India.

Musyoka, J, Charles, R, and Kaluli, J (1991) 'Inter-agency collaboration in the development of agricultural technologies at national and district level in Kenya',

Agricultural Research and Extension Network Paper No. 23, Overseas Development Institute, London.

Nahas, F (1991) 'Appropriate technologies for improved duck-rearing in Bangladesh – the experience of Friends in Village Development', paper presented at the Asian Regional Workshop 'NGOs, Natural Resources Management and Linkages with the Public Sector', 16 20 September 1991, Hyderabad, India.

Ndiweni, M, MacGarry, B, Chaguma, A, and Gumbo, D (1991) 'Involving farmers in rural technologies: case studies in Zimbabwean NGOs', *Agricultural Research and Extension Network Paper No. 25*, Overseas Development Institute, London.

Nunberg, B (1988) 'Public sector, management issues in structural adjustment lending, *World Bank Discussion Paper 99*, World Bank Publications, Washington DC.

Ribe, H, Carvalho, S, Liebanthal, R, Nicholas, P and Zuckerman, E (1990) 'How adjustment programs can help the poor: the World Bank's experience', *World Bank Discussion Paper 71*, World Bank, Washington DC.

Richards, P (1985) *Indigenous Agricultural Revolution: Ecology and Food Production in West Africa*, Hutchinson, London.

Satish, S and Farrington, J (1990) 'A research-based NGO in India: The Bharatiya Agro-Industries Foundation's cross-bred dairy programme', *Agricultural Research and Extension Network Paper No. 18*, Overseas Development Institute, London.

Satish, S, Vardhan, T J P S and Farrington, J (1991) 'Integrated pest management in Castor: a participatory programme involving NGOs, public sector research and extension agencies and farmers in Andhra Pradesh, India', paper presented at the Asian Regional Workshop 'NGOs, Natural Resources Management and Linkages with the Public Sector', 16–20 September 1991, Hyderabad, India.

Sethna and Shah (1991) 'AKRSP's experience of influencing policy on wastelands development in India', paper presented to the Asian Regional Workshop 'NGOs, Natural Resources Management and Linkages with the Public Sector', 16–20 September 1991, Hyderabad, India.

Shah, Parmesh and Mane, P m (1991) 'Networking in participatory training and extension: experiences of the Aga Khan Rural Support Programme in Gujaret State', paper presented to the Asian Regional Workshop 'NGOs, Natural Resources Management and Linkages with the Public Sector', 16–20 September 1991, Hyderabad, India.

Sollis, P (1991) 'Multilateral Agencies and NGOs in the Context of Policy Reform', paper presented to the Conference on Changing US and Multilateral Policy Toward Central America, 10–12 June 1992, Washington DC.

Sollows, J, Jonjuabsong, L and Hwai-Kham, Aroon (1991) 'NGO–government interaction in rice-fish farming and other aspects of sustainable agricultural development in Thailand', *Agricultural Research and Extension Network Paper No. 28*, Overseas Development Institute, London.

Sotomayor, O (1991) 'GIA and the new Chilean public sector: the dilemmas of successful NGO influence over the state', *Agricultural Research and Extension Network paper No. 30*, Overseas Development Institute, London.

Tendler, J (1982) 'Turning private voluntary organisations into development agencies: questions for evaluation', *Program Evaluation Discussion Paper No. 12*, USAID, Washington DC.

Vasimalai, M (1991) 'Livelihood promotion technology for the rural poor – the case of PRADAN', paper presented at the Asian Regional Workshop 'NGOs, Natural Resources Management and Linkages with the Public Sector', 16–20 September 1991, Hyderabad, India.

Watson, H R (1991) 'NGO–GO relationships: the Rural Life Centre's way', paper presented at the Asian Regional Workshop 'NGOs, Natural Resources Management and Linkages with the Public Sector', 16–20 September 1991, Hyderabad, India.

Wellard, K and Copestake, J G (eds) (1993) *Reluctant Partners? NGOs, the State and the Rural Poor in African Agricultural Change*, Routledge, London.

World Bank (1991a) *How the World Bank Works with Non-governmental Organisations*, World Bank Publications, Washington DC.

World Bank (1991b) *World Development Report 1991: The Challenge of Development*, Oxford University Press, Oxford.

World Bank (1989) *World Bank Work with Non-governmental Organisations: Recent Experience and Emerging Trends*, World Bank Publications, Washington DC.

Chapter 5

Dheandanoo, C (1991) 'Integrated education for mentally retarded children in Thailand: a new dimension', paper presented at the Tenth Asian Conference on Mental Retardation, Karachi, November. Hegarty, S (1990) *The Education of Children and Young People With Disabilities: Principles and Practice*, UNESCO, Paris.

Helander, E et al (1989) *Training in the Community for People With Disabilities*, World Health Organisation, Geneva.

National Statistical Office (1986) *Survey on Health, Welfare and Use of Traditional Medicine*, NSO, Bangkok.

Chapter 7

Evaluation Mission (1991) *Evaluation Mission Report*, MoA/FFHC, Addis Ababa.

Ministry of Agriculture (1990) *Guidelines for MoA/NGO Collaboration*, MoA–NGO Liaison Office, Addis Ababa.

Sandford, D (1992) *Community Conservation Proposal*, FFHC/MoA, Addis Ababa.

Sandford, D and Manzi (1988) *Evaluation Report*, FFHC Ethiopia, Addis Ababa.

Wolde, G (1992) 'NGO Trends in the agricultural sector in Ethiopia', paper presented at the workshop on 'Scaling-Up NGO Impact', SCF/IDPM, Manchester University, January 1992.

Chapter 8

Channock, M (1989), *Neither Customary nor Legal: African Customary Law in an Era of Family Law Reform*, Oxford University Press, Oxford.

Child Law Review Committee (1992), *CLRC Report Part One and Part Two*, Ministry of Labour and Social Welfare, Kampala, Uganda.

Dunn, A (1992) 'The social consequences of AIDS in Uganda', Overseas Department Working Paper No. 2, Save the Children Fund, London.

Mulenga, J (1988) 'The law of Uganda in relation to the child', paper given at the National Seminar on the Convention on the Rights of the Child, Kampala, Uganda.

New Vision (1988), *President Museveni's address at a National Seminar*, Kampala, Uganda, 13/6/88.

Perry Williams, J (1991) 'An assessment of the Child Law Review Committee, Uganda, 1989–1991', MSc Dissertation, University of Lancaster.

Sparrow, J (1992) 'The Child Care Open Learning Programme in Uganda', *Development in Practice*, vol. 2 (2), OXFAM, Oxford.

Uganda Government Statutory Instruments (1991) *The Babies and Childrens Homes Rules*, nos. 13 and 14, Kampala, Uganda.

UNICEF (1988), *Report of National Seminar on Rights of the Child*, UNICEF, Kampala, Uganda.

UN, United Nations, New York.

Chapter 9

Abed, F H (1987) 'Scaling-up in Bangladesh Rural Advancement Committee' in M Bamberger, ed., *Readings in Community Participation*, vol 2, World Bank, Washington DC.

Safiqul Islam and A M R Chowdhury (nd), 'From progress to development in Sulla', mimeo, BRAC, Dhaka.

Korten, D C and R Klauss (1984), *People-Centred Development*, Kumarian Press, West Hartford.

Korten, D C (1990, *Getting to the 21st Century: Voluntary Action and the Global Agenda*, Kumarian Press, West Hartford.

Lovell, C (1991) 'Scaling-up health: two decades of learning in BRAC', mimeo, BRAC, Dhaka.

Chapter 11

Billis, D (1988) *NGO Management: A Collaborative Approach to Training and Research*, Transnational Associations 6, Geneva.

Billis, D (1989) 'A theory of the voluntary sector: implications for policy and practice', Working Paper 5, Centre for Voluntary Organisation, London School of Economics, London.

Billis, D and Harris, M (1991) 'Taking the strain of change: UK local voluntary agencies enter the post-Thatcher period', paper presented at the ARNOVA Conference, Chicago, October 1992.

Billis, D and MacKeith, J (1992) *Organising NGO: Challenges and Trends* (provisional title), Centre for Voluntary Organisation, London School of Economics, London.

Brown, L D (1990) 'Bridging organisations and sustainable development', Working Paper 8, Institute for Development Research, Boston.

Brown, L D and Covey, J G (1989) 'Organisational development in social change organizations: some implications for practice' in Drexler, S W and Grant, J (eds) *The Emerging Practice of Organisational Development*, NLT Institute for Applied Behavioral Science.

Campbell, P (1987) *Management Development and Development Management for*

Voluntary Organisations, Occasional Paper No. 3, NGO Management Network, Geneva.

Cernea, M M (1988) 'Non-governmental organisations and local development', *World Bank Discussion Paper no. 40*, World Bank, Washington DC.

Chalker, L (1989) *The Role of NGOs in Today's World*, Cecil Jackson Cole Memorial Lecture, Commonwealth Institute, London.

Clark, J (1991) *Democratising Development: The Role of Voluntary Organisations*, Earthscan, London.

Department of Health (1989) *Caring for People: Community Care in the Next Decade and Beyond*, HMSO, London.

Dichter, T W (1987) *Development Management: Plain or Fancy? Sorting Out Some Muddles*, Technoserve, Connecticut.

Dolan, C (1992) 'Will British NGOs scale-up their advocacy role in the 1990s' (this volume).

Edwards, M and Hulme, D (1992) 'Scaling-up the developmental impact of NGOs: concepts and experiences' (this volume).

Fowler, A (1990) 'What is different about managing non-governmental organisations (NGOs) involved in Third World development?', *NGO Management*, 12, pp. 18–20.

Harris, M (1989) 'The governing body role: problems and perceptions in implementation', *Nonprofit and Voluntary Sector Quarterly*, 18 (4), pp. 317–334.

Harris, M (1990), 'Voluntary leaders in voluntary welfare agencies', *Social Policy and Administration*, 24 (2), pp. 156–167.

Hodgkinson, V, Lyman, R and associates (1989) *The Future of the Nonprofit Sector*, Jossey Bass, New York.

Hodson, R (1992) 'Small, medium or large? The rocky road to NGO growth' (this volume).

Kajese, K (1987) 'The agenda of future tasks for international and indigenous NGOs: views from the South', *World Development*, 15 (Supplement), pp. 79–86.

James, E (1989) *The Nonprofit Sector in International Perspective*, Oxford University Press, New York.

Korten, D C (1989) *The U.S. Voluntary Sector and Global Realities: Issues for the 1990s*, Institute for Development Research, Washington DC.

Kramer, R (1981) *Voluntary Agencies in the Welfare State*, University of California Press, Los Angeles.

Lipsky, M and Smith, S R (1990) 'Nonprofit Organisations, Government and the Welfare State', *Political Science Quarterly*, 104 (4), pp. 625–648.

MacKeith, J (1992) *Meeting Needs or Meeting Targets: The Relationship Between Fund-raising and Service-providing Functions in a Major UK Charity*, paper presented to the Third International Conference of Research on Voluntary and Nonprofit Organisations, Indiana University, March 1992.

Powell. W (ed) (1987) *The Nonprofit Sector: A Research Handbook*, Yale University Press, Yale.

Rowbottom, R W (1977) *Social Analysis*, Heinemann, London.

Van Til, J (1988) *Mapping the Third Sector: Voluntarism in a Changing Social Economy*, Foundation Center, New York.

Yound, D (1985) *Casebook of Management for Nonprofit Organisations*, Haworth Press, New York.

Chapter 12

Billis, David (1984a) 'The missing link: some challenges for research and practice in voluntary sector management', in Knight, B (ed) *Management in Voluntary Organisations*, Occasional Paper No. 6, Association for Researchers into Voluntary Action (ARVAC).

Billis, David (1984b) *Welfare Bureaucracies: Their Design and Change in Response to Social Problems*, Heinemann, London.

Billis, David (1989) *A Theory of the Voluntary Sector: Implications for Policy and Practice*, Centre for Voluntary Organisation, Working Paper 5, London School of Economics.

Billis, David and MacKeith, Joy (1992) 'Growth and change in NGOs: concepts and comparative experience', (this volume).

Campbell, P (1987) *Management Development and Development Management for Voluntary Organisations*, NGO Management Network, Geneva.

Connors, Tracy (1980) 'The boards of directors' in Connors, Tracy (ed) *The Non-Profit Organisation Handbook*, McGraw Hill, New York.

Fowler, A (1988) 'NGOs in Africa: achieving comparative advantage in relief and microdevelopment', *IDS Discussion Paper no. 249*, Institute for Development Studies, University of Sussex.

Handy, Charles (1981) *Improving Effectiveness in Voluntary Organisation*, Bedford Square Press, London.

Harris, Margaret (1989a) 'The governing body role: problems and perceptions in implementation', *Non-profit and Voluntary Sector Quarterly* 18 (4), pp. 317–323.

Harris, Margaret (1989b) *Management Committees in Practice: A study of Local Voluntary Leadership*, Centre for Voluntary Organisation Working Paper 7, London School of Economics, London.

International Council of Voluntary Agencies (1989) 'Building sustainable NGO partnerships: global solidarity and empowerment of the people', Santo Domingo, Dominica Republic.

Kramer, Ralph (1981) *Voluntary Agencies in the Welfare State*, University of California Press, Los Angeles.

MacKeith, Joy (1992) 'Meeting needs or meeting targets: the relationship between fund-raising and service functions in a major British charity', Conference on Research on Voluntary and Non-Profit Organisations, Indiana University.

Nathan Report (1990) *Effectiveness and the Voluntary Sector*, National Council of Voluntary Organisations.

Chapter 14

Araujo, M de (1990), *Na Margem do Lago: Um Estudo Sobre o Sindicalismo Rural*, Editora Massangana, FUNDAJ, Recife.

Aufderheide, P and Rich, B (1988), 'Environmental reform and the multilateral banks', *World Policy*, vol. 2.

Barros, H de (1985), 'Modernização agrícola autoritária e desestruturação do ecosistema', *Cadernos de Estudos Sociais*, Vol. 1 (1) January–June, FUNDAJ, Recife.

Branford, S and Glock, O (1985) *The Last Frontier: Fighting Over Land in the Amazon*, Zed Press, London.

Caminhar Juntos (1991), Bulletin of the Diocese of Juazeiro, July.

Cernea, M (1988a), 'Involuntary resettlement in development projects: policy guidelines in World Bank-financed projects', *World Bank Technical Paper No. 80*, Washington DC.

Cernea, M (1988b), 'Involuntary settlement and development', *Finance and Development*, September, pp. 44–46.

CHESF (1985) *Reservatorio de Itaparica: Plano de Desocupação*, Recife.

Esteva, G and Prakash, M (1992) 'Grassroots Resistance to Sustainable Development: Lessons from the Banks of the Narmada', *The Ecologist*, 22, 2, March/April, pp. 45–51.

Goodman, D and Hall, A (eds) (1990) *The Future of Amazonia: Destruction or Sustainable Development?* Macmillan, London.

Gross, A (1989) *Fight for the Forest: Chico Mendes in His Own Words*, Latin America Bureau, London.

Hall, A (1978), *Drought and Irrigation in North-East Brazil*, Cambridge University Press, Cambridge.

Hall, A (1989a) Field visit to Sobradinho region.

Hall, A (1989b) Interviews with Polosindical officials, Petrolândia.

Hall, A (1991), *Developing Amazonia: Deforestation and Social Conflict in Brazil's Carajás Programme*, Manchester University Press, Manchester.

Hallward, P (1992) 'The urgent need for a campaign against forced resettlement', *The Ecologist*, 22, 2, March/April, pp. 43–44.

IDB (1984) 'Project performance review. Sobradinho hydroelectric project', mimeo, Inter-American Development Bank, Washington DC.

Jornal do Comercio (1992) 'Colonos insistem por uma solução', 8 April, Recife.

Paul, S (1987) 'Community participation in development projects: the World Bank experience', *World Bank Discussion Paper 6*, Washington DC.

Revkin, A (1990) *The Burning Season*, Collins, London.

Rich, B (1989) 'The Greening of the Development Banks: Rhetoric and Reality', *The Ecologist*, Vol. 19, No. 2, March/April, pp. 44–52.

Scott, A (1990) *Ideology and the New Social Movements*, Unwin Hyman, London.

World Bank (1980) 'Social issues associated with involuntary resettlement in bank-financed projects', *Operation Manual Statement*, World Bank, February, Washington DC.

World Bank (1990) 'Operational Directive 4.30: Involuntary Resettlement', *Manual Transmittal Memorandum*, World Bank, 29 June, Washington DC.

Chapter 15

Alfaro, R M (1991) *Estrategia Educativa y Politica de Transferencia de INCIDES*, INCIDES, Lima.

Arca, J M (1991) 'Reflexiones sobre el manejo de la epidemia del colera en la Unidad Departmental de Salud de Lima Sur', *Salud Popular* no. 13, INSAP, Lima.

Carrasco, G, Robles, D and Carbonel, J (1988) *Methodologia de Trabajo con Organizaciones Populares*, Presidencia de la Republica/Instituto de Investigacion, Promocion, y Apoyo para el Desarrollo: Proyecto Nacional de Participacion Popular, Lima.

Fowler, A (1988) 'Non-governmental organisations in Africa: achieving comparative advantage in relief and micro-development', *IDS Discussion Paper* no. 249, Institute of Development Studies, University of Sussex.

Fowler, A (1991) 'Building partnerships between Northern and Southern development NGOs: issues for the 1990s', *Development in Practice*, OXFAM, Oxford

Mendoza, I (1991a) 'Las politicas de promocion en salud de las ONGD Peruana (1976–1989), *Salud Popular* no. 1 (1991), INSAP, Lima.

Mendoza, I (1991b) *ONGD y Salud, Tendencias Globales y Algunas Perspectivas para los Anos Noventa*, Lima.

Morgan, M, Monreal, M, Escobar, M and Escalante, N (1991) *Sistematizacion, Propuesta Metodologica y dos Experiencias: Peru y Colombia*, CELATS, Lima.

Tendler, J (1982) 'Turning private voluntary organisations into development agencies: questions for evaluation,' *Program Evaluation Discussion Paper* no. 12, USAID, Washington DC.

Chapter 16

Cairncross, S (1990) 'Water supply and the urban poor' in Hardoy, J et al (eds) *The Poor Die Young*, Earthscan, London.

Cairncross, S, Hardoy, J and Satterthwaite, D (1990) 'The urban context' in Hardoy, J et al (eds) *The Poor Die Young*, ibid.

Cochrane, G (1983) 'Policies for strengthening local government in developing countries', Staff Working Paper No. 582, World Bank, Washington DC.

FURPROVI and Stein, A (1990) 'FURPROVI: an example of community participation' in *Funding Community Level Initiatives: cases from Latin America*, IIED-AL, London.

Hardoy, J, Cairncross, S and Satterthwaite, D (1990) *The Poor Die Young*, op cit.

Hardoy, A, Hardoy, J and Shusterman, R (1991) 'Building community organisation: the history of a squatter settlement and its own organisations in Buenos Aires', *Environment and Urbanisation*, 3 (2).

Hurley, D (1990) *Income-Generation Schemes for the Urban Poor*, OXFAM, Oxford.

Stren, R (1989) 'Urban local government' in Stren, R and White, R (eds) *African Cities in Crisis*, Westview Press, Boulder.

UNCHS (1987) *Global Report on Human Settlements 1986*, Oxford University Press, Oxford.

United Nations (1991) *World Urbanisation Prospects 1990; estimates and projections of urban and rural populations and of urban agglomerations*, United Nations, New York.

Chapter 17

Much of the information in this paper comes from ACORD records and reports and its associates. In addition, the following sources have been used:

ACORD (1990) *Orientation Plan 1991–5*, ACORD, London.

ACORD (1991a) *ACORD's Gender Policy*, ACORD, London.

ACORD (1991b) *ACORD's Experience With Participatory Methodologies*, RAPP document no. 3, Volume 1, ACORD, London.

ACORD (1991c) *Africa in 1991 – Hope or Despair? The challenges for ACORD*, ACORD, London.

Birgegård, L-E (1987) 'A review of experience with integrated rural development (IRD)', Issue Paper no. 3, Swedish University of Agricultural Sciences, Uppsala.

Edwards, M and Hulme, D (1992) 'Scaling-up NGO impact: learning from experience', paper presented to the SCF/IPDM workshop on 'Scaling-up NGO impact learning from experience', University of Manchester, January 1992.

Fowler, A (1987) 'NGOs in Africa: achieving comparative advantage in relief and micro-development', paper presented to the conference on 'The role of indigenous NGOs in African recovery and development', 10–15 January 1988, Khartoum.

National Resistance Movement (1986) *Ten Point Programme*, National Resistance Movement, Kampala.

Ruttan, V W (1984) 'Integrated rural development programmes: a historical perspective', *World Development*, vol. 12, no. 4, pp. 393–401.

Chapter 18

Cernea, M (1988) *NGOs and Local Development*, World Bank, Washington DC.

Garilao, E (1987) 'Indigenous NGOs as strategic institutions', *World Development* (Supplement), vol. 15.

ICVA (1990) *Relations between Southern and Northern NGOs: Effective Partnerships for Sustainable Development*, ICVA, Geneva.

Lemaresquier, T (1987) 'Prospects for development education', *World Development* (Supplement), vol. 15.

LOK NITI (1988) 'NGOs and international development co-operation', *Journal of the Asian NGO Coalition*, vol. 5 (4).

Minear, L (1987) 'The other missions of NGOs; education and advocacy', *World Development* (Supplement), vol. 15.

Padron, M (1987) 'NGOs from development aid to development co-operation', *World Development* (Supplement), vol. 15.

Trivedy, R (1989) *Report of Malawi Action Research Project*, OXFAM, Oxford.

UNECA (1989) *People's Charter on Popular Participation*, UNECA, Addis Ababa.

Chapter 19

Arnold, S H (1988) 'Constrained crusaders? British charities and development education', *Development Policy Review*, 6 (3), pp. 183–209.

Charity Commission (1991) 'OXFAM: Report of an inquiry submitted to the Charity Commissioners', 8 April, London.

Clark, J (1991) *Democratising Development: the Role of Voluntary Organisations*, Earthscan, London.

Drabek, A G (ed) (1987) 'Development alternatives: the challenge for NGOs', *World Development*, 15 (supplement).

Gladstone, F (1989) 'Towards a plentiful planet', report on development education in Britain, National Council for Voluntary Organisations, London.

Hyden, G (1983) *No Shortcuts to Progress: African Development Management in Perspective*, Heinemann, London.

International Freedom Foundation (1989) 'A multitude of sins' and accompanying letter, 22 March, London, IFF.

Korten, D C (1987) 'Third generation strategies: a key to people-centred development', in Drabek, 1987.

Korten, D C (1989) 'Global realities: issues for the 1990s', draft for review and comment, Institute for Development Research, Massachusetts, Boston.

National Council of Voluntary Organisations (1989) *NCVO Response to the White Paper 'Charities: A Framework for the Future'*, National Council for Voluntary Organisations, London.

Toye, J (1987) *Dilemmas of Development*, Blackwell, Oxford.

World Bank (1990) *World Development Report 1990*, University Press, Oxford.

Index